THE ENGLISH LEGAL HERITAGE

Foreword by Lord Elwyn-Jones

Oyez Publishing

Editor's Note

In 1976 I was approached by John Stidolph, and invited to commission and edit a book which, in his words, would 'record English law as it exists today.' The book was not to be just another legal textbook but would contain illustrations in the form of photographs and reproductions of old prints in order, it was hoped, to make it a true celebration of English law and the English legal system and of appeal to lawyers and laymen alike. So *The English Legal Heritage* was born.

At almost the same time the Labour Government of the day responded to pressures from many quarters and set up a Royal Commission on Legal Services 'to enquire into the law and practice relating to the provision of legal services in England and Wales and to consider whether any, and if so what, changes are desirable in the public interest in the structure, organisation, training, regulation of and entry to the legal profession, including the arrangement for determining its remuneration, whether from private sources or public funds, and in the rules which prevent persons who are neither barristers nor solicitors from undertaking conveyancing and other legal business on behalf of other persons.' By coincidence as this book goes to press, so the Royal Commission too has completed its task and sent its recommendations to the Lord Chancellor. Whatever conclusions the Royal Commission has reached it is undoubted that there will be recommendations that will bring about change; just how radical that change will be is a matter of conjecture. Notwithstanding the existence of a Royal Commission the law has continued to develop in order to reflect modern day needs, and lawyers themselves are continually adapting themselves and their institutions to keep abreast of these changes. In the following pages we have attempted to describe the long and continuing process of the evolution of the English legal system, the influence that it has had on the development of the legal systems of former British colonies and the ways in which it too has been influenced – by the continuing growth of the common law in the Commonwealth, by the entry of the United Kingdom into the European Economic Community and by the different jurisdictions within the United Kingdom itself, namely those of Scotland (whose legal system, unlike its neighbours, is based on Roman law) and Northern Ireland.

Space has precluded us from even a passing mention of the laws and legal systems of the Isle of Man and the Channel Islands, and those same restraints have forced both editor and contributors to be highly selective in the treatment of their appointed subjects. Each section of *English Legal Heritage* is worthy of a book in its own right – indeed many books have been published on these subjects, some of which are listed on page 188 for those whose appetite has been whetted and wish to read further.

To the contributors, the publisher, the staff of New Law Journal and my husband, all of whom have exercised great patience and forbearance while the book has been in production my heartfelt thanks.

Judy Hodgson London June 1979

Created and produced by John Stidolph
Edited by Judy Hodgson LL.B.
Photography by Julian Allason JP
Picture research by Tom Williams
Designed by Paul Watkins

© Berkswell Publishing Co. Ltd. 1979
First published by Oyez Publishing 1979
ISBN 0 85120 401 5

Colour separations by Newsele Litho Ltd
Typesetting by Input Typesetting Ltd
Printed in England by Ebenezer Baylis & Son Ltd. Leicester and London

Frontispiece: The Opening of the Law Courts. The procession of judges through the Great Hall of the Royal Courts of Justice takes place after the Lord Chancellor's Breakfast every year early in October at the beginning of the Michaelmas Law Term

Contents

List of Contributors

Julian Allason photographed many of the scenes and personalities who illustrate this book. His work has appeared in many magazines including *Architectural Design* and *Vogue*. He was appointed a Justice of the Peace in 1974.

Andrew Arden is a barrister. He is consultant to the Legal Action Group and was formerly director of the Small Heath Community Law Centre, Birmingham.

Francis Cowper was called to the Bar at Gray's Inn and is now a Bencher of that Inn. He is also a member of Lincoln's Inn. In addition to this work as a law reporter in the House of Lords he is a regular contributor to UK law journals and writes the London Letter for the New York Law Journal.

Gavin Drewry BSc (SocSci) is a lecturer in government at Bedford College, University of London. His books include *Final Appeal: A Study of the House of Lords in its Judicial Capacity* (with Louis Blom-Cooper QC) and *Legislation and Public Policy*.

Frank Goldsworthy was for many years High Court reporter of the *Daily Express*.

R N G Harrison BA is a director of Butterworth Law Publishers Ltd, and was formerly editor of the *All England Law Reports*.

Judy Hodgson LLB is editor of the *New Law Journal*.

Professor Harry W Jones is Cardozo Professor of Jurisprudence at Columbia University.

The Rt Hon Lord Kilbrandon PC, LLD, DSci was a Senator at the College of Justice in Scotland and Lord of Session 1959–1971 when he was appointed a Lord of Appeal in Ordinary. He was chairman of the Scottish Law Commission and chairman of the Commission on the Constitution.

The Rt Hon Lord MacDermott PC, MC, LLD was a judge of the High Court of Northern Ireland and a Lord of Appeal in Ordinary. He was Lord Chief Justice of Northern Ireland 1951–71. A Unionist member of the Parliament of Northern Ireland he served as Attorney-General 1941–44. He was chairman of the Committee on the Supreme Court of Judicature of Northern Ireland which reported in 1969, and a member of the Gardiner Committee set up in 1974 to consider, in context of civil liberties and human rights, measures to deal with terrorism in Northern Ireland.

S W Magnus QC is a member of the Foreign Compensation Commission. He was a puisne judge of the High Court of Zambia and served as a Member of Parliament in Northern Rhodesia, which subsequently became Zambia, 1964–68.

L W Melville is a solicitor. After teaching law at the Law Society's College of Law he joined a leading firm of City solicitors to specialise in transactions in technology. His book on technology transfer is now in its third edition.

James Morton is a solicitor practising in London.

Michael Leyland Nash LLM is a lecturer in law at Norwich City College of Further and Higher Education.

The Hon Sir Basil Nield CBE, DL has combined careers in both politics and the law, achieving the distinction of being a judge of the High Court who has also been a Member of Parliament. He was the first judge and recorder of Manchester Crown Court and served as a judge of the Queen's Bench Division 1960–78.

Nigel Pascoe is a barrister and a member of the Western Circuit. He originated and edits the All England Quarterly Law Cassettes.

The Rt Hon Lord Rawlinson PC, QC was Solicitor-General from 1962-64, Attorney-General 1970-74, and chairman of the Senate of the Inns of Court and Bar 1975–76.

Gerald Sanctuary is a solicitor and executive director of the International Bar Association. He was formerly the Law Society's Secretary, Professional and Public Relations.

Foreword by Rt Hon Lord Elwyn-Jones CH

It is a brave undertaking to produce a book on the English Legal Heritage. There are a thousand years of history behind it, and it has become the heritage not only of the people of this country, but in varying degrees of one third of the population of the world. In visiting former British territories, it is indeed touching to see how faithful the allegiance is to the traditions which their lawyers learned initially in our Inns of Court.

While this book will clearly be attractive to the general reader, a glance down the list of contributors shows that it is also an authoritative work in which lawyers themselves will find value. Its publication is timely because the public has been increasingly concerned in questions of legal administration, a concern which was recognised in 1976 by the establishment of the Royal Commission on Legal Services.

There are illuminating chapters on Parliament, on European institutions and on the law as it is administered in different parts of the United Kingdom and the many areas of the world where the Common Law inheritance survives. The High Court and the system of appeals are admirably described but I wish there had been room for rather more about the work of the county courts and in particular about the significance of the widespread use of arbitrations before the Registrars. While the amounts at stake in these courts may be small, the numbers of cases are immense and it is here, as in the Magistrate's courts, that most ordinary citizens have their experience of the functioning of the law.

There is a helpful and topical chapter on Legal Aid and Advice. In the thirty years since the passing of the 1949 Act, nearly 3,000,000 people have been enabled, with the benefit of legal aid certificates, to pursue their rights in the courts, and many others have received advice under the scheme introduced in 1972. It was a matter of great satisfaction to me personally in 1979 to introduce the Legal Aid Act which, with Regulations, will represent a new package extending the benefits of legal aid and advice to many more people and their families.

Another recent development, well covered in this book, has been the growth of Law Centres in deprived urban communities where young lawyers are performing a valuable social service in helping to fill the unmet need for legal aid and advice. I hope that greater availability of legal services will increase people's confidence in the ability of the law and the legal system to redress their grievances, to protect their rights and to provide a framework for an ordered community.

It will be through such means that our Legal Heritage will be seen to belong not only to lawyers, but to us all.

A view of Inner Temple from the Gardens
showing Harcourt Buildings, Crown Office Row with
the tower of the Royal Courts of Justice projecting
above, the Inner Temple Hall and Library and a
corner of Paper Buildings

The interior of the New Hall, Lincoln's Inn which was opened by Queen Victoria in 1845

The interior of the Temple Church

1

The Development of Law in England

Michael Leyland Nash

Sources of English Law One of the main characteristics of English law is that it has developed in an evolutionary rather than a revolutionary way. The framework of the law-making bodies, the law-enforcing bodies and the law-interpreting bodies has been filled in gradually at different times and by different hands or brushes just as the framework might be fitted round a rather sprawling and panoramic picture. The result is impressive but in many ways piecemeal. Can we really decide now what this framework, this constitution is? How would the legal and administrative structure be described, after one thousand and more years of growth?

Common Law English law is a tangled skein and has come from many sources, some major and some minor, but if we apply the maxim 'Things are not always what they seem' to matters both present and historical, we shall not go far wrong. It is certainly true in one sense that William the Conqueror sent out travelling justices or justices in eyre to collect and collate the customs of the country, and that those he decided to make universal were *common* to the whole country. It is also true that he accepted in great part the Dooms of the Saxon Kings. It is certainly a consistent feature of English legal history to adapt and modify rather than to destroy and replace. The change has risen in most cases like yeast from below, rather than being imposed from above, although there have been some such impositions, rather too many for the liking of most people, in recent times. But, for the most part the law remains 'common', or originating in custom, rather than in code, or law imposed from above by a legislative body. The legislative body has of course often approved and ratified what was custom, and the courts have played an important role in absorbing customs, especially mercantile customs, into the main body of English law.

Decrees Kings had always made decrees; in fact they still make them, although strictly under the orders of their ministers. A dramatic modern example occurred in 1968, when, on the advice of her Prime Minister Harold Wilson, the Queen ordered the closure of the banks because of a gold crisis. The occasion for the decree could not have been more contrived for effect if it had been fictional, for it occurred at a very early hour in the morning, the Queen being roused from her bed to sign the decree in Council. In former days the monarch was

far more independent of ministers and was sometimes their intellectual superior.

Statute The most important source of law today is statute or Act of Parliament. This presupposes Parliament itself. Our own Parliament or Parlement (strictly a speaking place) somewhat resembled the European Assembly today. It could not pass laws. It could only fume, pontificate and advise. It had no real power except that of a pressure group or of several such groups. It looked forward, like the European Assembly today, to the time when its voice would be heard, and its decisions accorded the form of binding law. The system of electing representatives, worked out in the fifteenth century, lasted with only minor amendments until 1832. But being an elected body gave it some teeth, and it began to challenge the royal authority. It was very much a case of a creature growing as big as its creator, then growing bigger and finally devouring it. The monarchy, as durable as the phoenix, returned and for a short period acquiesced in the situation. It was Stuart recalcitrance which finally brought the matter to a crisis in 1688. The throne, the source and repository of legal authority in this country, was declared vacant on the flight of James II. Members of the former Parliament assembled themselves to resolve the situation. Legally the status of those institutions involved is most interesting, but it is a conundrum and insoluble. A Parliament cannot be so called unless it is called by royal authority (there was no Instrument of Government such as existed under the Commonwealth) so this gathering called itself a Convention. It offered the crown in the end to Mary, the elder daughter of James II, and her husband William III, the head of state of the Netherlands. The first action of the royal pair was to declare the Convention a Parliament. But, as can be seen, it is quite impossible for both sovereigns and Parliament to be legal, as each had to legitimise the other. Nevertheless the situation was legal in the pragmatic sense, as it always becomes in such situations.

As far as the sources of English law are concerned, we can say that from 1689, the date of the Bill of Rights, statute is the most important source of law in the land, and from then on Parliament or, strictly speaking, the Sovereign in Parliament, is the source and repository of legal authority. Even this cannot be entirely true, as there are times when Parliament is not sitting, and

particularly during such periods ministers have recourse to the royal prerogative.

It was William the Conqueror too who declared that England was a royal possession and that the king alone was 'owner' of every part and parcel of the land. This means that there can never be an absolute title to land in this country. It is always held ultimately 'of the Crown'. This is a matter of some convenience to those who wish to effect compulsory purchase, or, to give it its ancient name, eminent domain, which is the right of the Crown to repossess its land. This was not the case in France, where absolute ownership was possible. When the metro, the underground railway, was built in Paris, no owner of private land would allow it to be undermined, so the State had to construct the railway directly beneath the thoroughfares which it owned. In London, on the other hand, statutory authority gave the State power to go underground anywhere it chose. The most direct result, in English law, was that the chief civil court, the King's or Queen's Bench, was chiefly concerned at its inception with claims appertaining to royal lands.

On the criminal side private jurisdiction was dispensed with as soon as was practically possible. The great barons might pretend to the power of life and death over their tenants and serfs but the royal courts, travelling at first wherever the king went, grew strong receiving popular support and approval. They were less likely to be prejudiced in favour of the prosecutor. The separation of powers, insofar as it was possible, was early favoured, and went hand in hand with the jury system. A 'local' involvement in cases has always been attempted if possible. Except in rare instances a man was tried where he committed the offence, not in a distant vacuum. But this referred to finding of the facts; the finding of the law depended on the king's judge.

The magistracy, founded in the fourteenth century, was also given many functions, both civil and criminal to begin with, as was the coroner, a Crown man, as the name implies. Many of these functions have gone, and the magistrate, confirmed by the Lord Chancellor, is a royal appointment like all judges, and now concentrates almost entirely on minor criminal matters.

Equity There is no phrase more quasi-religious in law than 'Keeper of the King's Conscience'. Yet that is the supposed role of the Lord Chancellor, the chief law officer of England and Wales. The title dates from the time when the Lord Chancellor was also a cleric and the king's chief chaplain, and it is yet another extension of the 'divinity that does hedge a king' and the resultant legal fictions. If a citizen suffered a wrong or injustice, the king's conscience was pricked – he also suffered, and the wrong had to be redressed. That was done in early days by the king himself and then by his deputy in these matters, the Lord Chancellor. Marcus Gheeraerht's famous Rainbow portrait of Queen Elizabeth I at Hatfield house, shows her wearing a gown embroidered all over with pictures of eyes and ears, to show that she saw and heard all that went on in her kingdom. The monarch embodied the body politic. He or she knew all, ordained all. If any member of the body, a subject, suffered wrong, the head would know of it and seek to correct it. Such was (and remains) the theory. James I, conscious of this position as the chief judge, tried to sit

as a judge in the court, but was overruled. Although he was still a judge in theory, by this time such a practice had become 'unconstitutional' as well as inconvenient. It is thought that the last king to sit as a judge was Edward IV.

It is an amusing but telling touch even today that when the Queen goes into the City of London and passes the spot where Temple Bar once stood and is within the precincts of the Royal Courts of Justice, all work in the courts must cease 'for an agent cannot work in the presence of his principal'. Thus, as the Queen passes through, there is a moment of suspended animation, like the characters in some Japanese Noh play. It may seem farcical, but it is all part and parcel of the wish to remind those in authority that they do not hold a self-sustaining power, but that they are given it by someone who may herself be powerless.

This system of redress by the Lord Chancellor is known as equity, and it is one of those words we have adopted because they do not translate well from the Latin. The Latin *aequitas* means a 'levelling' and it is an

attempt to place the parties in a case on the same level, the same footing. Other synonyms are used, but none express exactly what is implied by equity, even though it may be called justice, natural law, fairness or the law of conscience or equality.

Equity developed its own peculiar remedies: rescission, specific performance, injunction and quantum meruit. The system developed side by side with the common law courts, the royal courts. But the courts of common law and equity were not the only courts–there were also the Ecclesiastical courts, the survivors of the old canon law courts of the pre-Reformation Catholic church. These were particularly concerned with family matters, with marriage, annulment, the custody of children and the interpretation of wills, as well as church property and the regulation of clerical discipline.

Then again there were the courts particularly rooted in mercantilism, with the customs of merchants, and there was a strong international bias to these courts, for their laws went back to places overseas, to the Laws of Wisby, the Laws of Oléron and the *Consolato del Mare*. In the eighteenth century Chief Justice Holt and Lord Mansfield did much to absorb these customs into English law proper.

Judicature Acts 1873–5 The plethora of jurisdictions, many of them overlapping, was finally reformed by the great Judicature Acts 1873–5. The courts were amalgamated: some found themselves with quite bizarre bedfellows – such as Probate, Divorce and Admiralty, the

third of the three new major divisions of the civil High Court. Whatever did these three, Probate, Divorce and Admiralty, known as 'Wills, Wives and Wrecks', have in common? The answer lies in their system of procedure, which was inquisitorial rather than accusatorial, and closely linked to the civil law of Europe.

Queen's Bench became the principal division of the new High Court, and Chancery (the Lord Chancellor's Court) the second division. The systems of law and equity were fused – all High Court judges were enabled to apply both systems. They were to apply the common law first, and if that resulted in an injustice, they were to apply equity. If law and equity clashed, equity would prevail – one of the sayings or maxims of equity.

The traditional keeper of the nation's state records, the Master of the Rolls, became the head of the Court of Appeal. Some great judges were to make their names here, among them Sir George Jessel, the first Master of the Rolls after the reform, whose face still stares down from the great panoramic picture of judges at the opening of the Royal Courts of Justice, now hanging in the Great Hall of those Courts in the Strand. The list also includes Lord Denning, the latest Master of the Rolls, the brilliant *enfant terrible* of thirty years on the Bench, a visionary in English law.

The ecclesiastical courts were stripped of most of their functions, but they still survive today to regulate the internal discipline of the clergy, even though few cases are heard. Because they are few, their notoriety is perhaps in inverse proportion. The three most notable

The Courts of King's Bench and Chancery in Westminster Hall. Mid 17th century. This is the earliest existing view of the Courts in Westminster Hall. King's Bench is on the left, Chancery on the right. They were divided by removable wooden partitions

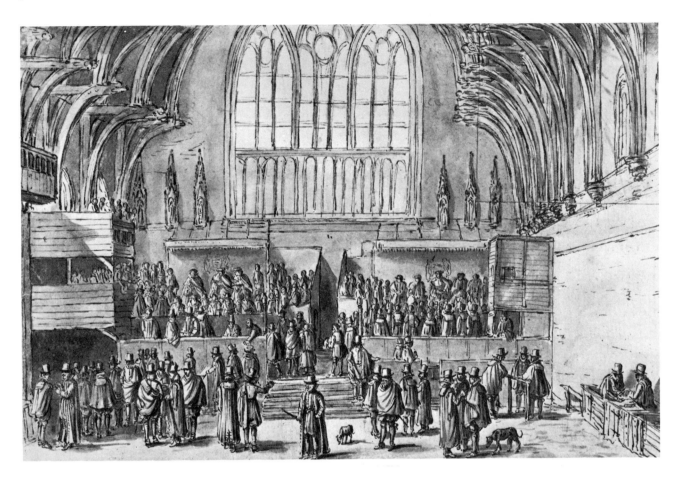

since 1875 have been those of Archdeacon Wakeford in 1921, the Vicar of Stiffkey in 1932, and the Vicar of Balham in 1963. In February 1921 Archdeacon Wakeford was found guilty in Lincoln Consistory Court of having committed adultery at the Bull at Peterborough with a 'woman unknown'. Wakeford maintained that he had put up at the Bull alone in order to prepare his sermons for Holy Week. On appeal the Judicial Committee of the Privy Council (a court retained to hear, inter alia, appeals from the classic professions) upheld the findings of the Consistory Court. There was a great deal of public sympathy for the Archdeacon, who ended his days in a poor asylum in 1930.

The case of the Reverend Harold F Davidson, Rector of Stiffkey in Norfolk, had a similarly dismal end, but attracted enormous notoriety at the time. Davidson, who was the twenty-eighth member of his family to enter Holy Orders, apparently found more vocation in trying to save the prostitutes of London than the souls of his little country parish. This led to scandal and he was eventually faced with five charges under section 2 of the Clergy Discipline Act 1892. He was found guilty, and on October 21, 1932 sentence of deprivation was pronounced upon him by the Bishop of Norwich, in which he was 'entirely removed deposed and degraded from [his] offices'. In medieval times the priest would have been literally stripped of his garments as deacon and priest; in modern times this unseemly charade has been discontinued. Davidson died a victim of a circus accident on July 30, 1937.

Legal Language and Documents It is as well to pause here to consider the language used in the courts, in legislative documents and in the system of law reports which were to provide the vital material for the doctrine of judicial precedent over seven centuries.

After the coming of the Normans the courts began to use the Norman-French language. Inevitably, in what was in many ways virtually a colony, the language became bastardized, and later ridiculed. (There is for example a case which emphasises the high point of ludicrousness, where a report mentions an incident in court in which the defendant 'jette un brickbat at le judge, que narrowly missed!')

Moreover the use of Norman-French was associated with a pretentious elite, out of touch with the people, a Brahmin-like caste which used French and Latin as a mystical barrier between themselves and common litigants who were amazed and bemused by it. If the Latin used in church became 'the blessed mutter of the Mass', in court it became a bewildering and often totally incorrect jargon.

The earliest statutes, the written legislation of Parliament, had been in Latin. Later, by 1275, some were in French while others were in Latin, but by 1309 French had become the more usual form. Reaction, probably brought about by the Hundred Years' War, came in 1362 when a statute required pleadings, which were then delivered orally in open court, to be in English instead of 'in the French tongue, which is much unknown in the realm'. It further enacted that they

should be entered and enrolled in Latin. The statute itself, ironically, is in French, and it was only after 1485 that statutes (as distinct from court pleadings) were in English. It is in Parliament that the last vestiges of Norman-French remain. The Lords Commissioners, when giving the Royal Assent, proclaim 'La Reyne le veult' or 'The Queen wishes it'. In the unlikely event of a royal veto (the last occasion being in 1708 when Queen Anne refused assent to the Scottish Militia Bill) they would proclaim 'La Reyne s'avisera' – the Queen will take advice, which is polite language for a rejection of the bill.

Thomas Carlyle, in his *Elucidations on the Letters and Speeches of Thomas Cromwell,* describes graphically how the Rump Parliament decided to abolish the use of Latin in legal proceedings:

March 25, 1652. 1st day of the New Year.
Above two years ago, when this Rump Parliament was in the flush of youthful vigour, it decided on reforming the laws of England, and appointed a working committee for that object, our learned friend Bulstrode one of them. [This was Bulstrode Whitelocke, a contemporary writer much consulted by Carlyle.] Which working committee finding the job heavy, gradually languished; and after some Acts for having law-proceedings transacted in the English tongue, and for other improvements of the like magnitude, died into comfortable sleep ...

The whole question of law reform, and the fact that it should be of a continuing nature, has concerned lawyers and non-lawyers alike for at least three centuries; and the progress, or lack of progress, always seems to strike familiar chords. Carlyle continues:

On my Lord General's [Cromwell's] return from Worcester, it has been poked up again; and now rubbing its eyes, set to work in good earnest ... Accordingly on March 25, 1652, first day of the New Year 1652 [this being 'The Little Parliament' so called], learned Bulstrode, in the name of the working Committee has suggested a variety of things: among others, some improvement in our method of transferring property—of enabling poor John Doe, who finds at present a terrible difficulty in doing so, to inform Richard Roe, 'I, John Doe do, in very fact, sell to thee Richard Roe, such and such a property according to the usual human meaning of the word *sell*; and it is hereby, let me again assure thee, indisputably sold to thee Richard by me John': which, my learned friend thinks, might really be an improvement. To which end he will introduce an Act: nay there shall farther be an Act for the Registry of Deeds in each County – if it please Heaven. 'Neglect to register your Sale of Land in this promised County Register within a given time', enacts the learned Bulstrode, 'such sale should be void. Be exact in registering it, the Land shall not be subject to any incumbrance'. Incumbrance, yes, but what is incumbrance? asks all the working Committee, with wide eyes, when they come actually to sit upon this Bill of Registry, and to hatch it into some kind of perfection: What is incumbrance? No mortal can tell. They sit debating it, painfully sifting it, for three months; three months by Booker's Almanac, and the Zodiac Horologe: March violets have become June roses; and still they debate what incumbrance is; and indeed, I think, could never fix it at all; and are perhaps debating it, if so doomed, in some twilight foggy section of Dante's Nether World, to all Eternity, at this hour! Are not these a set of men likely to reform English Law? Likely these to strip the accumulated owl-droppings and foul guano-mountains from your rockisland, and lay the reality bare – in the course of Eternities! ...

I add only, for the sake of chronology, that on the fourth day after this appearance of Bulstrode as a law-reformer,

Dinner in Hall in the Inner Temple. Students keeping Dining Terms dine in messes of four at long tables while the Treasurer and Benchers entertain their guests at Grand Night at the top tables. A few barristers dine at the small table on the right

occurred the famous Black Monday; fearfullest eclipse of the sun ever seen by mankind. Came on about nine in the morning; darker and darker: ploughmen unyoked their teams; stars came out, birds sorrowfully chirping took to roost, men in amazement to prayers; a day of much obscurity: Black Monday or Mirk Monday, March 29th, 1652. Much noised of by Lilly, Booker and the buzzard astrologer tribe. Betokening somewhat? Belike that Bulstrode and his Parliament will, in the name of law reform, and otherwise, make a Practical Gospel, or real Reign of God, in this England?

Before we leave this period for a moment, to compare the astonishing similarities with law reform today, we may also turn profitably to a speech made by Cromwell on the same subject, when speaking in state in the Painted Chamber at Westminster on September 17, 1656:

There are some things which respect the Estates of men; and there is one general Grievance in the Nation. It is the law ('Hear, hear!' from all quarters of the Nation). Not that the Laws are a grievance; but there are Laws that are a grievance; and the great grievance lies in the execution and administration. I think I may say it, I have as eminent judges in this land as have been had, or that the Nation has had, these many years. (Hale and others: yea!) Truly I could be particular as to the executive part of it, to administration of the law; but that would trouble you. But the truth of it is. There are wicked and abominable Laws, that it will be in your power to alter. To hang a man for sixpence, thirteen pence, I know not what; to hang for a trifle, and pardon murder – is in the ministration of the law, through the ill-framing of it. I have known in my experience abominable murders ac'quitted. And to come and see men lose their lives for petty matters: this is a thing that God will reckon up.

And again, on April 21, 1657:

I hope you will think sincerely, as before God, 'That the Laws must be regulated!' I hope you will. We have been often talking of them: and I remember well, in the old Parliament, that we were three months, and could not get over the word 'Incumbrances'; and then we thought there was little hope of regulating the Laws, when there was such a difficulty as to that. But surely the Laws need to be regulated. And I must needs say, I think it is a sacrifice acceptable to God, upon many accounts. And I am persuaded it is one thing that God looks for, and would have. I confess, if any man should ask me, 'Why, *how* would you have done it?' I confess I do not know How. But I think verily, at the least, the Delays in Suits, and the Excessiveness of Fees, and the Costliness of Suits, and those various things that I do not know what names they bear – I have heard talk of "Demurrers" and such-like things which I scarce know ... But I say certainly that the people are suffering greatly in this respect; they are so.

Had Cromwell risen from the grave in the 1970s he would have been astonished, or perhaps depressed, to find how many of the points he raised so pointedly in his blunt fashion were still being debated inside and outside of Parliament, and how many of them had still not properly been resolved.

The Legal Calendar A statute of 1731 provided that as from March 25, 1733 all pleadings, etc. except in the old Court of Admiralty, should be in English instead of in Latin. The date on which the Act was due to come into effect (March 25) was then considered—being before the introduction of the Gregorian Calendar in 1752—to be New Year's Day. The fixing of New Year's Day throughout English history (and particularly legal history) has been, to say the least, somewhat bizarre. The legal year was reckoned in England to start on Christ-

mas Day until 1066. From 1067 until 1155 the year began on January 1; from 1155 until 1751 it began on March 25; and since 1752 is has again been reckoned from January 1.

The terms and sittings of the courts and of the Inns of Court have likewise fluctuated, although mostly keeping their original names. The Inns of Court in their dining terms keep to the original four terms, which are as follows: Michaelmas, which begins the first Wednesday in November (Michaelmas being September 29); Hilary, beginning the third Wednesday in January (the Feast of St Hilary is January 13); Easter, which begins on the first Wednesday after Low Sunday and Trinity (beginning on the first Wednesday after Trinity Sunday). Each term is of twenty-three days' duration.

Law sittings in England and Wales commence on the Feast of St Hilary (if we take the post-1752 year beginning on January 1); and the term which begins on Michaelmas Day (September 29 or thereabouts) ends on the Feast of St Thomas the Apostle (December 21). Thus the legal and ecclesiastical years, dating from the time when many lawyers were also clerics, are still very much intertwined.

Legal Latin did not come to an end with the Act of 1731, needless to say. It was found that technical terms like *nisi prius*, *quare impedit*, *fieri facias*, and *habeas corpus*, were, as Blackstone put it, 'not capable of an English dress with any degree of seriousness', and so, two years

later, in 1732, another Act was passed to allow such words to be continued 'in the same language as hath been commonly used'.

Yet what sort of Latin was it, and how was it pronounced? There are said to be three forms of Latin: first, good Latin, such is allowed by grammarians and scholars; secondly, false or incongruous Latin, which in times past would abate original writs (although it would not make void any judicial writ, declaration or plea, etc); and thirdly, words of art, known only to the sages of the law, and not to grammarians, called Lawyers' Latin.

Indictments were in Latin (of a sort) until the enactment of the statute of 1731, and continued in Wales until a statute of 1732. According to Coke (5 Co Rep 121) when an indictment was in Latin it could be quashed for 'false Latin' if the words in question 'do not make sense in Latin, unless they were terms of art in English law'.

Maxims or sayings are usually in Latin because they are derived from Roman law, or because they were invented by mediaeval jurists in lawyers' Latin.

The Great Jurists One of the most characteristic features of English law is the doctrine of judicial precedent (following decided cases of higher courts or perhaps courts of the same level). This doctrine depends on a hierarchy of courts and on a good system of law reporting.

From about 1272 until 1536 the cases had been reported in what we now know as the *Year Books*. Their authors are anonymous for the most part, lost to us like their contemporaries who built the great cathedrals, but they have, like those same contemporaries, an enduring monument. These cases are still quoted in English courts where there is no modern precedent.

The Year Books Anthony Fitzherbert, a Tudor judge, compiled a grand abridgement of the *Year Books* in 1516. After 1536 private law reporters took over and the *Year Books* no longer appeared. The authors of these reports, which were to last until 1865, are of course known to us. They varied greatly in style and quality, but perhaps their greatest disadvantage, looking back, was that they were selective in a random manner. The reporters themselves at their discretion or whim reported what they thought were the best or most suitable cases. Sometimes they were not well-served by their assistants, who waited until their masters fell asleep in court and then fecklessly wrote comments in the margins. It was said of Espinasse, that 'he listened to one half of a case and reported the other half.'

But against this we must place the balance of the great case reporters, Plowden, Coke, Dyer and their like; and with them we must remember the great place occupied in the development of English law by legal writers and commentators.

Ranulf de Glanvil The first writer of note must be Ranulf de Glanvil, who was Chief Justiciary to Henry II. Lord Campbell, in his *Lives of the Lord Chancellors*, wrote that 'he must have thrown into the shade all others connected with the administration of the law.' Not only a skilful military commander, he presided with distinguished lustre in the *Aula Regis* (The Royal Court) and wrote a book on the law and constitution of England. Campbell, writing in 1845, could not resist adding a footnote that Coke (the great seventeenth century commentator) seemed to envy Glanvil, because his own exploits as ex-chief justice when Sheriff of Buckinghamshire could not compare with those of ex-chief justice Glanvil as crusader. Indeed, Glanvil, who accompanied Richard Coeur de Lion on crusade, died in the Holy Land, at Acre, in 1190.

The book referred to is the first classical text on the common law of England. It was called *Treatise on the Law and Customs of England*, but we cannot be sure that Glanvil wrote it. Maitland, the great nineteenth century legal historian, suggested that it was written by Hubert Walter, himself later Justiciar, but with Glanvil's consent and under his supervision. Perhaps, to use a modern phrase, we may say it was 'ghosted.' It deals in fourteen books with the law administered in the *Curia Regis*, the Royal Council. It was a major milestone in establishing the common law as a system in its own right, and it long remained the standard textbook of English law. About 1265 an attempt was made to produce a revised and up to date edition. We know Bracton, our next great writer, made extensive use of it, and an edition of it was introduced into Scotland in the early thirteenth century, under the name of *Regiam Majestatem*. The authorship of this book was doubtfully ascribed to Glanvil on the evidence of Roger of Hoveden (or Haveden), a chronicler who died in 1201.

Bracton Henry de Bracton (or Bratton) wrote, between 1235–59, *De Legibus et Consuetudinibus Angliae*, which was described by Maitland as 'the crown and flower of English mediaeval jurisprudence'. Bracton sat as judge in the king's central court, soon to be distinguished as the King's Bench, and the work of this court was beginning to make it clear that England was to have a native common law. It was the greatest and the most comprehensive treatise on English law till Blackstone wrote his *Commentaries* five centuries later. Bracton used as the foundation of his treatise some two thousand cases which he had collected from the Plea Rolls. It was the earliest attempt to treat the whole extent of the law in a manner at once systematic and practical, and it was moreover, true literature. It had an enormously 'good press', if one may express it that way. Unfortunately when mediaeval law fell into decay in the fifteenth century the system so expertly outlined and to some extent initiated by Bracton became more and more technical, and less and less rational, because it was based on a system of writs. A case could not be brought unless it could fit into a certain prescribed formula.

Bracton's true worth was recognized by Fitzherbert in the sixteenth century and Coke in the seventeenth.

Thomas Littleton A fifteenth century lawyer, Thomas Littleton is certainly worthy of mention. His birth and death dates have not been certainly established. According to some he was born in 1407 and according to others, as late as 1422. He probably died in 1481. He was Chief Justice of the Court of Common Pleas (the court involving land cases other than royal lands) and of the King's Bench. His fame rests upon a treatise which he wrote in law-French for law students, *The Tenures*. It long remained the principal authority on English property law. It has been called by Maitland, 'a thoroughly mediaeval work written in decadent colonial French', but it was nevertheless the greatest treatise since Bracton, and was also described, surely too fulsomely, by Coke as 'the most perfect and absolute work in English law not written in Latin'. If Bracton's work had been founded upon cases in the Plea Rolls, Littleton's was founded upon cases in the *Year Books*. Thus both books point to the early importance of case law or precedent. Littleton's work also showed the importance of rationalising these precedents, of extracting what is referred to as the *ratio decidendi*, the reason for the decision.

Effigies Viri is aurati nuper lacita coram clariß. EDOARDI COKI Capitalis Iuſticiarij Rege tenendâ aſsignat

Sir John Fortescue From the same period there also emerges the Lancastrian Chief Justice, Sir John Fortescue. Like Littleton, authorities differ as to his birth and death dates. Some authorities say he was born in about 1385 and some in 1394. His death occurred sometime between 1476 and 1479. The very doubt attached to these dates shows us the state and temper of the times. Fortescue wrote, for the guidance of the ill-starred Edward, Prince of Wales (son of Henry VI) *De Laudibus Legum Angliae* ('In Praise of English Law'). He compared favourably the English common law with the French civil law, and the English monarchy, already beginning to be constitutional, with the absolute monarchy of France, exhorting the prince to uphold the English version (though his father had been crowned king of both kingdoms). This work was first published in 1537, probably because of the birth of another Edward, who was heir to the throne and the son of Henry VIII. It is perhaps significant that he was the only lawyer to write a book for the guidance of a future king. Later attempts were left to royalty itself, such as the *Basilicon Doron* of James I, for Henry Frederick, Prince of Wales; and the instructions of Frederick, Prince of Wales to the son who was to become George III.

Anthony Fitzherbert was a Tudor judge of Common Pleas. He was born in 1470 and died in 1538. The *Year Books* were coming to an end, and Fitzherbert's *Graunde Abridgement* of 1516 superseded all previous abridgements and even the *Year Books* themselves, which ceased in 1536. This book used an enormous range of reports, including the great source known as *Bracton's Notebook*. It was the first important attempt to systematise the whole law and *Fitzherbert* became the 'bible' for many generations of lawyers. Fitzherbert also wrote other works, notably a book upon local government law in 1538.

Edmund Plowden Fitzherbert was followed, in this legal gallery, by Edmund Plowden (1518–85) who has been called 'the most learned lawyer in a century of learned lawyers', and who might have been the Lord Chancellor had he not remained a Roman Catholic. He was a barrister of the Middle Temple and the pioneer of the modern style of law report. Plowden was a meticulous man. Maitland records that he reported cases 'at length and lovingly'. He reported only points of law and only those points on which the court had given judgment. Moreover, he studied the record with such care, before the case was argued, that he could have argued it himself. After he had written the report he would submit it for correction to the judges and serjeants who had argued it.

He was also, for the day, a man of liberal religious persuasions. He was an MP during the reign of the Catholic Mary Tudor, yet he resigned, together with 39 other MPs, over the revival of the heresy laws in 1555. Like the Spanish humanist, Vitoria, he did not believe in the death penalty for differing religious belief.

Coke Plowden was followed by Coke, the subject of one of Maitland's most immortal phrases (or paraphrases): 'And then the Common Law took flesh in the person of Edward Coke'. Of Coke much could be written, and much has been written, by much more talented hands than those of the present writer. He was a colossus in the field of both law and politics, the first person to be called 'Lord Chief Justice of England'. He defended the common law against the claims of the royal prerogative and had a profound influence on the development of English law and the English constitution. It was he who dared to tell James I that he could not sit as a judge in person, even though in theory he might be the chief judge. Coke showed that judges were not merely or necessarily 'lions under the king's throne', although they could still be appointed and dismissed at that time at the royal pleasure.

Coke is best known for his reports. 'Our book cases are the best proof [of] what the law is', he wrote. Coke wrote his reports in thirteen parts. Eleven of these were published between 1600 and 1615, and the remaining two parts posthumously in 1655 and 1658. Sometimes Coke is carried away by his own pedantry. The well-known rule in *Pinnel's case* in 1601–2 is not the decision in *Pinnel's case*, but merely a commentary by Coke on the case.

Coke's research helped to link seventeenth century cases with those of mediaeval times. Even his great rival Francis Bacon, the Lord Chancellor, admitted: 'Had it not been for Sir Edward Coke's reports, the law by this time had almost been like a ship without ballast; for that the cases of modern experience are fled from those that are adjudged and ruled in former times'. The time would come of course when there would be too much ballast.

John Selden It is the legal chronology of Maitland which constantly links the great legal writers with one another. John Selden (1584–1654) was, according to Maitland, 'in all Europe among the very first to write legal history as it should be written'. He issued his version of Fortescue's *De Laudibus*, and *Fleta*, a summary of Bracton.

Matthew Hale Selden was followed by Matthew Hale (1609–76), mentioned by Carlyle in his commentary on Cromwell, a judge under Commonwealth and Restoration, a great judge and a great writer on the criminal law. Of him Maitland wrote that 'he sketched a map of English law which Blackstone was to colour'. He was a member of that committee on law reform about which Cromwell waxed eloquent in 1652, and his important work, *Pleas of the Crown,* was published posthumously.

Blackstone It is encouraging perhaps that Blackstone was a disappointed barrister and was later to be an indifferent judge. His talent lay in writing. Blackstone owed his fame at least partly to a philanthropist named Charles Viner (1678–1756) who founded the first common law professorship at Oxford, named the Vinerian professorship after him. Blackstone took up his appointment in 1758, two years after Viner's death, and he held it for eight years until 1766. Between 1765–9 he published his lectures as *Commentaries on the Laws of England* in four volumes, and these still remain the best general history of English law. Blackstone, although accepted as authoritative both here and in the newly emergent United States for several generations, was of course not without his flaws. He gave it as his opinion on one occasion that John Wilkes was disqualified from sitting in Parliament, only to be answered by Grenville, who, quoting from Blackstone's own *Commentaries,* showed that none of the causes of disqualification listed there applied to Wilkes.

Nevertheless, his works, because of their very comprehensive nature, were enormously influential and have been translated into French, Italian, German and Russian. Sir Carleton Kemp Allen, himself a most distinguished legal writer, commented, 'Blackstone's object was to present the law of England, not as a kind of black art veiled from the profane, but as a rational, coherent system comprehensible, important and of cultural value to any person of educated mind'.

William Murray, Lord Mansfield A most notable contemporary of Blackstone was William Murray, who became Lord Mansfield, and had an enormously long term (thirty-two years) as Lord Chief Justice. He in turned owed much to Sir John Holt (1642–1710) in the field of commercial law, or, as it was then called, the Law Merchant. The laws and customs of merchants had long been, strictly speaking, outside the pale of the English legal system proper. They were looked upon with something like suspicion, for they derived mostly from foreign parts, from Barcelona, the Atlantic coast of France, from Genoa, and the Baltic and the towns of the Hanseatic League. Holt realised that the common law rules must be given greater flexibility if they were to be adapted to the needs of commerce, and his decisions on the doctrine of the employer's liability for the faults of his employees and the liability of carriers were of great importance. To this day frequent reference is made to his judgment in *Coggs v Barnard* (1703), a leading case in the law of bailments.

However, Holt was willing to recognize the practices of merchants and traders to a limited extent, and the completion of this process is due to Mansfield. The great judge founded the English commercial law on the civil law (Roman law), which, in 1759, he declared to be the general source of mercantile law in the world. He sat with select juries of city merchants to decide which customs should become part of the law of England.

The permanent stamp of Mansfield upon Anglo-American law lies in the commercial field. When he assumed office in 1756 English law was land-centred and landbound in outlook and entrenched professional tradition. Mansfield was a visionary – there is perhaps at least one such judge in each century in England. In the seventeenth century it was Coke, in the nineteenth century it was to be Blackburn and Jessel (the two were perhaps of equal distinction in common law and equity respectively) and in the twentieth century Atkin and Denning, sharing equal honours. Mansfield saw beyond the narrow confine and sought to follow the continental experience of a specialized body of rules for commerce

and banking.

He was only overruled six times in thirty years as Lord Chief Justice, from 1756 to 1788. His pet hobbyhorse was the doctrine of consideration in contract (or the lack of it). He preferred the idea that contracts should be enforced because of moral obligation, an idea which we are bound to say finds twentieth century echoes in Lord Denning's ideas of promissory estoppel. This idea of Mansfield's was not irretrievably lost until the case of *Eastwood v Kenyon* in 1840.

Lord Blackburn Colin, Lord Blackburn (1813–96) spanned the nineteenth century as Mansfield spanned the second half of the eighteenth. A very learned lawyer and a disciple of Roman principles, he was also a great authority on the common law. Perhaps most law students will remember him for defining what was virtually a new tort in the case of *Rylands v Fletcher* in 1868. Certainly by that time he was sure enough of his status and authority to break with old rules and declare new ones, rather like Lord Denning in our own day. His celebrated judgment in *Taylor v Caldwell* (1863) which greatly eased the severe principle of contract known as the rule in *Paradine v Jane* (1647) was based very largely on Roman doctrines. He considered too that foreign jurists could be treated as authorities and referred to Pothier with great respect in the House of Lords in the case of *McClean v Clydesdale Banking Co* in 1883.

Sir George Jessel (1824–83) was Blackburn's opposite number in the courts of equity. He was so authoritative that, according to Professor Heuston, he was treated as an authority in his own day, in the sort of reverential way usually only accorded to the dead. In *Hammerton v Henry* (1876) he declared: 'There is no such thing as law which is uncertain – the notion of law means a certain rule of some kind ... the reason and spirit of cases make law, not the letter of particular precedents'. This is in the true tradition of equity, and Jessel affirmed these points in terms of which Lord Mansfield would have heartily approved.

An abiding difficulty has been the role of the judges as interpreters of Acts of Parliament and statutory instruments. These should of course be clear, but they are not always so. In considering the interpretation of statutes, Blackburn said, in *Young v Leamington Spa* (1883), 'We ought, in general, in construing an Act of Parliament to assume that the Legislature know the existing state of the law'. This more than faintly damning statement was perhaps partly responsible for the passing of the Interpretation Act in 1889.

Lord Atkin Two judges dominate the twentieth century, Lord Atkin and Lord Denning. James Richard, Baron Atkin, was born in Brisbane in 1867 and died in 1944. He was one of those figures like Cardinal Manning, who suddenly and perhaps rather unexpectedly, display a more liberal and reforming temperament the nearer they approach old age. Atkin was a great defining judge. It was he who enunciated the 'neighbour' principle in *Donoghue v Stevenson* in 1932, the case which finally established negligence as an independent tort, soon to become the most important of all torts. Equally intriguing (to those salacious enough to consider them) are those stories behind the great definition which have become part of legal lore. It is said that Atkin was staying in Sussex while working on the theme of his great judgment and went into Brighton on the weekend to carry out what we should now call a spot questionnaire on what the average or reasonable man thought about negligence. Unfortunately he included in his 'sample' a courting couple who denounced him to the police as a Peeping Tom. He was arrested and asked for his identity. On saying that he was a Lord of Appeal, the police were, perhaps naturally, sceptical and kept him in a cell until his identity was finally established by a distraught relative. Meanwhile, Lord Atkin, phlegmatic and stoical to the end, had used the time in the cell to write his judgment and was most grateful to the police.

Whatever the truth of the matter it is a delicious piece of legal lore as to how a great and very human judge came to write a very great judgment. Such stories are an aspect of law, as they are of other subjects, which cannot be entirely ignored, and, although they may be as apocryphal as the real identity of the snail in the ginger beer bottle, they assume a certain relevance in their own right.

Lord Denning Alfred Thompson, Baron Denning was born in 1899. His erudition has been matched only by his extraordinary humility and self-effacement. As the Master of the Rolls, he is the chief justice of the civil side of the Court of Appeal, and has held that office since 1962. Lord Denning demoted himself voluntarily from the House of Lords to this office in unprecedented fashion. He was demoted because, in the words of David Wyn Williams, in *The Spectator* (February 1, 1975) 'he wanted the power rather than the glory'. This is not in any way to gainsay his humility. He feels he is a torch-bearer and a visionary, which he is, but that he is only such to give justice to all who seek it, and that justice shall not be defeated because of technical rules. Like Mansfield and Jessel before him, it is the spirit and not the letter of the law which must prevail. Two of his judgments, which are legion in their importance and quotability, must suffice here to illustrate his mind. On May 20, 1975, Lord Denning gave judgment in favour of Miss Doris Nellor, aged 81, who had fought a seven-year legal battle to stop New Windsor Corporation building a multi-storey car park on Bachelor's Acre, a tarmac open space in the centre of Windsor. Speaking of the custom of preserving village greens, Lord Denning said:

The result is that in many village greens no one knows who is the owner of the land. But everyone knows that the villagers have a right to play games on it. If anyone should disturb or hinder the exercise of that right any one of the inhabitants can sue to enforce the right of all. And such a right, once acquired by custom, cannot be lost by disuse or abandonment. It can only be abolished or extinguished by Act of Parliament. And no statute can take away that right by a side wind.

Again, in 1975, in a very different case (*Schorsh Meier v Hennin*) Lord Denning insisted that the common law could not defeat itself by being so firmly entrenched that it could not change, no matter how old any rule was. He ruled that, because of the United Kingdom's commitment to the Treaty of Rome, a 350 year-old rule that payment of a High Court judgment must be in sterling should be overruled.

Thus, with these cases, one on ancient custom, and one on the laws of the European Economic Community, the history of English law seems to have come full circle. It has come from sources many and varied. It has distinguished between civil and criminal law by applying different sanctions and remedies and bringing the cases to court by different procedures, although an overlap area is recognized. Many men have contributed to it, the aristocrat and the commoner. Nor should we forget the role in its development played by some of our political rulers: Henry I, known as the lawgiver; Edward I, known as the English Justinian; Henry VIII, who reformed as well as destroyed; and James I, who was far more than the pedant of popular legend; and of course Cromwell, thundering in his bewildered way for law reform.

The common thread which seems to run through every century of English law is that it is based upon the Judaeo-Christian ethic, even though the English could not, even by their best friends, really be described as a religious people. We may perhaps reflect on the words of Lord Denning, who, in a radio conversation with Lord Scarman, in March 1977, said 'without religion there is no morality, and without morality there is no law'.

Below: The Central Criminal Court, Old Bailey, from a 19th century engraving. Old Bailey is the name of the street in which the Court building stood and from which it has now taken its name

Bottom: Lord Rawlinson, dressed in the wig and gown of a Queen's Counsel

2 THE LEGAL PROFESSIONS

The Administration of the Bar

Lord Rawlinson

Origins of the Bar The division of the English legal profession into two branches, barristers and solicitors, is very old. It already existed in 1292 when an Ordinance of Edward I instructed the judges to appoint a certain number of attorneys and apprentices to serve the courts. The attorneys were the forerunners of the modern solicitors, while the apprentices-at-law (*apprenticii-ad-legem*) evolved into the modern barristers. There was also at that time, and for many centuries afterwards, a senior rank of lawyer, a serjeant-at-law (from the Latin *serviens-ad-legem*, servant of the law). The serjeants were the principal advocates and it was from their ranks only that the common law judges were appointed. It was the ambition of every apprentice eventually to be appointed a serjeant by the Crown.

With the growth of the legal profession in the late thirteenth and fourteenth centuries there grew up on the western outskirts of the City of London voluntary associations of practising lawyers and students. The associations centred on various Inns (Latin *hospitia*) which meant a town house, or mansion, and in particular a mansion used as a hostel for students. The most important of these associations were the four Inns of Court, the Honourable Societies of Lincoln's Inn, Inner Temple, Middle Temple, and Gray's Inn.

The serjeants also had an Inn. This was located at three different places in the course of history – near Holborn Circus, in Chancery Lane, and in Fleet Street. An apprentice, or a barrister as he came to be called in the sixteenth century, on being appointed a serjeant left his Inn of Court and joined Serjeant's Inn where he remained for the rest of his life, whether practising at the Bar or being appointed a judge in one of the courts of common law. No more serjeants were appointed after 1875. The existing serjeants sold their Inn and returned to the Inns whence they had started their careers. Thus the Inns today have many members who are judges as well as barristers.

The precise origins of the Inns are lost in the mists of history, but all four were in existence in the latter half of the fourteenth century. The records of Lincoln's Inn, the Black Books, run continuously from 1422 to the present day. No charter, statute, or other written authority for the foundation of any of the Inns exists, but in 1608 James I granted to the Inner Temple and the Middle Temple jointly in fee simple the land which they had occupied as tenants for 250 years previously. This royal charter makes it clear that all four Inns are established for the same purpose and are of equal status. The two Temples are described as 'two out of those four colleges, the most famous in all Europe, as always abounding with persons devoted to the study of the aforesaid laws and experienced therein'.

The Inns of Court The four Inns of Court have the exclusive right, deriving from the authority of the judges, of calling persons to the Bar, thereby granting them rights of audience in all courts, and also the right to exercise discipline over members of the Bar. Thus the education of students and the maintenance of standards of professional conduct have always been among the most important of the Inns' functions. They also own extensive property in the centre of London, including their halls, libraries, other communal facilities, and extensive buildings, a large proportion of which is let to barristers as professional chambers.

Each Inn has three classes of members: students, barristers, and benchers, or Masters of the Bench, who form the governing body. There are about 70 to 100 benchers in each Inn, vacancies being filled by election by the existing members of the Bench. The benchers appoint one of their number to be Treasurer, or head of the Inn, each year. Each Inn has also a permanent administrative staff under an Under-Treasurer or Sub-Treasurer.

A barrister's Inn is his professional home throughout his career. He joins it as a student, is called to the Bar by its Treasurer, and remains a member whether he practices at the Bar or goes into another walk of life or is appointed a judge. For the rest of his life he can lunch or dine in the Hall with his fellow members, use the library and gardens, and join in the social life of the Inn.

The Barrister's Work The Bar of England and Wales is not a large profession. In 1977 there were about 4,000 barristers in practice, compared with about 34,000 solicitors. But it was twice the size it was twenty years previously. Such a rapid expansion has meant that the Bar of today is a very young Bar. In 1977 over half the members were of no more than ten years' call.

The Bar is the specialist branch of the legal profession. Barristers are principally the corps of advocates. They are 'lawyers' lawyers' whose services are not available directly to members of the public but only through the

THE MARCH PAST

THE ROLL CALL

THE CALL PARTY

A Dinner of the Senate of the Inns of Court
and the Bar held in Middle Temple Hall in the
presence of the Queen and the Duke of Edinburgh

Mr Kenneth Chard, in full regalia, when he was Head Porter, in Gray's Inn Hall

intervention of a solicitor. The layman with a legal problem seeks the advice of a solicitor who in nearly all cases can give him the advice or carry out the services he needs. Moreover, if it is a question of representing him in minor matters in the lower courts, the county courts or the magistrates' courts, the solicitor can do this also. But if there is a particularly difficult problem the solicitor will recommend his client to 'take counsel's opinion' and the problem will then be sent by the solicitor to a barrister specialising in the branch of the law concerned for his advice. Similarly if the client has to be represented in court (other than in minor matters in an inferior court) the solicitor will instruct a barrister to undertake the case. When it is necessary for the barrister to have a conference with the client, the solicitor will accompany the client to the barrister's chambers.

All practising barristers are required to have chambers and a clerk. In London, where about two-thirds of the Bar practise, the chambers are almost exclusively in the Inns of Court, and there are local Bars in the major provincial cities, usually grouped in buildings near the law courts. The average size of a set of chambers is now thirteen barristers. At the head will normally be a Queen's Counsel of some seniority who, although he is in no way the employer of the other members of chambers, is a person of considerable influence and authority. By the rules of their profession barristers must be independent practitioners and may not enter into partnership or into a contract of employment with other barristers.

Each member of the chambers is quite independent, earning his own individual fees and paying his own way. It is an exacting but an exciting life.

About one in ten practising barristers is a Queen's Counsel. This does not denote any special relationship with the Crown or with the state. It is merely the title of the senior rank in the profession. All barristers who are not Queen's Counsel are known as 'juniors' whatever their age. Queen's Counsel are instructed in the more difficult cases where particular specialist knowledge of the law involved and a high skill of advocacy are required. A Queen's Counsel normally works only with a junior, whom he is said to 'lead' in the case and who can take on the simpler aspects of the work. A Queen's Counsel is known colloquially as a 'silk' because he is entitled to wear a silk gown instead of the stuff one worn by a junior. A barrister who has succeeded in building up a large practice in about fifteen years will probably apply 'to take silk' to the Lord Chancellor, who advises the Queen on who should be granted it. The list is published on Maundy Thursday every year. Nowadays, there are usually about thirty names on it, which is about a third as many as have applied.

There are of course many people who have been called to the Bar but are not practising barristers. Apart from the enormous number who came from other Commonwealth countries and have gone home to practise after being called to the Bar in London, there are an unknown number of people resident in this country who are entitled to call themselves barristers and are members of an Inn of Court but have no right to appear in court or to give legal advice to the public. There is a distinction between a 'practising barrister', who may do those things, and a 'non-practising barrister', who may not. Quite a number of the latter do in fact use their qualification as a barrister as salaried employees in the legal departments of commercial concerns, or in the Civil Service or local government. These three groups of employed barristers have their own professional bodies, whose nominees are represented on the Senate and Bar Council.

The Independent Champion How is a practising barrister distinguised from a non-practising one? The short answer is that the former makes practice at the Bar his primary occupation and conducts his practice from chambers with a clerk. The second requirement may seem at first sight to be curious, but it is one of the requirements laid down by the Bar Council in order to maintain the independence and the standards of the profession. For the practising barrister is a person with legal knowledge and skills who is prepared to, and indeed must, put his or her abilities at the disposal of any member of the public who requires them. This is what the Bar calls 'the cab-rank principle'. Clearly the principle has to be circumscribed. The matter in which the client needs the services of the barrister must be in a field of law in which he holds himself out to practise. There would be little advantage to anyone if a barrister expert in the law of probate were compelled to defend in the Crown Court a man accused of murder. Again, a proper fee must be offered. In these days of legal aid, finding the fee is not the problem it once was.

The essential feature of the cab-rank principle is that the Bar should always be able to provide a champion to fight the cause of any man or woman, however humble or however important, whose rights, liberty or property are threatened. This principle applies both in criminal matters, when society is accusing one of its members of breaking a law considered necessary for civilised living; or in civil disputes, when one party alleges that another has caused him an injury, broken a contract with him, or done that which gives rise to a legal action. Although it is just as important in a country in which the rule of law is to prevail that the State or great corporate organisations should have their case adequately presented as it is that that the individual should not be illegally crushed, it is in fact in cases where the individual is up against the State or other large impersonal organisation that the duty of the advocate is seen at its clearest.

The Senate and the Bar Council Although similar in structure, function, and size, the Inns did not take any steps to act in concert until the middle of the nineteenth century. Education had traditionally been carried on in the halls of the Inns, where the students, along with other members, took their meals in common. A senior member of the Inn would be appointed 'reader' to be responsible for the training of the young. This training

consisted in part of mock trials, or moots. There were no examinations, call to the Bar being at the discretion of the Bench. Only in 1852 did the Inns jointly set up the Council of Legal Education, which instituted formal lectures and examinations for Bar students, although the latter did not become compulsory until 1872. In 1894 there was a further measure of co-operation with the establishment of a joint standing committee to examine and make recommendations upon matters of common concern, but the committee had no real power. In 1965 there was created a Senate of the Four Inns of Court to which were delegated executive powers in certain fields including discipline, educational policy and student welfare.

Although every barrister has always belonged to one or other of the Inns of Court, the Bar as a body was slow to set up its own representative institutions. Until the end of the nineteenth century the only representative organisations of barristers were the messes attached to the circuits into which England and Wales were divided for judicial purposes. In 1883 in response to a petition presented to him the Attorney-General called a meeting of the Bar (one thousand attended), and a Bar Committee was set up. This in turn was replaced in 1895 by a General Council of the Bar, with somewhat wider functions, though a proposal that it should concern itself with the enforcement of professional discipline was successfully resisted by the Inns. The Inns made a financial contribution to the new Council on the understanding

that it would not 'interfere with the property, jurisdiction, powers or privileges of the Inns'. Although it possessed no disciplinary powers the rulings of the new General Council of the Bar on matters of professional conduct were in fact accepted by the Bar in general. When the Senate of the Four Inns of Court was set up in 1966 the Bar Council was given representation on it.

These limited arrangements were not wholly satisfactory for there was overlapping of functions between the Senate and the Council. So a constitution was evolved for a new central governing body of the profession to be known as the Senate of the Inns of Court and the Bar. This new Senate took over from both the previous Senate and the General Council of the Bar on July 27, 1974.

The Senate as now constituted is made up essentially of (a) representatives appointed by the Benches of the Inns, and (b) representatives elected by the Bar. The Bar representatives also constitute an autonomous Bar Council which is not subject to directions from the Senate.

The Senate elects a President, Chairman, Vice-Chairman, and Treasurer. The Chairman is also Chairman of the Bar Council and when acting in that capacity he is known as Chairman of the Bar.

The work of the Senate is supervised by the following committees: Executive, Finance, Law Reform, Planning, Accommodation, Libraries, Trust Funds. The Council of Legal Education, which controls the Bar examinations and runs the Inns of Court School of Law, is a committee of the Senate.

The work of the Bar Council is supervised by the following committees: Bar, Professional Conduct, International Relations, Fees and Legal Aid, Young Barristers, Taxation and Retirement Benefits. The Bar Council and its committees are concerned with representing the Bar's interests vis-à-vis Government departments, the solicitors' branch of the profession, the judiciary, foreign Bars and others outside the profession. The constitution charges the Bar Council generally with the function of maintaining the standards, honour and independence of the Bar and promoting, preserving, and improving its services.

The Senate employs a Secretary and other administrative staff with offices in Gray's Inn. The services of the secretariat are available to the Senate and the Bar Council and their committees and to the Inns.

Professional Conduct and Discipline One of the most important duties of the Senate and the Bar Council is the maintenance of high standards of professional conduct. There is no comprehensive written code of conduct for a barrister, but there is a generally accepted tradition of ethical behaviour and sets of rules on various aspects of practice. The establishment and the amendment of rules of conduct and etiquette are in the hands of the Bar itself acting through the Professional Conduct Committee, whose decisions are subject to approval by the Bar Council. The Professional Conduct Committee has a triple function. First, it gives rulings on what it thinks is the correct conduct of a barrister in certain

circumstances, either in response to particular questions put up by barristers or on matters which it considers need to be regulated. Secondly, it investigates complaints of misconduct made against barristers. If after examination there appears to be a prima facie case of misconduct the Committee may direct that the complaint shall form the subject of a charge before a disciplinary tribunal, or, in minor cases, the Chairman of the Committee may admonish the culprit. Thirdly, in cases of incompetence or breach of professional etiquette falling in either event short of misconduct the Committee may arrange for appropriate advice to be given to the barrister concerned. The Professional Conduct Committee has a lay representative as one of its members.

Disciplinary powers over barristers are, by resolution of the judges and with the concurrence of the Inns, exercised in accordance with the Senate regulations. A charge of professional misconduct against a barrister is heard by a disciplinary tribunal appointed by the President of the Senate. A tribunal consists of not less than five nor more than seven persons, one of whom must be a lay representative and one may be a judge, the remainder being barristers. The hearing is in private unless the Chairman, at the request of the accused, directs that it be in public. The accused may, if he wishes, be represented by counsel. A barrister found guilty of misconduct may be sentenced to be disbarred, suspended from practice for a period, ordered to repay or forego fees, or reprimanded. A sentence of disbarment or suspension must be published within the profession and to the press, and a lesser sentence may be so published.

A barrister who has been found guilty by a tribunal may appeal against finding or sentence to the judges. He does this by petitioning the Lord Chancellor to appoint High Court judges as 'visitors' to his Inn; it is normal for three judges to be so appointed to hear the appeal.

A Great and Noble Calling A young man or woman coming to the Bar will not find the path to success easy. Advocacy is a talent as well as a skill, and it is rarely very speedily learnt. It calls for courage, judgment, sensibility, application – and, it has been said, an excellent digestion! It is one of the few callings left wherein a man or woman throughout their career rests solely upon their own independent efforts. No one, at any time, is the barrister's master once he or she begins to practise. The barrister must ever maintain and demonstrate rare integrity, respectful to the court, but servant to no one.

A great nineteenth century lawyer described the Bar as 'a great and noble calling ... upon which depend in no small degree the rights and liberties both of individuals and nations. To elicit truth by intellectual struggle and conflict, to supply just weights and balances to the scales of justice by laying before justice all the considerations on every side of every question that ought to weigh; to stand forward for the weak, the miserable, the degraded, and even the guilty; and on great occasions, when public liberties are in question, to assert the same right, the privilege, and duty of free, undaunted, open speaking of truth – that is the right, that is the duty, that is the privilege of our profession'.

THE BAR

Life in Chambers

Nigel Pascoe

7.15 am Paddington. £1 to park the car and the best part of £10 for Taunton or Bristol.

'*The Times*, please ... thank you'. Platform 3.

'Morning ... excuse me, is anyone sitting here for breakfast?'

No, nothing in the Law Reports this morning but remember to check Tuesday's *Times* for identification case later this week. See that Richard Roe QC has made the circuit bench ... that will shake a few timorous solicitors in East Anglia. Breakfast over, check cross-examination of last witness last night ... prepare the next one. Flag the two authorities for the submission ... prepare draft notes for tomorrow's final speech.

'Will you share a taxi?' 'No need, my solicitor's meeting me at the station. Come on, I'll fix you a lift.' 10 o'clock, through the court door, chorus of 'Morning sir' from friendly, well-fed police officers and ageing ushers. Young articled clerk already in the robing room with a further proof and the dread news that 'the defendant would like a word with you before giving evidence.'

Morning in court, its custom never staled by infinite variety. Judge a little tetchy this morning? 'You know, Mr X, that question was rather clumsily phrased.' 12.58 pm. 'Is that a convenient moment' ... rise ... bow ... out ... race for the telephone to ring chambers. 'John ... part heard ... bound to go into Thursday unless the submission succeeds ... no, it won't. But I'll ring at close of play. Mr Emmett? What does he want? John, I finished those papers on Monday. Yes. I put them out for typing. Look just tell him very politely they're on their way, will you? OK. Oh, and John, there's a set of papers on my desk for Carters. They want an advice quickly on a landlord and tenant issue. Well ask my pupil to have a look at it will you? Many thanks.' Bye.

'Ham salad please. That's very kind of you, I'll have a bitter lemon. Now look David, can't we agree the next witness? I don't really want him. And he doesn't add anything to your case. Incidentally I have a couple of authorities for my submission ... they're in court ... by all means have a look. What do you mean? Of course I'm going to submit! You never know with Tommy ... it might come off.'

A long, hot afternoon. The prosecution close their case at 3.30 pm. 'Your Honour there is a matter of law ... it might take a few minutes ... ' Suddenly, as the argument takes shape on your feet the marvellously exhilarating feeling that he's coming round ... The infinite satisfaction of realising that your opponent just isn't on top of your authorities and that the evidence really is deficient ... Suddenly, 'Anything more you want to say Mr X ... I accede to the defence submission ... it seems to me I am bound by the Court of Appeal decision in ...... bring the jury back please.'

'John? We're out! Look, I can do that death by danger tomorrow at the Bailey. Oh, it's out. Where? Where's that? Norfolk! Oh I see, paid brief before the justices.

Perfectly alright. Well done John. Yes – any messages, on my desk. Goodnight.'

Return train. Cup of tea. In on time. *Evening Standard*. Traffic already streaming out of London and hold up against the traffic at Hyde Park Corner. Chambers, 7.00 pm. Check post, must remember to contact my spondee to dine in Hall ... thought I'd paid that subscription ... three sets of papers ... correct typing ... dictate one opinion ... check tomorrow's brief has no law in it – thank goodness, no. Leave Chambers 7.45 ... home 8.20. 'Sorry, darling – I couldn't get away before.'

Dinner. Tomorrow's brief. Asleep by 12.00.

And so on, day after day for the circuiteers. Not surprisingly more and more are leaving the outer suburbs of London to live on circuit. Provincial chambers are finding an ever increasing number of desperate young men knocking on their doors anxious for a home. But of course that is not the whole picture. Barristers without circuit practices for the most part are still centred in London. It is not possible to describe a typical set of chambers to an outsider for they will vary enormously, with the personality of the head of chambers, the chief clerk and of course the type of work. But the life of a London practitioner, leaving aside for a moment his particular speciality, has a number of common characteristics which have not varied for centuries. He needs, for example, the camaraderie of chambers not simply as a diversion from papers but to perform more effectively as a lawyer. Thus coffee at 11.00 at the Temple Table is not simply a welcome chance for legal gossip but an opportunity to pick the brains of a fellow member of chambers. Barristers regularly wander round their chambers in the late afternoon, trying out, for example, a difficult quantum on a number of others. 'Edward, you're usually pretty reliable ... age 42, multiple injuries, including two crushed vertebrae and a broken thigh, ... four months in hospital ... 15% disability ... ' At lunch of course a further chance to talk shop, yet it is the attractions of contemporary politics which often then excite that characteristically cynical humour that the Bar possesses in abundance.

Afterwards, if the weather is fine, a stroll perhaps in one of the most peaceful parts of London, say Gray's Inn or the Inner Temple Gardens. At the end of the day, for some, a few minutes over a glass of wine in El Vino's or The Devereux.

Within that framework a great deal of work can be done nevertheless. It is still probably true that a leading junior in his early forties works harder than virtually any other member of the community, although the joint depredations of the Inland Revenue and rising legal expenses have taken a more than healthy toll. At the other end of the ladder, young barristers still endure the uncertainty of those last months of pupillage, uncertain whether there will be a place in those chambers at its end. Sadly, too often there is not.

It would be quite wrong to assume that the Bar does not care about the increasing problem of accommodation. Desperate efforts are being made to try to find homes for an increasing pool of young men anxious to run the risks which have always been inherent in the career. Never perhaps has there been a greater need for a trained body of professional advocates, even if they fear to drown in the new oceans of statute which flow unchecked on the doors of the lawyer. I have sought to capture a little of the flavour of this most rewarding of occupations. A stranger who breaks through the barrier will find as ever enormous good humour, fellowship and the unending fascination of forensic encounter. He will learn that barristers have gas bills as large as any other member of the community and that they are increasingly concerned with the need to cut their expenses and retain their standards. He will find that politically they are surprisingly diverse and yet united in condemnation of the sharp, the rude or the pretentious. He will note with wry pleasure the genuflections towards the Bench and the more candid opinions after court hours. He may, as he wanders down Middle Temple Lane or across the Temple courtyard towards King's Bench Walk, understand a little of the corporate life which survives surprisingly well, and that despite the rising costs of everything from wig and gown to red tape. Perhaps he will visit the best law libraries in the world or, with a spare evening, try the different delights of the Bar Musical or Bar Theatrical Society. And as he leaves perhaps a 20th century production of *Twelfth Night* again in Middle Temple Hall, he may be surprised at the number of lights still burning about the Temple. Men and women of all ages are earning their living the hard way. For my part, I would not change it for a king's ransom.

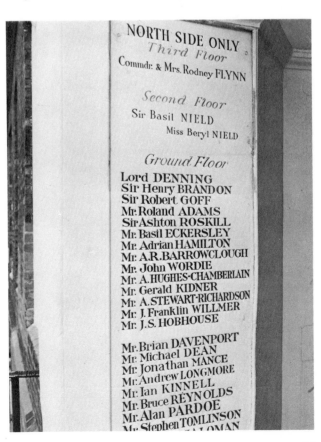

North Side Only
Third Floor
Commdr. & Mrs. Rodney FLYNN

Second Floor
Sir Basil NIELD
Miss Beryl NIELD

Ground Floor
Lord DENNING
Sir Henry BRANDON
Sir Robert GOFF
Mr. Roland ADAMS
Sir Ashton ROSKILL
Mr. Basil ECKERSLEY
Mr. Adrian HAMILTON
Mr. A.R. BARROWCLOUGH
Mr. John WORDIE
Mr. A. HUGHES-CHAMBERLAIN
Mr. Gerald KIDNER
Mr. A. STEWART-RICHARDSON
Mr. J. Franklin WILLMER
Mr. J.S. HOBHOUSE

Mr. Brian DAVENPORT
Mr. Michael DEAN
Mr. Jonathan MANCE
Mr. Andrew LONGMORE
Mr. Ian KINNELL
Mr. Bruce REYNOLDS
Mr. Alan PARDOE
Mr. Stephen TOMLINSON

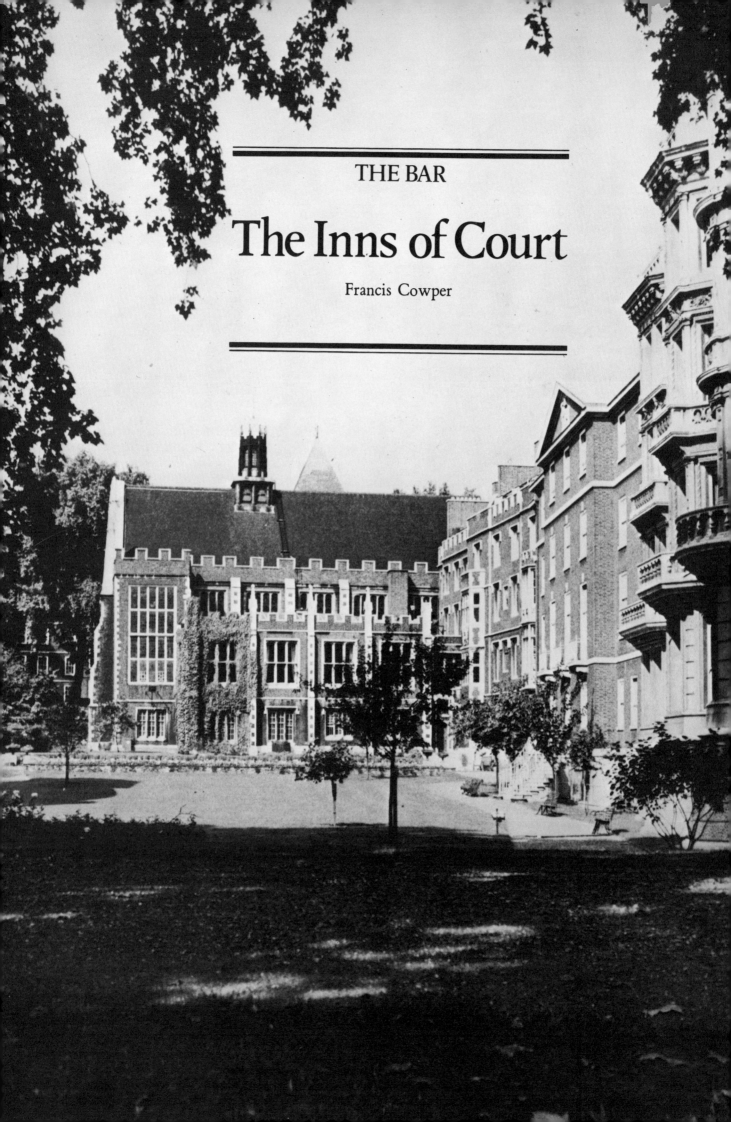

THE BAR

The Inns of Court

Francis Cowper

The Inns of Court are unique. They are not merely schools of law. They are not merely lawyers' trade unions. They are not merely convivial social clubs. But they blend all three functions in the recognition that their members should be whole men, not just legal technicians, on the one hand, or hunters of fees and full employment, on the other.

No one knows their origin. Some guesses place it in Edward I's designs to stabilize the legal profession in the late 13th century. Certainly they were in existence by the mid 14th century. Their earliest extant records are those of Lincoln's Inn commencing in 1422, the year of the death of Henry V. One persuasive conjecture as to their original purpose was that bodies of lawyers, coming to London for the then relatively short law terms, took over a number of large houses as residential clubs which were used during the law vacations for the instruction of pupils. It may be so. Certainly by the 15th century a whole legal quarter had grown up along the suburban boundary between the commercial City of London and the royal City of Westminster where the judges sat in the King's palace.

Nor were Lincoln's Inn, the Inner Temple, the Middle Temple and Gray's Inn the only institutions of their kind. At the height of their development they formed the centre of an integrated legal profession, a network of interrelated confraternities, with a dozen Inns of Chancery below them and the two Serjeants' Inns above. The Inns of Chancery, Staple Inn, Barnard's Inn, Clifford's Inn, Clements Inn, New Inn and the rest, subordinate to the Inns of Court, but internally autonomous, were in the nature of preparatory colleges from which transfer to an Inn of Court was a natural transition. To the Serjeants' Inns migrated the men who accepted the degree of serjeant-at-law, *serviens ad legem*, leaders of the Bar ripe for promotion to the common law Bench. Nothing in English institutions is ever completely tidy and the distinction between the barrister, the specialist advocate, on the one hand, and the attorney or solicitor, the legal man of business and day to day adviser of his clients, on the other, was slow in defining itself, but for general purposes one may say that the Inns of Chancery came to do for attorneys and solicitors what the Inns of Court did for the Bar.

The system admirably exemplified the English genius for effective practical improvisation rather than long term planning dependent upon a whole complex of assumptions and estimates of future contingencies and imponderables. Over the centuries the Inns of Court have adapted themselves to the changing conditions of society. Until the Civil War in the 17th century the instruction given in the Inns was almost wholly oral. The qualification to sit on the governing body of an Inn of Court was to hold one of the biannual Readings, courses of lectures onto which were grafted discussions, moots, or mock trials, and more informal bolts or siftings of doubtful points of law. Members of the Inn at all levels were expected to participate, the more senior assisting in the instruction of their juniors.

The Inns were residential colleges, communities living under scholastic discipline, and the great Hall of each was at once lecture room, dining room, club room, and, on the occasion of festivities like the keeping of Christmas, theatre and ballroom too. Not only prospective professional lawyers became members of the Inns. Many rich young men were entered there to acquire enough law to manage their estates, act as Justices of the Peace or follow employment in the public service. They were expected to acquire not only law but also social accomplishments and the Christmas celebrations, which lasted till Candlemass on February 2nd, often centred round a mock prince and his court, serving the double purpose of inculcating courtly and diplomatic etiquette and providing an occasion for broad fun in topical satire and parody. When a Lord of Misrule took over, the excesses of the students' rags often gave grave concern to the governing Benchers.

The Civil War in the 17th century broke the continuity of the old order and attempts to reestablish it after the King's Restoration in 1660 gradually faded away. The framework of readings and moots disintegrated. The Inns of Court ceased to be residential colleges, and only dining in Hall as a qualification for call to the Bar carried on the tradition of the old community spirit. Printed books were now multiplied and a student, no longer depending on lecturers, read for the Bar. Legal education went underground and private pupillage became the accepted method of instruction. Throughout the 18th century the Inns of Chancery were steadily losing their grip on the professional lives of the attorneys and solicitors and becoming mere dining clubs, until in the 1830's the Law Society arose to take over their former functions, leaving them to wither away in total inutility. In particular the Law Society put professional qualification on the firm footing of those written examinations in which the pragmatic Victorians had so much faith.

Meanwhile the Inns of Court pursued their leisurely, gentlemanly way, producing an able and incorrupt Bar and, through it, an able and incorrupt, if somewhat Olympian, Bench. But the earnest, tidy, reformist spirit of the times and the quickening tempo of life in an increasingly industrialised nation could scarcely be expected to leave alone those enchanted islands of quiet in the heart of the modern whirlwind. Soon after the middle of the century examinations for call to the Bar were gradually introduced. In the 1870's the entire court system was remodelled and the serjeants-at-law, long professionally ailing and losing ground to the Queen's Counsel, were shorn of all their privileges. Leaving behind only the memory of their separate Inns, they returned, each man, to his original Inn of Court.

Such being the collective background of the Inns of Court, what of their individual developments? The Temples, we know, take their name from the Knights Templar, the monastic military Order which, after being the backbone of the crusading armies in the Holy Land, fell foul of the French king and, on his instigation, was suppressed by papal authority in the early 14th century. Soon afterwards the lawyers moved into their London house beside the Thames. Whether Lincoln's Inn, halfway up Chancery Lane, takes its name from

Henry de Lacy, Earl of Lincoln, or from a certain Serjeant Lincoln the learned have not finally made up their minds. Gray's Inn, formerly the manor house of Purpoole, is called after the Lords de Gray of Wilton. But the actual foundations of the Inns as legal societies remain veiled in the mists of history.

The history of the Inns is written in their stones and bricks, recording a living and unbroken continuity – the original Round Church of the Templars, where the worn and battered effigies of the Knights lie between time and eternity; the little 15th century Hall of Lincoln's Inn, where Sir Thomas More learnt the law; the sober yet exuberant Elizabethan Hall of the Middle Temple; the great green tree shaded expanses of the Walks of Gray's Inn, as the 18th century laid them out behind their tall graceful iron gates; the 19th and 20th century chambers added here and there, some better, some worse, reflecting the fluctuating tastes of generations of Benchers. Sometimes an influential and modernising Bencher like Lord Grimthorpe of Lincoln's Inn in the late 19th century would be tearing down and replacing old buildings in the name of sound structural policy and good economics. After devastation in the bombardments during the last war there was a frenzy of wholesale reconstruction. In his later years Charles Lamb, born in Crown Office Row in the Inner Temple, was lamenting the prosaic utilitarian alterations which had eroded the stately collegiate atmosphere of the Inns of his 18th century childhood when the scarcely trade-polluted waters of the Thames touched the gardens. Now the river is pushed back beyond the great Embankment loud with the ceaseless discordant din of mechanical traffic flow. Yet, subject as they are, like all living things, to successive changes and though the outer world besieges them, the Inns have still remained recognisably themselves, each with its own distinct and unduplicated personality.

The Inns still train the Bar of England, now by providing a specialist finish to that knowledge of the law which the student has acquired at a university or elsewhere. By requiring him to dine in Hall and encouraging him to participate in after dinner moots, they induct him into the corporate spirit of the profession. They provide the libraries which he shares with the practising members of the Bar. They help the student to find men who will accept him as a pupil and impart to him the practical knowledge of court work without which even the most meticulous mastery of legal theory is mere bookworm stuff.

For the London based practitioner the Inns provide the working chambers where the Bar carry on their profession. They provide lunches in their Halls where barristers, coming straight from court or from their desks, and students from lecture rooms and libraries meet and mix at the long refectory tables. During the dining terms the barristers, as well as the students, are encouraged to dine in Hall promoting the constant habit of association which personalises the Bar and promotes a sense of corporate unity. The two Temples share the Temple Church. Lincoln's Inn and Gray's Inn each has its Chapel. Bar and students share in common activities – debates, lectures, concerts, theatricals, or tennis and croquet in the gardens.

Lincoln's Inn Each Inn has its own separate and distinct personality. Thus two historical accidents have especially influenced the development of Lincoln's Inn. First, in 1734, Lord Chancellor Talbot established his court at the upper end of its Hall, leaving only the lower part for dining and the other purposes of the Inn's communal life. Thereafter until the new Law Courts were opened in 1882 the Chancery judges sat within the Inn for, as the work of the Court increased and Vice-Chancellors were appointed to assist the Lord Chancellor, court rooms were erected close to the Hall to accommodate them. This meant that the Inn became a magnet for Chancery practitioners who moved in the rarified atmosphere of equity, that juster sort of justice, so much more esoteric than the rough and tumble practice of the common law. In the first chapter of *Bleak House*, with the Lord Chancellor sitting in the old Hall in the midst of a London fog, Dickens draws a remarkable picture of the mystique of equity practice moving in a learned labyrinth of trusts, settlements of great estates and the custody of infants, the Lord Chancellor's wards of court. The presence of so many learned men practising so refined and complex an art imparted to the Inn an atmosphere of a certain fastidious superiority, diluted though it was, since no Inn is all of a piece, by more robust matters attached to other branches of the law.

The cramped conditions in the old Hall used partly as a court eventually induced the Inn to build another, and in 1843 a very large and imposing neo-Tudor structure, with a fine library annexed to it, arose on the south-west part of the garden. Queen Victoria opened it in great state and the prestige of the Inn rose correspondingly.

In the first World War two small bombs fell within the precincts of Lincoln's Inn, and made such an impression on its cloistered inmates that two little plaques were set up recording the exact date and time of their explosion and the fact that they shattered windows 'and did other material damage'. In the second World War the Temple and Gray's Inn were devastated but Lincoln's Inn escaped relatively lightly, its two Halls and its library surviving intact. Consequently both in outward appearance and in the continuing rhythm of its life it has changed less than the other three Inns. Its Hall at dinner time, its library, its barristers' common room maintain very perceptibly a collegiate atmosphere and the table talk is excellent and wide ranging. Some of the rituals of dining have fallen into disuse but permission to smoke after dinner is still discreetly given by the lighting of a candle in a tall silver candlestick. One touching custom dates only from the first World War. Ever since then a mess of four has been laid for those who never came back. First it was a very junior mess at the Bar tables. Now, complete with a great silver rose bowl, it is the senior mess.

At dinner there is a very marked distinction between the Benchers, the Bar and the students, particularly noticeable in so large a Hall. Each Bencher entering is

Below: The statue of Sir Thomas More stands over the doorway of a solicitor's office in Carey Street facing the Royal Courts of Justice

Bottom: A corner of the library in Lincoln's Inn reserved for the use of benchers

announced by name and bows to the company standing, who bow in return. The junior Bencher recites the resounding graces before and after the meal. When he has intoned, 'God be praised for all his benefits. God preserve the Queen, the Church and this Honourable Society and grant us his peace evermore', the Benchers retire to their private room, each bowing as he goes. The Bar sitting at tables parallel to that of the Benchers linger over their port and their coffee. The students, distinctly separated from the Bar by the great length of the Hall, linger less long, unless there is a debate, a lecture or a moot.

Gray's Inn Perhaps Gray's Inn presents the greatest contrast to Lincoln's Inn. Sited beyond the northern extremity of Chancery Lane on the far side of Holborn, it was the remotest of all the Inns from the courts sitting at Westminster and, until late in the 17th century, it looked out over open country to the Hampstead and Highgate hills. Its day of glory came under the Tudors, when with new men like Thomas Cromwell, the Cecils and the Bacons, Nicholas and Francis, among its members, it was in the forefront of the changes which obliterated the mediaeval polity. In the Civil War its members were split almost evenly between King and Parliament and in the restless and conspiratorial England of the Restoration it was again divided, but a decline was setting in and it gradually ceased to be a breeding ground for the judiciary. Sir John Holt, Chief Justice under William and Mary, and Lord Raymond, Chief Justice under George I, were indeed trained at Gray's Inn, but as the 18th century progressed it became more and more of a backwater and by the middle of the 19th century its somnolence was almost complete. Calls to the Bar were numbered in ones and twos. When the new Law Courts in the Strand arose between Lincoln's Inn and the Temple the obvious convenience of immediate proximity to them drew the last of the practising Bar to those Inns, so that the chambers in Gray's Inn were abandoned to solicitors and architects.

But at this low ebb an energetic policy of revitalisation turned the tide. Scholarships were established. Moots, long abandoned in all the Inns, were recommenced at Gray's Inn and gradually the membership began to grow again. In its depressed days men without privileges or connections, who had to make their own way by their own efforts, had gravitated to Gray's Inn, men like the future Lord Justice Lush, who started in London practice as a poor solicitor's clerk up from the country and who, after he came to the Bar, won universal esteem for his talents and his character. So now men who had to make their own way still turned to Gray's Inn in increasing numbers. One of them proved to be a meteor whose brilliance illuminated a revolutionary change in its fortunes.

F E Smith, tall, dark, handsome, resolute, a ruthless pursuer of success and glittering prizes in politics as well as at the Bar, imparted to Gray's Inn his own dynamism and self-confidence. He became the first Lord Chancellor bred at Gray's Inn since Francis Bacon. Under his influence at the turn of the century Gray's Inn set its

Below: Two gateways to Lincoln's Inn. Left: A 19th century engraving of the Chancery Lane gate. Right: The main entrance from Lincoln's Inn Fields

Bottom: Gray's Inn Chapel and Hall from Gray's Inn Square

LINCOLN'S INN GATE.

Students queuing on the steps at Gray's Inn before dinner on Call Night

internal affairs in order, and by good housekeeping got the better of servants and tradesmen who had been systematically cheating it.

It was in this period that a providential windfall consolidated the renewed recognition of Gray's Inn. One of its few eminent members in mid Victorian times had been Lord Justice Holker, a Lancashire man who had made a very large fortune at the Bar. He died childless leaving a widow who survived him for many years and after her death there came to the Inn from his estate an inheritance large enough to dispel a very great part of its financial anxieties.

Misfortune and revival had given Gray's Inn a character all its own, a curious combination of tenacity to its traditions, a robust and friendly informality among its members and a more intimate bond between the Benchers, the Bar and the students than was found in the other Inns. The seating at the long refectory tables was by seniority in messes of four and there were complex rules governing the obligations of members to toast one another individually and collectively by messes. Alleged breaches of custom were adjudicated upon by the senior barrister in Hall, 'Mr Senior', after the Benchers had retired to their private room, and the standard fine for a breach was a bottle of port. It was for Mr Senior to give permission to smoke after an application by 'Mr Junior', the junior student, shouted across the Hall, often through a barrage of counter-shouting. Any evening in Hall might produce a spontaneous celebration with songs and recitations of all descriptions and assorted party tricks. There could be no greater contrast with the decorous proceedings at Lincoln's Inn.

The spontaneous spirit of the ordinary members of Gray's Inn found expression in the founding of a magazine, *Graya*, not by the Benchers, but on the initiative of a group of barristers. The first editor was a retired journalist who in middle age was called to the Bar and entered practice. *Graya* still appears.

Till the outbreak of the second World War Gray's Inn was a peaceful harmony of predominantly late 17th and 18th century buildings. In the bombardments it was devastated. But it rose again and the first building to be completed was its well loved Elizabethan Hall, burnt from roof to cellar but now reproduced almost in replica, so that those who knew it of old were conscious of scarcely any difference.

The postwar 'student explosion' brought the young life of the Society into particular prominence and in the 1960's the Benchers, conscious of the problem perplexing the profession in finding chambers for a rapidly expanding Bar initiated a policy of persuading practitioners to return to the Inn. Despite the doubts at first inspired by the distance from the Law Courts more and more groups of barristers, especially the young, are successfully finding their feet in chambers made available to them in the Society.

Inner Temple Court 1796. The Round Church of the Temple in the centre with Farrar's Building on the left and, on the right, the first of a row of shops which ran along the south face of Temple Church

The Temple At the lower end of Chancery Lane, beside the Thames, the twin Temples, the Inner Temple and the Middle Temple, were markedly different from Gray's Inn, perched at the top of Holborn Hill, and Lincoln's Inn, looking westward across Lincoln's Inn Fields, the great square which had once been fields indeed. There is a Georgian openness about Gray's Inn, and Lincoln's Inn too is full of light and air. The Temples, built on a site sloping down to the river, developed as a maze or warren of irregular courts and alleys with the strange Round Church of the Templars at its heart.

No one knows when the two Societies were founded or why precisely they co-existed as separate bodies or when the lawyers started adopting the conventional buildings to their own purposes. We do know that they were there in the time of Chaucer, for one of his Canterbury pilgrims was steward to one of the Temple Societies. Certainly the Inner Temple is 'inner' in the sense that it lies topographically in closer proximity to the Church, though the two Societies share the use of it, the south half of the spacious choir annexed to the Round being assigned to the Inner Temple and the north half to the Middle Temple.

Inner Temple The structure of life in the Inner Temple did not differ in essence from that of the other Inns. The senior members, the practitioners, concerned themselves with the instruction of the students by readings and moots. For their recreations there was the elaborate and extravagant ritual beauty of the masques and revels in the Hall. There was often trouble with turbulent students and sometimes political trouble, as when, during the revolt of the Earl of Essex in 1601, the Inner Temple bought a considerable quantity of arms and armour for the defence of the Queen and afterwards found itself financially embarrassed by the cost. A recurring preoccupation was the City of London's claim to jurisdiction over the Inn, consistently resisted by the members. Twice, when the Lord Mayor, invited to dine in the Hall, had insisted on coming in state, the City Sword, borne aloft as a symbol of his authority, was beaten down by the younger members. When in a frosty January in 1679 a tremendous fire broke out in the heart of the Temple, the Lord Mayor, imagining that now was the time to make good the City's claim, arrived with its Sword erect, the Inner Templars, turning from the blaze, beat it down again. The Mayor sulkily retired to a Fleet Street tavern and revenged himself by turning back the City fire engines.

All but the eastern part of the Temple had escaped the Great Fire of London in 1660; it had stopped short of the Church. Between these and other fires and the need to accommodate an expanding membership there was much building and rebuilding during the 16th and 17th centuries. Hare Court, built on the Outer Garden, commemorates Nicholas Hare, a very active 16th century bencher. In 1609 a light and airy building with an open gallery at the top rose on the site of the present Paper Buildings. Next to it, along the river wall to the east the King's Bench Office was built in 1621. Beyond that, all along the Inn's eastern boundary, King's Bench, Walk arose. The first chambers on the site of the present Mitre Court Buildings did not go up till 1701.

As the old system of legal education withered after the destructive intrusion of the Civil War and the tide of resident student turbulence receded, a cloistered peace came to pervade the Inner Temple. In the late 17th century its terraced garden was filled with jessamins, peaches, nectarines, cherries, plums, laurels, junipers, hollies and bay trees. Behind the angle of King's Bench Walk was a hidden garden for the Benchers with lawns, paths, and a lion's head fountain under a cherry tree. The Niblett Hall built between the wars of 1914 and 1939, now stands on the site.

Of the Inner Temple in the late 18th century we have a perfect picture thanks to the chance that a barrister's clerk produced a son who was a literary genius. Charles Lamb, born in Crown Office Row in 1725, painted the whole setting in describing 'The Old Benchers of the Inner Temple', especially the 'cheerful, liberal look' of the great garden and the surrounding buildings. His lifetime produced several utilitarian disimprovements, but it was the later 19th century that contrived many grim and gloomy inroads among Spenser's 'bricky towers, the which on Thames' broad ages back do ride.'

Buildings in The Inner Temple. From left to right, Harcourt Buildings, Crown Office Row and the Hall. A glimpse can be seen of Elm Court

Paper Buildings burnt down in 1838 (when, it is said, a future judge, after dining in Hall put a lighted candle under his bed in mistake for another object) was replaced in ponderous, monotonous uninspired stone. The western half of Crown Office Row went the same way. Dr Johnson's Buildings in Inner Temple Lane, Mitre Court Buildings and Harcourt Buildings followed suit. In 1870 the charming old Inner Temple Hall was replaced by a somewhat unpleasing substitute in Law Courts gothic. Matching it to the east was a new range of buildings incorporating the library and the Benchers' rooms. The library clock tower was rather like a miniature Big Ben.

The 19th century saw the progressive development of the chambers system for the Bar. One-man chambers remained, but it was becoming more and more usual for men to group together in twos, threes or half dozens. As in all the Inns, there were many residents who brought a sort of village life to the whole complex of courts and buildings when the busy day's work was over.

Below: Middle Temple Hall from the north. The view has hardly altered since this early 19th century engraving was made

Bottom: Middle Temple Hall interior before it was bombed in the Second World War. The hall has been completely restored to its original form but the chandeliers have been replaced by floodlights

The life of the Temple had not the cloistered calm of Lincoln's Inn. This was the realm of the common law, the bustling business of disputes over broken heads, broken contracts, street accidents, libel and slander and, of course, crime. It was in this atmosphere that the famous leaders of the Bar flourished, providing copy for the newspaper reporters by their speeches and their cross-examinations. Such a life produced robust characters like the keen yachtsman who built a dinghy in his one-man chambers in Crown Office Row, where he both lived and practised, and launched it at the Temple Stairs, or the King's Counsel whose pupil parties in King's Bench Walk were famous in the 1920's. After lashings of drink, everyone would stand on the tables, a sack of rats would be opened and emptied and terriers would be let loose to hunt them through the chambers. Such high jinks were exceptional but they were possible.

A view of Fountain Court, Temple. An engraving by Fletcher after a painting by Joseph Nichols which hangs in the Benchers' Smoking Room in Middle Temple. Middle Temple Hall is on the right of the fountain and court which was laid out in 1681

Middle Temple The Middle Temple life was very like that in the Inner Temple, though it lacked the great expanses of tree-shadowed King's Bench Walk. Its buildings were more of a huddle, Elm Court, now vanished, between Pump Court and the back of Crown Office Row, Essex Court and Brick Court divided from each other by a pleasant red brick 18th century building. But the glory of the Middle Temple was and is its great Elizabethan Hall with its double hammer beams and its intricately carved gallery. The coloured effigy tomb of its builder, Edmund Plowden, stands in the Temple Church on the north side. He was the greatest lawyer of his time, but he sacrificed his career to his steadfastness in his faith as a Roman Catholic. When Elizabeth I came to the throne he was just about to receive the degree of serjeant–at–law, but his refusal to conform to the Queen's Established Church barred him from that and any other future promotion. Instead of migrating to Serjeants' Inn and becoming a judge he remained a member of the Middle Temple and it was he who was put in charge of the rebuilding of the Hall. It is his monument. That Hall, the fountain beside it, surrounded by trees, and the terrace overlooking the Inn's garden remain one of the most charming spots in any of the Inns.

The memories of the Middle Temple's past cluster thickly round the Hall. Here Shakespeare's *Twelfth Night* was played in his lifetime. Lawyers like Clarendon, Hardwicke, Blackstone and Eldon join hand with literary men like Evelyn, Fielding, Cowper, Sheridan and Thackeray, public men like Pym and Burke, adventurers like Raleigh and Drake.

The first World War did not radically alter the life of the Temple, though between the wars the top hat was abandoned, save by the older and more conservative men and was replaced by the black homburg 'Anthony Eden'. In 1922 women began to be called to the Bar, but their impact was then slight and spasmodic.

Then came the devastation of the second World War. In successive bombardments the Temple Church, the Inner Temple Hall and Library, Crown Office Row, Fig Tree Court, Elm Court, the south side of Pump Court, the building which divided Essex Court from Brick Court were either burnt to the bare walls or reduced to rubble. The gothic Victorian Middle Temple Library on the west side of the garden was too badly blasted to survive. Middle Temple Hall narrowly escaped. Early in the war its east wall was blown in. In one of the last bombardments a shower of fire bombs destroyed the outer roof but the flames were checked in time to save the splendid beams. After the war the Temple gradually recovered. The Church and the Middle Temple Hall were restored with loving care. The Middle Temple Library was moved to another site. The Inner Temple hall rose again in a sort of neo-Caroline style, the library and administrative buildings in blameless modern Georgian. In the reconstructed chambers modern comforts replaced the Dickensian picturesque of their predecessors.

47

Top: The nave of the Temple Church. On either side
lie the 13th century effigies of Knights Templars. The
walls of the Church are decorated with grotesque
gothic heads said to represent souls in heaven and souls
in hell (above)

Right: The charming house occupied by the Master of
the Temple. Originally built by Wren, it was
destroyed in 1941 and rebuilt after the war. Quite one
of London's most desirable tied cottages, it is in the
gift of the Crown

Above right: King's Bench Walk, named after the
King's Bench office which stood on the site until
burned down in 1677. Car parking is zealously
supervised by the dutiful Frank Jordan (extreme right)

The Inns Today The postwar period brought many changes to the life of the Inns of Court. The combination of the extension of popular education, the extraordinary increase in crime and of the spread of litigiousness following on the institution of legal aid, swelled the ranks of the students, clamorous for new 'amenities' and privileges and impatient of discipline and restrictions, while the numbers of the practising Bar grew beyond precedent.

The problem of introducing so many aspirants to the practical skills of advocacy, as pupils to established practitioners, became acute, since practice is a very different thing from book learning and not every able, busy man is an effective teacher. So too the problem of finding physical accommodation in chambers for newcomers presented enormous difficulties. Where formerly it was normal to have a dozen men working in a set of chambers, it now became usual to have twenty or thirty. All this affected the atmosphere of work in the Inns which, with the social dominance of the motor car and the increased demand for parking space within their boundaries, much diminished their cloistered calm. Relaxations in the conventions of dress and demeanour, especially among the students, modified the tone and atmosphere of life in the Inns. So did the increasing female presence.

Lunching and, even more, dining in the great Halls of the Inns remains the central bond of their cohesion and continuity; the dinners, occasions of formal ritual as well as conviviality, an outward expression of adherence to common standards, the lunches informal and friendly as members come in from court, chambers or library as and when they can. Both foster, focus and solidify the constant habit of personal association which has created a common public spirit in the Bar enabling its members to 'strive mightily but eat and drink as friends', so that they are not a mere loose association of 'lone wolves' intent only on the opportunism of profit and advancement. Many disruptive factors of our time militate against both the discipline and the camaraderie of such institutions but their function and their advantages are clear.

Because our Bench and Bar are incorrupt we tend to take it for granted that that is part of the natural order of things. But it is a most extraordinary achievement. A mere qualification factory for technicians is a thing relatively easy. It can be organised by any one of a dozen systems of lectures or instruction, even a correspondence course. But for those who seek legal assistance or a just adjudication of their disputes, perhaps in the face of powerful interests or of the State, the personal qualities of honour, courage and integrity are paramount.

The present function of the Inns is to personalise the Bar, to superimpose on the technical legal skills the personal elements which must dominate them. In that spirit for six centuries the Inns have adapted themselves by their own innate instincts to the changing character of many successive states of society, from the beginning keeping alive the idea of the 'free and lawful man'. It is essential to our society that they should do so still.

The Profession of a Solicitor

Gerald Sanctuary

In England and Wales today there are about 32,000 solicitors with practising certificates. No doubt there are several others who practise law but who do not need to hold a certificate, or who have moved into other fields of endeavour. Solicitors represent the largest branch of the legal profession, and the majority of them are in private practice, some as principals, but many as assistants. A growing minority, however, are working for the Government, for local authorities, and in commerce and industry. There are more solicitors in the South-East of the country than in other parts, and many in London, but firms of varying sizes can be found throughout England and Wales.

This section will describe the work of The Law Society, the solicitors' professional association, and also the way in which a city and a country practice operate. There is also an examination of the work of salaried solicitors, in public and private employment.

The Law Society The Society was set up in 1825, at a time when practising attorneys were becoming gradually more respectable. The landowners and the growing middle class increasingly had need of advisers, people who could help with the management of their private fortunes. They also sought ways of preserving these fortunes, and passing them on intact to the next generation. Because a large number of attorneys then practised without any qualification or marked degree of learning, those who founded The Law Society took an early decision to encourage, and later insist upon, the passing of examinations by all those who wished to become members and to call themselves 'Solicitors of the Supreme Court'.

It was this insistence upon educational standards of entry, and the gradual development of professional rules of conduct, that steadily established the solicitor as a respectable 'man of affairs'. Galsworthy's John Forsyte and his son, Soames, were drawn from life, solicitors who made a comfortable living by settling the problems and keeping the confidences of the ruling section of English society. One early rule was that a solicitor was not permitted to 'tout' for business. It was recognised also that his first duty was to his client, not to himself; if there was any conflict between his own interest and that of his client, then it was – and still is – his duty to say so and to advise the client to seek separate advice.

The Law Society now exists by virtue of the grant of a Royal Charter. It possesses considerable powers of government over the profession it represents, all granted to it by Parliament over the 150 years of its history. When it was first founded, its few members together subscribed sufficient money to buy a piece of land, in Chancery Lane in the heart of legal London, and there they built The Law Society's Hall, which stands there today, its solemn pillars and dignified stone facing across the street toward the Public Record Office. In later years the building was extended, and today it houses a large professional staff, an excellent members' library and rooms where meetings can be held and meals eaten.

A Council of seventy members governs The Law Society. The majority of its members are elected by the Society's 30,000 members throughout the country—not all solicitors are members, even though they are governed by the rules; a small minority are appointed by the elected members, because they possess some specialist experience that is of value to the Council in its deliberations. The Council is divided into a number of committees who make or recommend policy decisions. The Council meets eleven times a year, and the standard of debates in its Chamber often reaches a high level. Each year a president is elected, and it is normal for him to receive the honour of knighthood in the Birthday Honours List. Past presidents tend to stay on the Council for several years after their term of office, which is extremely onerous. There are some bodies whose presidents perform formal and ceremonial functions, but it is normal for the president of The Law Society to be in his room at the Hall every day of the working week, closely involved with day-to-day decisions, meeting and entertaining visitors from overseas and from other organisations. He is also expected to visit and speak to meetings of many of the 121 local law societies throughout the country.

Local law societies are entirely independent of The Law Society. Their representatives come to meetings held nationally and also attend the Society's national conference which is usually held in October each year. Several of the local societies are older than The Law Society, and a few were formed at the end of the eighteenth century. They vary a great deal in size, some of the London societies having over 800 members, while the Aberystwyth Society has only 12.

Education and Training From the days when educational qualifications were first introduced, it has been thought right that any would-be solicitor should combine practical with theoretical training. For this reason he or she is expected to spend a period in articles, that is working in a solicitor's office. The ideal articles will give the student experience in commercial, trust and conveyancing work, accounts, litigation and general office procedure. In the best offices the student spends some time in each of the office departments, and this enables him or her to understand the practical application of the law.

Examinations are set by The Law Society, and a very large number of the students prepare for them at one of the College of Law centres, which are situated in London, Guildford and Cheshire. Students who already have a law degree (and this now represents over three-quarters of the annual intake) are exempted from some of The Law Society examinations as are some of those who enter the profession, for example as a mature student, or as an already qualified Fellow of the Institute of Legal Executives. The examinations are held twice each year, and at present the profession is growing at the rate of about 1,200 a year.

The Education and Training Committee of the Council of The Law Society decides education policy, appoints examiners and deals with the problems posed by particular cases. If, for example, a student is convicted of some crime during training, this will almost certainly lead to an appearance – after the court conviction – before the Education and Training Committee. Those whose escapades come into the category of a student prank will probably receive a caution, delivered with due solemnity; but those who have been convicted of dishonesty will almost certainly be barred from taking The Society's examinations. The public have come to rely upon a solicitor's honesty, and this is the reason for a policy that can sometimes seem rather harsh.

With the College of Law, The Society arranges and encourages solicitors to attend regular further training courses. Each year there are lectures at the Society's Hall, repeated throughout the country as crash courses, dealing with changes in the law resulting from recent legislation and judicial decisions. Some of the Groups of The Law Society also organise training courses for their members.

Having qualified, the new solicitor attends at The Law Society for an admission ceremony. As well as the certificate of qualification, he or she is handed a *Guide to Professional Conduct*, which gives details of all the rules that must now be followed. In essence, these are that a solicitor must:

1 Keep his own and his clients' money entirely separate;
2 Honour all undertakings (i.e. promises) given in his professional capacity;
3 Refrain from advertising his services;
4 Maintain complete confidentiality in respect of all his clients' affairs, and behave generally in a professional manner.

This is not the end of the obligations which bind solicitors. All those who hold a practising certificate must contribute to The Society's compensation fund, which exists to repay anyone who has suffered as a result of a solicitor's dishonesty. All principals in private practice are also required to join The Law Society's indemnity insurance scheme, which provides minimum insurance cover against the risks of negligence.

Discipline and Complaints Solicitors deal with people's problems. For this reason, the profession is regularly called upon to act and advise at a moment of crisis in a client's life. Strong feelings, anxiety and tension may be present. More difficult still, it is rare for each person in a situation of conflict to obtain what he wants. In a dispute over property, some form of compromise may be advised. In a divorce, there will often be a dispute over the custody of children and the payment of maintenance. When it is alleged that there has been a breach of contract, or an unfair dismissal, there are almost always two sides to the story, two conflicting claims. When the legal aspect is finally settled, one or both of the clients involved may be left with a sense of grievance, and may look round for someone to blame. He may feel that his solicitor has done a poor job, has delayed unduly, or has failed to understand his needs. When this happens, he may decide to complain to The Law Society about the solicitor's behaviour.

There are, of course, other reasons for complaints. Solicitors do sometimes make mistakes; a very few are dishonest. The Law Society has created a Professional Purposes Department to deal with complaints against solicitors, and to institute any necessary action. Rather more than half this department's work involves helping and advising solicitors who find themselves faced with professional problems; the rest is concerned with complaints and matters of discipline.

The Law Society has no power to fine solicitors, or to strike them off the Roll of Solicitors. It can administer a rebuke, and can require a solicitor to give advance notice of his intention to apply for his next practising certificate, retaining for itself a discretion whether or not the certificate will be granted. In the case of serious offences against the rules of professional conduct, The Society acts as 'prosecutor' before a body known as the Disciplinary Tribunal. This tribunal was created by Act of Parliament; its members are appointed by the Master of the Rolls, a senior judge with a special responsibility for the solicitors' branch of the legal profession. The tribunal is composed of solicitors and lay members. It has the power to administer fines, and to strike a solicitor off the Roll; an appeal from its decisions is to the Master of the Rolls.

Since 1974 there has been an independent check on the way in which The Law Society carries out its functions in relation to complaints against solicitors. Parliament has created the post of Lay Observer (sometimes called The Law Society's ombudsman), an official paid from public funds and occupying rooms in the Royal Courts of Justice in the Strand. He is responsible to the Lord Chancellor to whom he reports annually. The Lay Observer has no power to investigate complaints from the beginning, although he receives a number of letters from the public asking him to do so. His function is to review The Law Society's own work. If he receives a complaint, usually to the effect that The Society has not behaved fairly, he asks to see the file. He will also invite the complainant to explain the reasons why he is dissatisfied. If he has questions, he will put these to The Law Society, and they will be answered. During his first four years of work, according to his annual reports, he concluded that in the great majority of cases referred to him The Society had behaved reasonably.

Remuneration Certificates Another statutory function of The Law Society is its certification of solicitors' bills for what is known as non-contentious work. The great majority of solicitors' work falls into this category, for 'contentious business' is work done only in connection with a court action. To illustrate this, if a major claim is made for damages, and settled after a year's argument and negotiation, the work is still regarded as 'non-contentious' if no writ has been issued. Under the Solicitors' Remuneration Order 1972 any client who feels that a bill for non-contentious work delivered by his solicitor is unfair or unreasonable can require the solicitor to obtain a certificate from The Law Society, stating whether in its opinion the sum is fair or reasonable, or what other sum would be fair and reasonable. This opinion is given in a remuneration certificate, for which The Society makes no charge to the client. A client

The crest and main doorway to the Law Society's Hall in Chancery Lane. The main hall and Palladian front were opened in 1831

cannot ask for a certificate after a bill has been delivered and paid.

On the whole, scale charges do not apply to much of solicitors' work, but all bills have to be fair and reasonable. Eight factors are taken into account by The Law Society, and by a court if the bill is 'taxed' or assessed by it. These are:

1 the complexity of the matter or the difficulty or novelty of the questions raised;
2 the skill, labour, specialised knowledge and responsibility involved;
3 the time spent on the business;
4 the number and importance of the documents prepared or perused, without regard to length;
5 the place where and the circumstances in which the business or any part thereof is transacted;
6 the amount or value of any money or property involved;
7 whether any land involved is registered land within the meaning of the Land Registration Act 1926; and
8 the importance of the matter to the client.

The Law Society's Non-Contentious Business Department has a great deal to do in addition to the certification of bills. Every year it makes proposals to the Chancellor of the Exchequer for changes in Revenue Law. Solicitors are in a good position to see the ways in which the law of taxation affects their clients. For example, the heavy burden placed on family businesses and on farms by the Capital Transfer Tax, and the problems faced by self-employed people trying to make pension provision for themselves, have been the subject of suggestions for reform. Evidence is also given to Government Departments and to Royal Commissions, often in response to a request to The Law Society for help. As the solicitors' professional association, The Society also gives a considerable amount of help to the profession in regard to the day-to-day problems met in their practices.

Law Reform The Society also maintains a Law Reform Department, which reviews all new legislation and selects Parliamentary Bills on which it seems appropriate to comment. Many Members of Parliament are glad to have the advice of The Society when they are preparing amendments for Bills passing through Committees at the House of Commons. The Society sometimes makes proposals for law reform on its own initiative, especially when it is found – by solicitors in private practice – that a particular piece of legislation is not working as had been intended.

Publications, Press and Publicity Every professional association needs a regular publication for its members, and to act as its public mouthpiece. The Law Society publishes a weekly *Gazette*, which contains a great deal of professional information and articles on legal subjects. The *Gazette* is published in competition with two other weekly journals, each independently owned, the *New Law Journal* and the *Solicitors' Journal*.

We live today in an age of communication. If Soames Forsyte had been asked by another solicitor whether the Law Society had need of a press office, or should pay attention to its public relations, he would have doubted the man's sanity. The Society's role, he would have said, was to provide for the education and training of solicitors, and to deal with matters of discipline when there was a breach of professional conduct. Even today, the phrase 'public relations' sounds offensive to the ears of many solicitors. Nevertheless, The Law Society now possesses a Professional and Public Relations Committee, and a department to do its will.

In the first place, there is a press office. The telephone is constantly in use, with enquiries from local and national newspapers, and from radio and television stations. A comment may be sought on a proposed change in the law; a spokesman may be required to answer a politician's charge that solicitors charge higher fees than they should; or an article requested on some aspect of the law brought into the news following some local or national scandal.

Working on the principle that people who understand something of the law have a better appreciation of the role of lawyers, The Law Society has gradually established for itself a reputation for producing teaching aids for use in schools. There are filmstrips, wallcharts, specimen document kits, books and other publications. The most successful are the filmstrips, which come with a recorded commentary, and the specimen document kits. All young people who leave school are soon faced with the problem of finding a job, and before long they want to marry and buy – or rent – a home of their own. They tend to sign documents without reading them and often without understanding them. There is now a remedy for this problem, and Law Society materials have been sold to at least one in six secondary schools in the country.

Civil Legal Aid The Law Society runs the civil Legal Aid Scheme, on behalf of the Government. Legal aid is available, to those whose means entitle them to receive it, in both criminal and civil matters. Generally speaking, the public tend to associate legal aid with crime, because there are many newspaper reports which state that 'the defendant was granted legal aid'. Criminal legal aid is administered by the Home Office, and is normally granted by the magistrates' court at which the case is first heard. The civil Legal Aid Scheme, however, is administered by The Law Society. This has been the case since 1948. Over recent years, the proportion of the population entitled to receive Legal Advice and Assistance under the Legal Aid Scheme has dropped because of the effects of inflation. Although there is now no legal aid for undefended divorce proceedings, it is still possible for people to obtain preliminary advice and assistance from a solicitor while they are preparing their statements and completing the necessary forms.

The Law Society operates a committee to administer the civil Legal Aid Scheme. On it sit representatives of the Bar, and of the Lord Chancellor's Office, to which The Society is responsible. There is also the Lord Chancellor's Advisory Committee, an official body which comments upon the operation of the Scheme and makes suggestions for ways in which it may be improved. There is a permanent staff at The Society's Hall responsible for administering the Scheme and fourteen legal aid areas covering the whole of the country.

The EEC Even before Britain signed the Treaty of Rome and became a member of the Common Market, there existed a Solicitors' European Group, run by The Law Society for its members interested in work and business matters on the Continent. Since British entry, almost every aspect of The Law Society's work has been effected in some way by the impact of EEC law. An International Relations Committee deals regularly with such matters as the rights of audience of British lawyers in European courts, and with reciprocal arrangements covering our own courts. The same committee is also involved in other international work; there are frequent visits to other European lawyers' associations and a particularly close relationship with the American Bar Association and the Law Societies of Australia and New Zealand.

Representing the Profession We live in an age when authority is little respected. In spite of this, The Law Society's utterances are accorded a good deal of attention by Government, by other professional bodies and by the mass media. Fundamentally, though, The Society remains a professional association. Although it certainly tries to operate in the national interest, its first task is to represent its members. It would be impossible to perform a trade union function, if only because the majority of solicitors are self-employed, but The Society is often involved in negotiation over the fees that

The Work of Solicitors

A City Practice The city with the largest number of solicitors is, of course, London. Several firms in the City of London, in Holborn and in Westminster have more than 20 partners and hundreds of employees. Their practices are mainly commercial, that is they work for public companies and institutions rather than for private individuals. In the other major cities, Manchester, Birmingham, Liverpool, Leeds, Cardiff, Plymouth and Newcastle, there are also substantial firms whose work is mainly done on behalf of commercial clients.

The typical city firm, then, will have many partners, each specialising in some aspect of the legal work brought in by clients. In all probability, the partners will hold a regular monthly meeting, probably in the evening after the day's work is over. Some of the partners will be quite close friends, but others may have only a slight acquaintance with one another. Most likely, the firm will have resulted from the amalgamation of two or three firms over the past ten years. With the problem of growing overhead costs, many firms have felt it wise to amalgamate with others having a different clientele, partly in order to be able to offer a more comprehensive service, and partly to make the enlarged firm more efficient, and more profitable, than the separate units could become before being merged together.

The city firm will not have abandoned all work for individual clients, many of whom will be on the boards, or senior members of the management teams, of company clients. The firm will be divided into different departments, at least one partner being responsible for each. For example, there may well be a department doing nothing but company flotations, reorganisations and mergers. For much of the time the staff of this department will be involved in the complex but regular work of preparing new share issues, settling the form of agreements and notices for despatch to shareholders, and agreeing with another firm of solicitors the clauses of a formal agreement embodying the new arrangements. A flurry of activity may follow the decision of a company client to make – or to defend – a take-over bid. The form and the accuracy of public statements must be carefully checked; the client must be advised on the legality of the intended bid, the despatch of notices, and the legal consequences of any new proposals. Stand outside the offices of a large firm of city solicitors late at night, and you will be able to see the lights burning in rooms where members of the staff are working against time to have an agreement ready for signature early the next day.

It is not likely that the partners will be burning the midnight oil in this way, but they may well be with the clients themselves, discussing moves and countermoves, and trying to anticipate what 'the other side' will do next. The solicitor who is in close touch with his clients' intentions, and with the men who make decisions, is better placed to advise competently as the situation develops. It is by no means always a battle that has to be fought: two major companies, one in Britain and another overseas, may have agreed to co-operate in a

solicitors earn and the conditions under which they work. In 1973, the Government of the day proposed that the basis on which solicitors' fees for conveyancing work were calculated should be changed. At that time, there was a scale in operation, and some politicians and sections of the national press claimed that it was inappropriate. The Law Society replied that a scale had the great advantage of ensuring that people knew exactly what expense they were likely to have to meet when buying or selling a house, but eventually it negotiated with the then Lord Chancellor, Lord Hailsham, a change which resulted in the present system under which solicitors charge whatever is fair and reasonable in all the circumstances.

Other negotiations between The Society and the Government of the day have taken place over the fees allowed by the courts in litigation, and the administration of the courts themselves. There is a procedure under which The Society may complain to the Lord Chancellor over the behaviour of an individual magistrate, or even a judge.

Many solicitors hold The Law Society in some awe, no doubt because of its disciplinary powers. Some are active in opposing its policies, and there is more than one other association of solicitors in existence. The largest of these, the British Legal Association, claims 2,000 members, and is more noticeable by the public statements it makes than for the work done for its members. It is not at all surprising that, in spite of its efforts, there should be a body of solicitors who do not agree with all that The Law Society does. Attempts to persuade its opponents to join ranks and to express their views from within the main professional body have not been taken up.

The interior of the offices of a firm of City solicitors. The variety of work undertaken means that the list of partners is long. From the central typing area corridors and doors lead to the partners' offices in a layout not dissimilar to that of any modern business premises

Opposite: The Law Society's premises in Chancery Lane offer extensive facilities to members. Seen here are (top) the Reading Room and (bottom) the Library

venture that will bring large profits to them both. This agreement must be put into writing, and it is for the solicitors to do this. Visits may have to be paid to other countries, interviews hurriedly arranged with the officials of foreign governments, and with the lawyers for the other organisations involved. Even if both parties are speaking the same language, it is likely that the law of more than one country will apply. The firm will send a partner, or a senior solicitor on the staff, who is familiar with this type of agreement, and probably also with the legal and political difficulties which will have to be overcome.

Since Britain's entry into the European Economic Community, more city firms have become involved in Common Market work. Several have established offices on the Continent of Europe, in Paris, Brussels and in some of the major German cities. Others have close links with European lawyers. Most of our Common Market partners have laws very different from our own, deriving from the *Code Napoleon*. All agreements have to take account of the law of Britain, of the other country involved, and of the growing volume of Common Market law.

The firm will have several other departments, handling commercial conveyancing, general litigation, trust and probate work, and other matters. Some firms have a

specialist function, dealing particularly with major insurance claims, with the registration of patents, or with the legal problems that arise following aircraft accidents, or collisions at sea. In each department there will be one or more assistant solicitors, probably qualified within the past five years, who are taking the opportunity to gain experience before seeking a partnership of their own.

There will also be several articled clerks, who are students in training to become solicitors. The usual practice is for these clerks to be moved from one department to another every three or six months. The Law Society requires that every solicitor should not only have proved his or her academic ability, but also have gained direct experience of everyday work in an office before qualifying. Articled clerks are paid a modest wage; most claim that it is not enough, but their principals (the solicitors to whom they are articled) will probably reply that for much of the time they are in the office they are being taught, not doing productive work. Today the average firm will receive far more applications from people who seek articles than they can possibly accommodate in their offices.

In addition to the work done directly for clients, the office has to be run, kept clean and warm, the rent has to be paid and a hundred administrative decisions taken

The Royal Courts of Justice and the Strand where
Temple Bar used to stand until it caused too great an
obstacle to traffic

every week. Most of the larger firms now have an office manager responsible for this work. There will also be a substantial accounts section, dealing not only with the firm's own affairs but also with receiving and paying out client's money. The strict rules that apply to the whole of the profession must be kept, and every year the firm's accounts must be audited to ensure that everything is in order. There are many other tasks, including the payment of wages and insurance, the purchase of new equipment and the hiring of new staff.

Most of the larger firms now have a system of time costing. A calculation is first made of the actual cost of work done; all the partners, and the staff, keep a note of the time they spend on a piece of work. This is then related to the earnings of that person, and an estimate is made of the fee that is later to be charged to the client. Payments made on the client's behalf are similarly noted. When the matter is completed, the work and the payments are collated, and a bill prepared. If the case has taken a long time, it is quite possible that the client will have been asked to make payments on account.

It has become a practice for several of the larger city firms to become involved in the work of a neighbourhood law centre. Within a few miles of the centre of the main cities there are areas where the number of solicitors' offices is few, and there is a great deal of unmet legal need. The involvement of the large firms with the work of these centres tends to vary; in some cases, the firm will make a regular payment to a law centre to help it carry on its work, which is mainly for people who are in dispute with landlords, in difficulties with the police, or experiencing problems with traders, hire purchase companies or employers. It would not be practicable for the large firm to do this work, simply because the clients could not afford to pay for it. Many of them will be entitled to legal aid under Legal Advice and Assistance Scheme, and law centres receive funds from this source. The money obtained in this way, however, is not normally enough to run the centre, and outside support is necessary.

Several firms prefer to give direct, practical help. One of the partners may be a member of the management committee of the law centre, and some of the assistant solicitors may take on the task of attending there in the evenings and at weekends, and giving advice to people who call. By contrast with the average firm of solicitors, whose clients are normally in contact during the day, law centres find that much of their work is done at times when their clients can get to them—in the evenings.

Life for the partners of these large firms is no bed of roses. It is no accident that the firm carries a very large sum by way of negligence insurance, for the smallest mistake, even a typing error, could lead to the loss of hundreds of thousands of pounds. If this were to happen, the firm would be negligent, and the partners would be held individually liable for the loss caused. It is most unlikely that they are rich men, and without the protection of negligence insurance they would not be able to sleep comfortably at nights.

The partners' work is not confined to the office; it is more than likely that evenings will involve them in meetings, domestic and foreign travel, and social occasions. A firm does not acquire clients automatically, but at the same time, solicitors are not allowed to advertise their services. Obviously, the partners' involvement in social and other community activity is necessary if they are to become known, and to maintain their business.

A Country Practice Let us now consider a very different type of law practice, that of a firm in a county town, many miles from the major population centres. The firm has three partners, and they operate what is known as a general practice. Their clients are all known personally to them, and the firm has acted for the same families and businesses for many years. Fortunately the partners own the freehold of the office they occupy, and although this has the advantage of reducing the firm's overheads, it creates some difficulties when the possibility of introducing a new partner is raised. He might be asked to buy his share of the freehold, yet it is more or less impossible to find a young man (or woman) able to do this. The partners have therefore been considering the possibility of an amalgamation, but no steps have yet been taken.

The partners, who all run their cars partly at the expense of the firm, drive in each day from their homes, and none of them takes more than twenty minutes over the journey. Not for them the daily travel by train to and from a large railway station. Like the partners of the city firm, they expect to spend a good deal of their time involved in community activity, and very likely each of them is involved in running various local charitable and sporting organisations.

This may conjure up a vision of relative ease and luxury, but this is far from being so. The firm has many problems, and all three partners are worried. Owing to the running inflation of the past four or five years, they have found that staff salaries and other expenses have risen sharply. Their fees have not come in as quickly, or at the level, they have planned. What is more, they find that an ever-increasing amount of cash is needed to finance the practice, settle expenses on behalf of clients and pay salaries. Profits during the past year were about as much as the year before, but it is obvious that they must retain a good deal of their own cash in the business because they already have a substantial office account overdraft at the bank. They cannot of course use any of their clients' money for their own purposes, even though there may be a hefty credit balance on the client's account.

Before we turn to the solution of their difficulties, let us consider the type of practice the partners are running. There is a good deal of conveyancing work, transferring land and houses to and from their clients. Because of the national economic recession, there is rather less of this work than there was, but it is nevertheless profitable for the most part. In addition to conveyancing there is a substantial amount of probate and trust work to be done. All three partners do both types of work, though the most senior of them tends to delegate as much as he can to his senior managing clerk, a man of 63 years. Today he would be called a legal executive.

Many of the firm's clients have appointed one or more of the partners as executors and trustees of their wills. As each winter comes, a telephone call brings the news that one of these clients has died. Immediately, the will is brought out from the safe, and one of the partners reads it. There may be some provision about cremation, and many testators these days express wishes about the use of their bodies for medical research or for a transplant. Normally this is all that is noted, except the fact of the appointment of executors, whose task it is to arrange the funeral and other matters. The days when the family solicitor solemnly reads the will have all but gone, and the normal practice is now to make copies of the document and send them, some time after the funeral, to the people interested. The assets are gathered in, the payment of capital transfer tax is arranged, probably with the help of the local bank manager, and the debts and legacies are duly paid. When there is a continuing trust, the partner dealing with the matter obtains advice on re-investment, and discusses with the beneficiaries under the will – probably the widow and her children – what their needs are, and will be. It is a very personal service, and after a time each partner gets to know how best to provide it.

The firm also does a good deal of litigation, much of it in the matrimonial courts. Even in country areas a high proportion of marriages end in divorce, and this takes up much of the time of one of the partners of the firm, and the young legal executive who has recently come to work for him. Most divorce cases today are undefended, but this still means that there is a good deal of work to do, especially negotiating maintenance payments, the division of property and arrangements for the custody of children. Passions run high and a feeling of resentment is often present, sometimes directed at the solicitor himself; the reason is that very few parties to a court action get exactly what they want, and if the solicitor is not careful he may find himself being blamed for a law that his client feels is unfair.

The essence of any successful law practice, and certainly a country one, is effective communication with the client. If one of the partners fails to keep in regular contact with his clients he has no-one but himself to blame if they become dissatisfied and think that it is he, and the other people involved, who is holding things up. In fact delay is as frustrating to the solicitor as it is to his client, but he has probably become more used to it. He may sometimes find himself doing everything he can to slow down a particular transaction, simply because it does not suit the client to go quickly. If his client, Mr Wilkes, has not yet found exactly the house he wants he will tell the solicitor to find some reason for delaying the exchange of contracts for the sale of his present house. To the purchaser and his solicitor, this may very well look like unconscionable delay and it may well suit Mr Wilkes to blame his solicitors rather than himself.

In the town where this country practice operates, there is a magistrates' court and also a county court. All members of the firm are entitled to appear in both courts, but it is often left to one of them to do all the advocacy work. Sometimes this is done with the help of

legal aid. In an average week there may be a few prosecutions to be defended, for clients charged with driving offences, or possibly breaches of local regulations. Occasionally a more serious charge may be brought, and when this happens the partner concerned will have to decide whether or not to brief a barrister to appear. In making this decision, much will depend on his own experience in dealing with this type of case. If it is likely to go to the Crown Court, then he will certainly ask a barrister to appear on his client's behalf.

There will be other occasions on which a barrister must be consulted. A client may have a particularly complicated transaction in mind, with tax implications, relating to the transfer of his family business, or farm, to his sons. It may be his wish to continue to live in his present home, yet he will probably be content to hand over the running of the business. What steps are necessary? Should the family company be wound up? What will be the effect of transferring its shares? How can the owner ensure a reasonable income for himself and his wife during his intended retirement? And what is to be done to provide for one of his daughters whose husband has turned out to be no good and left her with two children to bring up on her own? These problems have personal as well as legal solutions. They must be discussed fully with the client, and it may well be necessary to seek expert technical advice from tax counsel, that is, a barrister well versed in the latest provisions of the Finance Acts.

The firm is not only dealing with such matters as these, but also with a wide variety of small problems, some for clients whom they do not feel they can possibly charge an economic fee. This brings us back to the problem now faced by them: how to adjust the firm's income so as to bring in a reasonable profit, while at the same time enabling them to finance salaries, overheads and the many payments they are making on behalf of their clients. Until now each partner, or one of the clerks working for him, has assessed bills on a hit-or-miss basis, looking quickly through each file and coming to a general conclusion of the amount of a fee that he considers reasonable. On reviewing this method, they realise that it simply will not serve them any longer. It is essential, they realise, to find out what it is costing them to do the work. With the help of their accountants, and a publication, *The Expense of Time*, supplied by The Law Society, they find that although some of their work is reasonably profitable, much of it is actually being done at a loss. This realisation brings the prospect of amalgamation with another nearby firm nearer, especially when it is realised that the partners of that firm are doing a good deal of similar work which could with advantage be done more economically by a medium-sized department, rather than by one man on his own.

The pressure of events and the partners' wish to maintain their practice and their own standard of living, brings them with some feelings of regret to decide that the proposed amalgamation is the only answer, that modern accounting and costing methods will have to be adopted, and that larger premises will have to be obtained, or maybe built. They face the prospect of having

The offices of a country solicitor are more traditional than those shown in the previous illustration. A solicitor and his articled clerk are likely to have to undertake most of the work themselves

to sell the freehold they own, but are at least reassured by the fact that this will leave them with enough cash to ensure that the new and enlarged partnership will have sufficient capital to expand the business and achieve a better profit.

Commerce and Industry There is an ever-increasing number of solicitors now working in commerce and industry. There are many attractions to this type of work: in the first place, the solicitor is free of the anxieties about overheads and rising costs that concern his brethren in private practice. Admittedly, he gives up something of his independence by becoming the employee of a large organisation, but there is the additional comfort of a reliable pension, a regular salary and the prospect, if he does well, of promotion.

The attitude of companies varies: some like to employ a large legal staff, usually headed by a senior solicitor of many years experience. Frequently, there may be barristers as well as solicitors working in such a department. Some companies, on the other hand, prefer to instruct independent firms of solicitors to do most of their legal work, relying on a relatively small internal staff of lawyers. Other companies take a middle course, using

their own legal department for national and international contract work, but instructing firms of solicitors, for example, to deal with conveyancing, major litigation and debt collection.

In recent years there has been a great deal of legislation dealing with employment. More and more employees are entitled to substantial compensation if they are thrown out of work through redundancy or dismissed. To make matters more complicated, it is now quite possible for an employee to claim that he or she has been 'constructively dismissed', that is, the job has been so altered that it no longer effectively exists. Many industrial tribunals, and the Employment Appeal Tribunal, have been set up, and it is often necessary to place complex legal arguments before these bodies. The result of a single case may affect many hundreds of workers in a factory or office, and solicitors working in commerce and industry now find themselves doing a great deal of this type of work.

The solicitor working in commerce is part of an organisation devoted to the making of a profit. The same is of course true of an ordinary firm of solicitors, but in fact they are also providing a service; by contrast, most companies are selling goods, and none of them are

subject to the rules of conduct that bind solicitors. For these reasons, the solicitor employed by a large manufacturing company, for example, can find himself subject to pressures that are not exerted on private practitioners. It may be, for example, that it is in the commercial interests of a company to take a particular action. On careful investigation, the company solicitor comes to the conclusion that this action would not be legal, and he so informs the managing director of the firm. Considerable disappointment, possibly anger results; the solicitor may be invited to look again at the situation, and ordered to search for any possible ways in which the desired objective can be achieved. If he is relatively junior in the organisation, anxious to make his way up the ladder of promotion and to keep on the right side of those who appointed him, he will be in a very real dilemma. It is at this moment that the advice of his colleagues, and possibly of his professional organisation, will be of the greatest support to him. If he is in any doubt as to the correctness of his opinion, then of course he will be wise to seek further advice, but if he is certain that the law prevents the proposed action being taken, he has no alternative but to advise against it.

There are other moments when the solicitor's professional integrity may be tested, and these are by no means only when he is a junior member of the staff. Many members of the profession find themselves on the boards of companies, having earned promotion to this position. It is a brave man who stands out against all his business colleagues, insisting that they cannot go ahead with a potentially profitable project that is near to their hearts. Occasionally, the only action open to the solicitor will be resignation.

It would be quite wrong, however, to give the impression that the life of a solicitor working in commerce is fraught with high moral decisions. On the contrary, he will often find himself dealing with relatively mundane matters, such as service contracts, patent rights, commercial agreements and the relationship between different units within a large group of companies. At all times he is in close contact with colleagues in the same organisation. He knows, however, that he has a professional qualification that binds him to behave in a particular way. Also, there are many solicitors who take the opportunity to move from the employ of a commercial organisation to private practice, and vice versa; the whole profession is the stronger for this facility.

National and Local Government Just as the number of solicitors in commerce and industry is growing, so is that of the profession in national and local government. In all the main Departments of State there are solicitors working in legal sections, most especially in those which have to do with primarily legal matters. For example, the Land Registry has several solicitors on its staff, as does the Public Trustee Office, though both these bodies have an independent status. There are also solicitors – and barristers – working in the Army Office, for the Royal Air Force and for the Royal Navy. They can also be found in sections of the Home Office, the Department of Education and Science, the Lord Chancellor's

Department and in many other Government departments.

Several thousands of solicitors are at work in local government. There was a time when the chief executive of every local authority was a solicitor, and although this is not always so today, there are nevertheless many members of the profession appointed to the most senior post. Local authorities have many statutory powers, and possess the authority to make regulations that will have the force of the law in their own areas. The duties of the authorities, and the regulations they make, have to be understood and reviewed by the legal staff.

As with solicitors employed in commerce, the members of the profession working in local government are subject to special pressures. They are responsible to committees whose members have been elected and who operate from a political point of view. The solicitor employee, whatever his personal views, is not allowed to give advice or make decisions on a political basis. On the contrary, his task is to advise on the law as it is, though of course he can tender his opinion on the means whereby it can be changed, if this is what his political masters desire.

Another special area of difficulty can arise when strike action is proposed, particularly by a union to which the solicitor belongs. Under normal circumstances a solicitor does not strike; his duty is first to his client, not to his own interest. Also, he is an officer of the court, and it will render him liable to disciplinary action if he ignores a court summons or simply fails to turn up to deal with a case which is about to be heard and for which he is responsible. One can easily imagine the difficulty in which a solicitor is placed, working for a council whose members are strong supporters of the trade union movement, when his own union orders him to strike because of a dispute. On the one hand he is in danger of disciplinary action by his professional body, and on the other he faces the prospect of being sacked by his employers if he fails to respond to a strike call. Fortunately, The Law Society is very well aware of the dilemma in which a solicitor can be placed, and special rules have been made regarding the conduct of trials and other matters which, if followed, greatly reduce the potential dangers. For example, a solicitor whose task it is to appear in court may ask an independent firm of solicitors to take on his function during the period of a strike, thus ensuring that the case goes forward, but allowing him to obey his union's instructions.

Once again, it should not be thought that solicitors working in local government are regularly facing such difficulties as described above. In fact, they will be dealing regularly with the acquisition of property for new buildings, or for roads, approving the form of public notices, undertaking prosecutions in the local magistrates courts and performing a wide variety of other work for which they are qualified. Most of them will have started their professional career in local government, and will have moved from place to place in order to obtain advancement. It is a good and satisfying career, and as with other fields in which solicitors work, there are high rewards for those who succeed.

SOLICITORS

Public Legal Services

Andrew Arden

In other chapters, the way the law works has been described in some detail. But there is one problem which has not yet been touched upon. That is the problem that some people have, both in gaining access to a lawyer and in paying for his services. This is a problem encountered by many people: those who are poor, unfamiliar with what the law can do for them and living in areas where there may be no lawyers working at all. It is with these people, their problems and the legal services that are available to help them, that we are concerned in this chapter.

From the sort of work which has been described as the normal material handled in the office of the average solicitor – whether in a town or in the country – it would be easy to think that the poor did not have much need for lawyers. Those who have no money or property are not too concerned about making wills. Nor, indeed, will they be performing commercial transactions on which they will require a lawyer's advice. The contracts that they make are likely to be of such little value that the cost of a lawyer's services would be disproportionate even if something goes wrong.

In fact, the law touches the life of each and every member of society. Just as drivers are constantly subject to the laws of the road when they are in their cars, so also are we all surrounded by a plethora of regulations and controls on our behaviour. In addition, there is a mass of rights or privileges to which individuals may be entitled, designed to balance out some of the least acceptable social inequalities and secure a decent standard of living for every member of society.

If we are to achieve a truly equal society, one which is as just as we like to claim, then everybody must have an equal chance of obtaining assistance when they come into contact, and most especially when they come into conflict, with these laws. This might seem, at first glance, a comparatively simple proposition and an ideal which it ought not to be too difficult to achieve. After all, many people today have heard of legal aid and one would think that if it does not reach enough people, the answer is to make it more readily available.

Unfortunately, this has proved not to be the case. Legal aid does no more than make the services of a single solicitor, and sometimes a barrister, available to an individual client. But the problems of the poor, those living in deprived areas, are so massive and often so complex, frequently affecting not just one individual but a whole class of the population, that they often need much greater resources than can be provided by a lawyer acting on his own.

Before we look at what services are available for these problems, it is necessary to understand what they are. It is also necessary to understand why it is that the traditional solicitor in private practice may not be able to cope with them. We are not here concerned, in the main, with legal assistance to those charged with criminal offences. This work is part of the traditional role of the lawyer and although there are circumstances when the service may be less than what is needed, by and large criminal defence work only occasionally touches the lives of a whole community or a whole section of the population. The problems with which we are concerned are those which constantly underlie the lives of very many people.

The Problems of the Poor The areas of law with which we are dealing are now usually called 'welfare law.' They are the offspring of the welfare state. Some are direct welfare laws, those which deal with the provision of welfare rights; others fall within a class called protective legislation, those literally designed to protect the rights of certain people, such as employment and housing laws. Let us take an example which, although dramatic, is a far from uncommon tale of what can happen to people caught in what is aptly described as the 'poverty trap'.

A man loses his job. It may be through no fault of his own, it may have come about through some vagary of the economy or by a change of policy. It may even be because the housing in which he has been living is in poor condition and he has suffered through ill health so that he is no longer fit for his work. He may already have been in financial difficulties: living in poor quality housing is very expensive – there are high heating costs because of damp and draughts, internal decoration does not last, clothing and furniture are damaged. When he falls out of work, he may be entitled to unemployment benefit, or he may need supplementary benefit. In either case, it is a safe bet that he will not receive adequate subsistence for himself and his family. It is likely that he will fall behind with rent, rates or mortgage repayments. There will not be enough money with which to feed and clothe the children properly. The family will be under strain: matrimonial difficulties may ensue. At this stage, a social worker, concerned about the children, may decide to take them into care. This will intensify the strain on the parents. Eviction may follow. Because the children are not living with them, the parents will be rehoused in a smaller property, one that may not be big enough to accommodate the children. And because there is nowhere for them to go to, the authorities may decide to keep the children in care. The family has broken up entirely. Nor would it be surprising if, at this point, the parents themselves reached the end of their tethers with each other and divorce followed.

This story may seem exceptional. It is a story which is unlikely ever to get into the newspapers. No one point in the story reveals anything sufficiently interesting to call it 'news'. But taken together there is a heartbreaking tale: and yet it is one that is going on every day in many of Britain's deprived areas. The question is: what could a lawyer do for them? For at every stage in that story there was something which a welfare lawyer might have been able to do which might have averted the sequence of events.

The loss of job may not have been fair, or the amount of redundancy money offered inadequate. Reinstatement or compensation could be fought for. The condition of the family home may be a matter for legal proceedings, either against the local authority or against a private landlord. Damages might be sought for the extra costs of living caused by the disrepair. If there is a mort-

gage, an arrangement might be made on the client's behalf to pay only interest and suspend repayments of capital until the family is out of financial difficulty. Similarly, compromises might be sought with the landlord or the local authority before the rent and rates arrears become too high. And the lawyer will need to look into whether the client is receiving his rent and rates rebates or allowances. If the client is living on supplementary benefit, there are additional entitlements which he may not even know he can claim, for example for clothing. The decision of the social worker may be premature and, properly advised and represented, may be resisted. In the same way, it may be possible to combat the eviction proceedings or arrange for a possession order to be suspended. And, even then, a decision to rehouse the family in such a way that the children could not be released from care is another decision which articulate and informed representation might avert.

The irony of all this is twofold: first of all, it is extremely unlikely that the people involved, the clients, will be aware that there are all these provisions for their benefit which might be used, nor are they likely to be aware that a lawyer could help in so many ways. Secondly, only a trained welfare lawyer would himself be aware of all these possibilities. For the sorts of subject in which lawyers are trained, reflected in the sorts of work which they have been described as doing, do not include to any considerable extent in many of the matters relevant to the story we have just read. Indeed, the only point at which the average lawyer would be automatically competent to assist would be on the divorce.

Apart from these three examples of welfare law, housing, employment and welfare benefits, there are other areas of law which affect large parts of the population: for example, consumer protection laws, laws governing race relations and sex discrimination, immigration controls. At the time of writing, there are one and a half million unemployed; 40 per cent of the privately rented accommodation in the country lacks one or more of the basic living amenities, 30 per cent is in substantial disrepair, just under 25 per cent is unfit for human habitation by legal standards. In the field of welfare benefits, astonishingly high percentages of people entitled to claim do not do so, mostly because they do not know about their rights or how to exercise them. These are contained in massive blocks of complicated legislation beyond the reach and comprehension of the very people they are designed to affect or benefit. When the legal rights of such large sections of the population are going wholly by default, then it is a time for general concern.

Mere access to a lawyer on its own is not going to be enough if people do not know that they have rights in the first place. Furthermore, even today, many people do not appreciate that they can obtain the services of a lawyer under one or other of the legal aid or advice systems. But these are admittedly comparatively easy problems to solve by the use of publicity. There are other reasons why conventional legal practice is ill-suited to cope with these problems. For a start, lawyers have not traditionally been trained in these subjects, nor have they regarded them as normal areas of their work.

This is easy to understand: legal aid has not been with us long. Lawyers in private practice must make a living. People with the problems we have been discussing do not have the money to pay for a lawyer. And because, for these reasons, lawyers do not do this sort of work, it is not appreciated that they can help.

Secondly, there is the problem of finding a lawyer: lawyers' offices are, for the most part, in the commercial centres of a town. Even if the client knows how to find a lawyer, there are more difficulties getting to him. The lawyer's office will only be open during normal office hours. Many people are reluctant or cannot afford to take the time off work that will be needed. They might be afraid of losing their jobs, or else may be embarrassed to admit they have legal problems. When the client gets to the lawyer's office, he finds a business-like atmosphere and reception which makes him feel, not unnaturally, ill at ease. When he meets the solicitor, the chances are that the solicitor will be a middle-class man without experience or comprehension of living conditions as the client knows them. The client will sense this lack of understanding. It will frustrate him, make it increasingly difficult for him to make himself clear; he will leave feeling that he has inadequately expressed himself, the chances are that he will blame himself for all this and the visit to the solicitor, instead of alleviating his fears and worries, intensifies them and makes him despair of getting any help anywhere.

Of course most solicitors in private practice seek to do their best by every client, regardless of class or the nature of the case. But experience may easily have left him, like the client, in ignorance of the possibilities contained in, for example, the public health or housing legislation, or social security laws. Nevertheless there are serious efforts underway to try and redress this imbalance. Lawyers have long recognised that these problems exist and have always contributed to the schemes which have tried to bridge that gap between the help people need and the resources for assistance which are available.

At the present time, there are a large number of different schemes in operation seeking to bring legal services to those who are most in need. A review of what is presently available is also a review of what has been done in the past and, to a lesser extent, of what can be done in the future.

Legal Aid and Advice The legal aid scheme is the best known system for bringing help to those who cannot afford to pay for a lawyer. There are two parts to it: legal aid and legal advice. We are talking here about both civil and criminal matters. It is perhaps most logical to start with legal advice.

There have been several systems in operation in the past under which people have been able to get a slice of a lawyer's time for not very considerable sums of money. The most recent scheme to be introduced, by solicitors themselves, is the £5 initial interview. The local solicitors lists, which are now available in public libraries, Citizens' Advice Bureaux and from other advice giving agencies, contain information about firms willing to act

for legally aided clients and about those who will give an exploratory initial interview of up to 30 minutes for a maximum fee of £5. Under the Green Form Scheme (or the £25 scheme) a person can get up to £25 of a solicitor's work, including possibly such charges as for postage, telephone or photocopying, and this work will be provided either free or for a graduated contribution from the client which depends upon a rough-and-ready means test administered by the solicitor himself. A solicitor can do any kind of legal work under the scheme except represent a client in court or before most tribunals. If legal aid itself is not available for a court appearance, and it is only exceptionally available for a tribunal appearance, the lawyer may, if he can keep the cost within the scheme or is not too concerned about charging for every hour of his work, assist a client to present his own case before the court or tribunal. In matrimonial cases, the work which a lawyer may do under this scheme can be up to £45. If he needs to exceed these limits he can apply for an extension to the Law Society. The Green Form scheme is most used for giving preliminary advice, helping to complete legal aid applications, doing preparatory work, perhaps writing a letter or two or making a telephone call, and can also be used to obtain other specialist advice, from a surveyor, or a doctor, for example, provided that it is for the purpose of determining the client's legal position. Its most serious deficiencies are that a solicitor cannot work many hours for the sums involved and that the point at which contributions are required is unrealistically low. However, those in receipt of supplementary benefit and similarly low incomes will not have to pay a contribution at all.

Once court action is involved, full legal aid will be needed. If it is a criminal matter, then it is only available for those defending a case and it is granted or refused by the criminal court before whom the matter comes up. It is not uncommon for a magistrates' court to refuse legal aid for hearings before it and even to refuse to grant legal aid for a case which will be heard in a Crown Court before a judge and jury. The Crown Court can then reconsider the matter itself and they are generally not ungenerous in grants of legal aid.

The civil Legal Aid Scheme is administered by The Law Society. It is available to anyone taking or defending civil proceedings, with certain exceptions and providing they qualify under the means test. To obtain it, an application must be filed stating the nature of the case being taken or defended, a statement of the litigant's own account of the matter and the information on which the means test is based. The client may either select a solicitor of his or her own choice, or else leave it to the Law Society to allot one. The application form may be obtained from the Law Society or from most solicitors and many advice agencies.

This system, too, has certain serious deficiencies. First of all, it does not normally apply to tribunal work, even although a large number of rights are determined in front of tribunals, such as employment tribunals, rent tribunals, national insurance and supplementary benefit tribunals. The theory for this is that tribunals are

supposed to be an informal means of justice. But most people – including some lawyers – find them just as intimidating as a court, and if a person is nervous in putting his case, he is just as likely to be nervous in a tribunal as in a court. Lawyers are permitted to appear before tribunals, even though legal aid is not available. Thus it is not uncommon to find, for example, an employer or a landlord who has been able to afford legal representation but an employee or tenant who has not.

Secondly, as with the Green Form Scheme, the levels at which people qualify are low and there is a not substantial slice of the population who are deemed not to be poor enough to qualify for legal aid and yet who cannot realistically afford to pay a lawyer. Changes introduced in April 1979 have gone some way towards ameliorating the situation. Even when legal aid is granted, there may be a hefty contribution to pay. When it is granted,

however, it works in this way: the lawyer continues to act on the client's instructions, but the Law Society pays lawyer's fees at the end of the day out of the legal aid fund.

This, however, leads to a further problem. Even when a person wins a case and a court orders the losing side to pay the winner's costs, there may be a difference between what the law allows one side to charge the other, and what the law allows a solicitor to charge his own client. This may not make much sense to the layman. The result, however, is that there is still a difference to be made up by the winning client. This is also true when the client is legally aided: The Law Society, as administrator of the Scheme, must pay the difference. And, if the legally aided client wins any money from the other side, The Law Society is permitted to pass this difference on to the client. This is called 'the statutory charge.' The effect of it may be illustrated in a simple example: a woman sues her husband in divorce proceedings for a share in the matrimonial home. She wins, perhaps, a share worth £3,000. The husband may be ordered to pay her costs. If the case has been long and complicated, the costs may run into four figures. The difference between what the husband pays of her costs and what the Law Society has to pay her solicitors may itself be several hundred pounds. And that will come out of her share of the matrimonial home.

The last major problem is that in the main it is only the services of a lawyer in private practice which are provided under legal aid, and that brings into consideration all of the factors mentioned in the earlier part of this section. In addition, it is worth mentioning that legal aid pays solicitors at a noticeably lower rate than would a private paying client, so that there is no incentive for solicitors to specialise in this sort of work and they are, indeed, expected to subsidise it out of higher-paying work. This, of course, means that legal aid work has a low priority in most practices and encourages the dissipation of experience in the problems most likely to be encountered by those seeking legal aid.

Nonetheless, there are a few firms, most of them in London, which have set themselves up to specialise in welfare law problems and which have sought to break down the barriers described earlier. Some of these firms are branches of other, more conventional practices, so that they are, to some extent, still subsidised by private practice. Others do almost nothing but legal aid, although most find it necessary to take on some conveyancing in order to make it pay. These firms, especially those which concentrate almost exclusively on legal aid work, have found that it is possible in a fairly short time to build up expertise in welfare law. They make a valuable contribution to the problems of the welfare law client and can pride themselves on maximising the use of the legal aid system in a way that achieves a very considerable effect.

Nor has this specialisation been confined to solicitors. A small number of barristers have set themselves up in chambers to specialise in this sort of work. All of the comments which were made earlier about the class, background and training of solicitors can be made with even greater force about barristers. Indeed, barristers pride themselves on their distance from their clients, although those few who have abandoned the traditional detachment of their profession have found that they have lost nothing of value to a case and, indeed, gained the greater insight which has often meant that little extra effort which turns the balance during a hearing.

The Legal Action Group Strictly speaking, this does not give a direct service to the public. Nonetheless, it would be wrong to leave this organisation out of a description of facilities available in welfare law. It was founded in 1972 by a group of lawyers who were discontented with the slight provision available in this area of law. They determined to lobby for improvements and greater facilities and one of their major contributions was to publish the *Bulletin*, which now comes out monthly,

and which both serves to keep concerned members of the profession in touch with what is going on in the development of legal services in welfare law and also to inform them, in a way that the traditional legal journals have not, about the law in these specialised subjects. It runs training courses, both for lawyers and lay advisers, on such matters as housing, employment, social security and the legal aid system itself. It publishes booklets about matters too long or too specialised for its *Bulletin* and it has a number of local branches which perpetuate this work in local settings, in addition to contributing to the knowledge and direction of the national organisation.

LAG has been extremely influential in this area, especially in legal aid and in the setting up of law centres, which will be discussed at the end of this chapter, and this influence and the specialised knowledge it has built up were recognised in the appointment of its first Director, Susan Marsden-Smedley, to the Royal Commission on Legal Services. In addition to the matters mentioned above, it keeps an up-to-date list of the sorts of agencies which provide welfare law facilities and which we will now go on to describe.

Legal Advice Centres There are, in fact, very few full-time agencies which describe themselves as legal advice centres. A legal advice centre provides just that, legal advice, but does not provide legal representation. Legal advice centres are often confused with law centres, which do provide representation and which operate in that respect like any other firm of solicitors. Most legal advice centres are a part of another agency, group or organisation which seeks to provide assistance to people living in the area in which it works by organising legal advice sessions run by volunteer lawyers at the sorts of time and in the sorts of place which are most convenient to the people they are trying to help, in the evenings or at weekends. All manner of agencies organise these sessions: from Church groups to community organisations, from residents' associations to advice centres run by the local authority social services departments in a few districts.

They are invariably free and the lawyers who man the sessions give their services gratuitously. They are usually advertised and well-known locally and often in very heavy demand. Many have colourful, shop-front premises. The two main difficulties are, first of all, that as the lawyers are mere volunteers they attend to this work in addition to their paid jobs and are frequently already tired by the time they turn to their legal advice session clients. Secondly, they have no power to represent people in the way that lawyers normally can: they cannot issue proceedings or even write letters in a personal capacity threatening to sue. They may write a letter for the client himself to send, or on behalf of the agency, but if the matter is not resolved by correspondence, the client must be referred to a solicitor in private practice. Usually their work is confined to advising people on what their position is in law and trying to help them come to a decision about what to do in their own particular circumstances.

Citizens' Advice Bureaux These are the best known of the advice agencies. They have been around for a long time. Their task, too, is primarily that of advising people of their rights or their legal position, rather than actually representing them in sorting out their problems. Most of them now run legal advice sessions on the lines described above, but a few employ full-time lawyers whose job is partly to see clients and partly to provide the other, lay, advice workers with a lawyer to turn to for professional guidance in the course of their advice giving. They may represent people before tribunals, but not in court actions. They, too, provide their services free of charge. But, again, when a matter is approaching court action, it must be transferred to a practising lawyer.

Other Specialist Agencies The agencies just described try to provide a wide range of advice. There are some agencies which provide advice, and sometimes actual assistance and representation, but only in limited areas of work. For example, there are now centres specialising in helping people with their financial problems. There are also a large number of Housing Aid and Action Centres, some funded by local authorities, others funded from alternative sources, such as Shelter, the national housing organisation which has become the spokesman for the homeless.

These housing centres rarely employ the services of a lawyer, but usually have a close working relationship either with the local authority legal departments, if they are themselves funded by the authority, or with solicitors in private practice in their areas. The degree of experience built up by the workers in these centres who are without legal training is such that it often exceeds the experience and knowledge of solicitors in practice. But the knowledge is usually confined to housing problems so that they can have some difficulty assisting in any broader way those of their clients who are within that poverty trap described above.

Other sorts of specialist agency seek to help people with welfare rights problems: local Claimants' Unions and local branches of the Child Poverty Action Group. CPAG itself maintains a legal department at its national headquarters, the Citizens' Rights Office, which can act for a client, although it will generally only do so where cases raise points of general importance as there is only one full-time lawyer on the staff. It also publishes material of value to welfare rights workers, especially its *National Welfare Benefits Handbook* which is produced almost every year, edited by Ruth Lister. The CRO also undertakes a certain amount of tribunal representation, as do the local branches.

One important resource in the field of welfare law is that provided by the trades unions. Most of them offer a legal facility to their members, as well as training in their rights and how to exercise them. This legal facility usually extends to representation, whether before tribunals or in courts. However, they mainly concern themselves with problems arising from employment rather than all the problems of a legal nature which confront their members.

Neighbourhood or Community Law Centres Law centres represent the most recent development in the provision of legal services to people in deprived areas and they certainly constitute the most exciting development. The difference between them and other local agencies has already been described: they can act for people in the same way as a lawyer. They have full-time, salaried lawyers on their staffs. They are allowed to advertise their services in the community, contrary to the normal rule against 'touting' for work. Many of them operate from offices with shop-fronts in which they can display information about rights, local matters of relevance and about the service they provide. They generally work only for clients living within a specified 'catchment area'. They seek and achieve an informal atmosphere in which the client feels at home, and are situated in the areas where there is the greatest need. Those which are open to the public are open outside ordinary office hours so that people can drop in at times which are convenient to them whether it is during the day, in the evenings or at weekends.

Law Centres do not charge for their services. They are managed by representatives of the local community in which each operates, and are funded in a variety of different ways: by central government, local authorities, and even by charitable bodies. They too use the services of volunteer lawyers at their late sessions, but the work of these lawyers is less confined than in a conventional legal advice centre because the law centre can actually take on, handle and follow through its cases. Thus the volunteer lawyer can start off a case in a late session which is then taken up by the centre itself and conducted on the client's behalf in court.

A law centre's solicitors frequently appear in local courts, although they can, like any other solicitor, instruct a barrister if they wish. Barristers too are employed in law centres, They work closely with the solicitors and can also appear in all the courts in which a barrister has the right of audience. In addition, many law centres employ community workers, and all of them devote some of their staff time to the problems of the community as a whole. By working in particular neighbourhoods, they build up a knowledge of what problems most seriously affect large sections of that community. They come to look at problems not just as lawyers on individual cases, but with a much broader perspective. For example, one law centre is engaged on working on behalf of a large number of people in its community in trying to get the conditions of the roads and pavements in the area improved: this is not a problem affecting just one client, but all those living in the area. Yet it is a problem which no single individual could afford to tackle on his own, even with legal assistance.

Some law centres have what is called a 'closed-door' policy. This means that they concentrate exclusively on working on issues with a broad impact in the community. They rely on other agencies in their areas to keep in touch with them as to what concerns the people in the area, or on their own contact with people living there. They devote a lot of their attention to educating the community, as to what rights they have and as to how to exercise them. They may run full courses, or publish information materials. They seek out and work in depth on matters of general importance. They may take selected 'test cases' or use avenues of law other than courts for their clients' benefit. Other law centres have an 'open-door' policy: they help quite literally anyone who comes in off the street, provided that the problem is of the sort they are equipped and permitted to tackle. Law centres do not handle every type of case: they do not usually do divorce work, they rarely do conveyancing, only a few do adult criminal work – in those areas where it constitutes a major community problem in its own right. Generally, they try to keep away from the sort of work with which a solicitor in private practice is most familiar and at home.

There are two reasons for this: first of all, The Law Society is the governing body which determines whether a law centre ought to have a waiver from the normal practice rules, specifically that relating to advertising. It imposes conditions about the sort of work a centre will do before agreeing to the waiver. It seeks to protect its members from what they believe might be unfair competition from a free, and advertised service. This is unlikely to be the case, in any event, because the clients of a law centre are by and large people who would not go to a private solicitor anyway and who could not afford to do so. Secondly, law centres which are open to the public have far, far too much work to handle as it is, without taking on the sorts of work which private practice is used to dealing with. Indeed, most law centres have to decide on their priorities and refer to private practitioners some cases which affect the poorer members of each community, and which may even affect large numbers of people in the community. In this way, rather than detract from the work of private practice, it has been the experience of all solicitors where a law centre opens up that work for private practice is increased.

It is often hard for people who come for help to a law centre to understand why the centre cannot assist them. It is just as hard for the staff to turn away people clearly in need, knowing that they will either let their particular problem go by default or else may have to pay a solicitor. But there is no law centre open to the public which can adequately handle all the work which comes in. It is for this reason that many law centres increasingly turn to a closed-door policy or reduce the amount of casework in order to concentrate on broader questions, or on acting for whole groups of people with a common problem at one time. It has been the experience here and in other countries where law centres have operated that the more casework which is done, the greater will be the demand for it in the future. And if two lawyers cannot handle the work this year, four will still be in difficulties the next. It is easy to see why this should be so: law centres cover populations ranging from the tens to the hundreds of thousands. As their reputations grow locally, so does the work. There is an infinite pool of problems if they are tackled on an individual basis.

The management committees of law centres have the final say in their operation, for example on such questions as which areas of work they will take on or treat as priorities. The majority of the management committee will be local representatives, perhaps from tenants' or residents' associations or from other agencies. There will also be a representative of the local law society, who forms the liaison with the private practice profession in the area, and perhaps a councillor or two, or a representative from a social services department. The management committee employs all the staff, including the lawyers, in the centre.

Although the centres never charge for their own work, they may use the legal aid scheme or the Green Form scheme, or they may ask a client to pay for the cost, for example, of a barrister at court or some other such specialist service. If they win, they are entitled to charge costs to the other side in the normal way. Generally, all the staff are given some training in the problems affecting each community. The centres seek to break down internal divisions between staff as much as they seek to dissolve the distance between themselves and their clients. They recognise that everybody's task is equally relevant, necessary and important to the end product. They have brought a new degree of professionalism to welfare law work and its clients that has until recently been sadly lacking, and that most of the other facilities for the provision of this resource do not have the capacity to give.

The law centres working group is the national organisation to which all law centres belong. There are at present only about 30 such centres in the country but it is to be hoped that the valuable role they fulfill will mean that they achieve the highest priority in the future development of legal services to those who are otherwise without adequate assistance in this complex society.

Conclusion It is sometimes felt, on both sides, that those lawyers who work in this area of law full-time are not a part of the conventional profession. To some extent that is true and, perhaps, a necessary attitude if old-fashioned barriers are to be broken down. On the other hand, these lawyers too are products of the profession and to that extent the legal profession may take some pride in the progress which has been made towards redressing the imbalance. There is a long way to go before we can talk of a truly just system. Some would say that it cannot be achieved without changing many aspects of the substance of the law itself. But in the meantime, work with communities or with individual clients can both serve to avoid a lot of immediate hardship and also to pinpoint a number of the actual problems of society today. Whatever sort of society we have or are likely to have, there will always be some regulation of it and that is likely to mean that there will always be lawyers. It is to be hoped that they will continue to contribute to reform and to the improvement of society in as broad a way as their perspective permits and that they will not be tightly confined to maintaining the existing *status quo*.

Design'd & Engrav'd by W. Hogarth ———   The BENCH.   Publish'd as the Act directs, 4 Sep. 1758.

Of the different meaning of the Words Character, Caracatura *and* Outrè *in Painting and Drawing.* ——
This Plate would have been better explain'd had the Author lived a Week longer.

There are hardly any two things more essentially different than **Character** and **Caracatura** nevertheless
they are usually confounded and mistaken for each other: on which account this Explanation is attempted.
It has ever been allow'd that, when a **Character** is strongly mark'd in the living Face, it may be consider'd as
an Index of the mind, to express which with any degree of justness in Painting, requires the utmost Efforts of a great
Master. Now that which has, of late Years, got the name of **Caracatura**, is, or ought to be totally divested of every
Stroke that hath a tendency to good Drawing: it may be said to be a Species of Lines that are produc'd rather by the
hand of chance than of Skill; for the early Scrawlings of a Child which do but barely hint an Idea of an Human
Face, will always be found to be like some Person or other, and will often form such a Comical Resemblance
as in all probability the most eminent **Caracaturers** of these times will not be able to equal with Design, be
cause their Ideas of Objects are so much more perfect than Childrens, that they will unavoidably introduce some
kind of Drawing; for all the humourous Effects of the fashionable manner of **Caracaturing** chiefly depend on
the surprize we are under at finding our selves caught with any sort of Similitude in objects absolutely remote in their kind. Let it be observ'd the more remote in their Nature the greater is the Excellence of these
Pieces; as a proof of this, I remember a famous **Caracatura** of a certain Italian Singer, that struck at
first sight, which consisted only of a Streight perpendicular Stroke with a Dot over it. As to the French
word **Outrè** it is different from the foregoing, and signifies nothing more than the exagérated
outlines of a Figure, all the parts of which may be in other respects a perfect and true Picture of
Nature. A Giant *or a Dwarf* may be call'd a common Man **Outrè**. So any part as a Nose, or a Leg, made
or less bigger than it ought to be, is that part **Outrè**. † which is all that is to be understood by this word, so
injudiciously us'd to the prejudice of **Character**. ———

                                                                    † See Excess, Analysis of Beauty. Chap. 6.

THE BENCH

The Judiciary

Gavin Drewry

Serjeant Buzfuz, who had proceeded with such volubility that his face was perfectly crimson, here paused for breath. The silence awoke Mr Justice Stareleigh, who immediately wrote down something with a pen without any ink in it, and looked unusually profound, to impress the jury that he always thought most deeply with his eyes shut. Serjeant Buzfuz proceeded.

Charles Dickens, *Pickwick Papers*

It is profoundly to be hoped that even in the comparatively remote era of Victorian Britain there were few judges as silly and somnolent as Mr Justice Stareleigh, who presided over the celebrated fictional trial of Bardell against Pickwick. Dickens did not much like lawyers and judges. Nor did he like the law's delays. His later novel, *Bleak House*, incorporates a fierce denunciation of the dilatory processes of the Court of Chancery, an institution destined soon to lose its historic identity in the major reforms of the courts which took place in the 1870s. In the hyperbolic words of a twentieth century biographer of Dickens, Una Pope-Hennessey:

The fly-wheel of the story of *Bleak House* is the Court of Chancery: all cogs move in connection with it. Principal and lesser persons alike are all drawn into the machinery and are one by one lethalised (*sic*) by the monster operating as Justice and Equity. The villain of the piece is the Law, protector of the Vested Interest. The Lord Chancellor and his Court represent the apparatus of evil.

Another famous 19th century critic of courts and judiciary was the librettist, W S Gilbert, a man whose own early attempts to make a living at the Bar had ended in ignominious failure. The short piece, *Trial by Jury*, has among its characters a comical judge who makes no secret of the 'jobbery' which brought about his appointment.

We may be tempted at this point to say that times have changed and eliminated, or at least drastically diminished many of the evils of which Dickens and his contemporaries so vociferously complained. At the same time, however, it is important to note than many of the targets of today's critics – costs, delays, professional restrictive practices, unnecessary obscurity of court rituals and legal language – are much the same as they have always been. And although many of the attributes of the judiciary today are different from those of a century ago, many are not. The basic job specification of a judge in England – listening to evidence, applying and interpreting (and occasionally repairing) the law enacted by Parliament, and developing the judge-made common law – have never altered and probably never will. The universal essence of the judicial process as judges themselves see it is applying the law as it is and not as the judge himself feels it ought to be. This requires a judge to be cautious, often downright conservative, in acknowledging social change. And this inherent professional conservatism has always drawn adverse criticism from those who are themselves anxious to change the social order, as well as from those who equate such conservatism with party-political

The English Judges

Judge	Number Serving (1979)	Salary (1979)	Where they sit
Lord High Chancellor	1	£22,228	Occasionally in House of Lords and Privy Council
Lord Chief Justice	1	£29,792	Presides over Criminal Division of Court of Appeal and Queen's Bench Divisional Court
Master of the Rolls	1	£27,261	Presides over Civil Division of Court of Appeal
President of the Family Division	1	£25,961	Presides over Family Division of High Court
Lords of Appeal in Ordinary	9	£27,261	House of Lords and Privy Council
Lords Justices of Appeal	16	£24,799	Court of Appeal
Vice-Chancellor	1	£23,886	Responsible for organisation and management of the Chancery Division of the High Court

High Court Judges:
  Queen's Bench
  Chancery
  Family
	
	47
	11
	16
		
		} £23,386
			Trial judges in their respective divisions and in the more important Crown Courts. Some also sit in Divisional Courts and Court of Appeal

Circuit Judges	305	£16,015	Trials and appeals in Crown Courts. Civil work in county courts
Recorders	360	£66 a day	Part time in Crown Courts

Stipendiary magistrates:
  London (Chief)
  London
  Provincial cities
	
	1
	41
	11
		
		£16,015
		£14,202
		£14,202
			Magistrates in London and some other large cities such as Birmingham and Manchester

Lay magistrates (Justices of the Peace)	28,000 (approx)	Expenses only	Magistrates and juvenile justices in courts throughout England and Wales. Some appellate work in Crown Courts

n.b. Judicial salaries were increased by 12½% in June 1979 with retrospective effect from April 1, 1979.

Conservatism. We will encounter some manifestations of this kind of criticism later in the chapter.

One major topic to be considered in this chapter is the process of appointing judges. The actual procedures have not changed much. English judges themselves still tend to come from privileged social backgrounds; once appointed, they still do much the same kind of job as their forebears; but one change that has taken place is that the party political basis for making judicial appointments all but disappeared in the first three decades of this century. It is with the appointment of judges that I shall begin; but first it is necessary to give a brief description of the principal judicial offices themselves.

Varieties of Judge English judges come, figuratively as well as literally, in a wide variety of different shapes and sizes, corresponding to the wide range of different types of court and embodying a distinct hierarchy in rank. The table opposite shows that hierarchy in descending rank-order.

The weight of numbers clearly lies in the bottom half of the table, particularly with the lay magistracy (justices of the peace), who try some 97.5 per cent of all criminal cases and are responsible for committing (i.e. carrying out a preliminary review of the case to see if it is strong enough to go to trial) the remaining 2.5 per cent, comprising the most serious types of offence, for trial by jury in the Crown Courts. Magistrates' courts also deal with some civil matters, including ancillary matrimonial proceedings, and with cases concerning juveniles alleged to have committed offences or to be in need of care and control. Magistrates are appointed by the Lord Chancellor, who is advised by local committees set up for the purpose. Although they are not lawyers by training, newly appointed magistrates are now required to undergo a short course of instruction and observation, with particular reference to court procedure and sentencing technique; in court they have the services of a legally trained clerk who has to negotiate the narrow and rocky channel between his proper function of giving advice and the improper one of trespassing upon the magistrates' own responsibility for taking the actual decision in a case.

Although magistrates cannot be ignored in a chapter on the English judiciary, if only because the legal system would seize-up overnight if they were to disappear or go on strike, our main concern is with the judges in the top half of the table. It is in the High Court, and more particularly, in the higher appellate courts that the decisions are made whose effects ripple outwards to create new law or new perspectives upon old law.

The Lord Chancellor The judges of the superior courts (including circuit judges and recorders) are appointed by the Queen on the advice of the Lord Chancellor (or in some cases, the Prime Minister – who will usually take his cue from the Lord Chancellor), and a word needs to be said about this curious office. Britain does not have a Ministry of Justice. Many 'law and order' functions, such as the police, come under the

responsibility of the Home Office; no particular minister has responsibility for law reform, though since 1965 there has been a standing advisory body called the Law Commission, which is answerable to the Lord Chancellor; the latter also appoints judges, magistrates and the chairmen of administrative tribunals (which have specialised quasi-judicial functions but are not, strictly speaking, courts). He himself is a constitutional hybrid. First, he is a Cabinet minister, the Government's chief spokesman in the House of Lords and in charge of a small government department run by a team of civil servants. Secondly, he himself is head of the judiciary: he can, and sometimes does, preside over the House of Lords, in its judicial capacity as final court of appeal from the courts of the United Kingdom, and over the Judicial Committee of the Privy Council, which is still the final appeal court for a number of Commonwealth countries. Thirdly, he has the powers of judicial patronage, already mentioned. Fourthly, he sits on the Woolsack to chair the House of Lords when it sits in its legislative capacity.

Apart from being a standing insult to those constitutional experts who still subscribe to a fundamentalist position on 'separation of powers', this is clearly a formidable combination of jobs for any middle-aged man to take on. The aspect that has tended to go by the board in recent years is the task of sitting in person to hear appeals; apart from anything else, the judicial House of Lords has taken to sitting in a committee room away from the Chamber of the House, and does so at times when the House is simultaneously sitting in its legislative capacity. Formerly, judicial business was transacted in the Chamber before each day's legislative business began. Now the Lord Chancellor has to face the fact that he cannot be in two places at once. Nevertheless, the present Lord Chancellor, Lord Hailsham, who has served in two Conservative governments, makes a point of sitting judicially as often as he possibly can. His Labour predecessors, Lord Gardiner and Lord Elwyn-Jones, were much less eager to don the mantle of judge.

Given the importance attached to the non-political character of the judiciary (discussed below) it is ostensibly a good idea if the Lord Chancellor, though a government minister, is someone slightly detached from the more rabid manifestations of party politics. In this regard, too, Lord Hailsham's tenure of office has been a slight departure from modern convention; although an outstandingly able lawyer, he was a flamboyant figure in Conservative Party politics in the 1960s, and had even been a major contender for the leadership of the Party when Harold Macmillan suddenly stepped down as Prime Minister in 1963.

Appointment of Judges So much for the head of the judiciary and the appointer of judges. What of the judges themselves? The bare qualifications for judicial office are simply stated, but taken by themselves they mean very little. High Court judges must be barristers of at least ten years standing in the profession; Lords Justices of Appeal must either have served as High

Court judges or be barristers of fifteen years' standing; Lords of Appeals in Ordinary must be barristers (or Scottish advocates – it is invariable practice to have at least two Lords of Appeal with Scottish backgrounds, since the House of Lords has a substantial jurisdiction in hearing appeals from Scotland) of fifteen years standing, or have held high judicial office (eg as Lord Chief Justice or Master of the Rolls) for at least two years. Lords of Appeal, assuming they are not already peers, are given life peerages on appointment to enable them to sit in the House of Lords. (There is no restriction upon their taking part in the legislative business of the House – apart from a convention that they should try to avoid issues of party political controversy – another affront to fanatical devotees of separation of powers.)

The first thing to notice is that all these top judicial jobs are reserved for barristers. There are rather fewer than 4,000 barristers in practice, and the reason which is usually given for restricting judicial appointments to this small circle is that word can quickly spread around the profession, and back to the Lord Chancellor's vigilant ear, about who has the requisite professional skills and moral integrity to be worthy of elevation to the Bench. If solicitors, who outnumber barristers by about eight to one, became eligible for senior judgeships then (it is argued) it would be much harder to maintain the necessary quality control, particularly as another carefully nurtured barristers' monopoly prevents solicitors from appearing as advocates in the higher courts and thereby having the chance to make a favourable impression upon the judges and the powers-that-be. This is somewhat hard on solicitors. It also gives rise to some disquiet of a more general character on the part of those who have doubts in principle about the virtues of a self-perpetuating oligarchy, and those who point out that the number of judgeships and other posts for which barristers alone are eligible has risen out of all proportion to the small size of the Bar, and that there is a risk of serious dilution of talent.

Some of the inter-professional tensions that can arise on this subject were seen in the debates on the Courts Bill in the parliamentary session 1970–1971. This measure brought about a major restructuring of the courts of intermediate jurisdiction (most notably, replacing the old system of local assizes and quarter sessions by a completely new network of Crown Courts, staffed by full-time circuit judges and part-time recorders). The Bill was based upon a report of a Royal Commission chaired by Lord Beeching, a man who had already acquired public fame (or notoriety) for his work in recommending the closure of uneconomic railway lines. The Report had recommended by a majority that solicitors as well as barristers should be eligible for appointment as circuit judges and recorders. The government disagreed. Solicitors fought back and the Lord Chancellor had to mediate in what was fast becoming an unedifying squabble between the two branches of the legal profession. The issue was resolved by a slightly ungainly compromise. Barristers *and* solicitors of ten years' standing were made eligible to become recorders, and now recorders of three years' standing can become

circuit judges. Not many solicitors have in fact been appointed as recorders. It surely cannot be long before the ranks of the higher judiciary are opened to suitably qualified solicitors: it is interesting to note that the present Lord Chief Justice, Lord Widgery, began his career as a solicitor, though he later atoned for his youthful folly by serving the requisite fifteen years at the Bar before becoming a High Court judge.

When considering appointments to judgeships it is necessary to say something about pay and conditions of service. It will be seen from the table that judges earn salaries which are, by the general standards of the British public service, quite high: top judges earn about the same as the Cabinet ministers and civil service permanent secretaries who run government departments. But the salaries are a good deal lower than top management posts in industry and commerce; a few years ago a High Court Judge, Sir Henry Fisher, was widely criticised for breaking with convention by leaving the Bench after only two years to take up a lucrative post in a merchant bank. More crucially, judgeships attract a much lower income than successful practice at the Bar. The invitation to join the Bench generally comes when a successful barrister is in his later forties or early fifties and earning a handsome living; if he has not been a success then the invitation would probably not have come at all. But there are few who can resist the tempting prospect of joining the *corps d' élite* of the legal world, and the knighthood and the prestige and the pension that go with it. The same kudos does not attach to circuit judgeships, and these posts are not a stepping stone to higher judicial office; fears are sometimes expressed that these lesser judicial posts may only be accepted by barristers who have achieved modest success and are willing to opt for a quiet life and guaranteed pension. Such fears may be exaggerated, though criticism of the judiciary tends to focus on the lower end of the hierarchy.

One of the attractions of judicial life is job security, which is founded upon long established principles of constitutional law. Written into legislation dating back to the Act of Settlement 1701, is the principle that senior judges hold office 'during good behaviour' and in the event of misconduct can be removed only on an address to the Queen by both Houses of Parliament. In theory, judges below the level of the High Court can be removed through the exercise of the Lord Chancellor's discretion, though in practice they also enjoy a good security of tenure. The salaries of the judiciary are a standing charge on the Consolidated Fund and cannot be altered by Parliament through the annual Estimates. There is now a compulsory retirement age of 75 for members of the higher judiciary, 72 for circuit judges, and 70 for justices of the peace.

Removal of Judges Parliament is not supposed to criticise particular judges except on a motion for their removal. Between 1700 and 1963 the conduct of seventeen High Court judges was the subject of critical motions in Parliament; but only one, an Irish judge, Sir Jonah Barrington, was actually removed, in 1830, for embezzling money which had been paid into court.

The phrase 'good behaviour' has never been precisely defined. In 1906, 347 Members of Parliament put down a motion criticising Mr Justice Grantham for grossly partisan conduct in the trial of disputed election petitions. The then Attorney-General quoted Sir Robert Peel as having said that the only grounds for removing a judge were 'corruption, partisanship, intentional moral delinquency'. Grantham, widely regarded as a bad judge, and one with an undisguised partisan prejudice in favour of the Conservative party, escaped removal, though his reputation undoubtedly suffered damage.

At the end of 1973, 197 Labour Members of Parliament put down a motion for the removal of the President of the controversial National Industrial Relations Court (since abolished – see below), Sir John Donaldson, but the motion was not debated. If it had been, Sir John would almost certainly have survived since the allegations against him, even if found proven, would not have fulfilled the very strict criteria for removal.

One small inroad into the principle of irremoveability was made by the Administration of Justice Act 1973, a section of which provides that the Lord Chancellor, following consultations with senior judges, can vacate a judicial appointment if satisfied that the judge concerned is unable to perform his duties because of a permanent incapacity of health, and is too ill to take the necessary step of resigning. This arose out of the unfortunate case of Lord Justice Winn who in 1970 had suffered a grievous stroke, and whose illness seriously depleted the manpower of the Court of Appeal for several months until he recovered sufficiently to resign and could then be replaced.

It should, in any event, be pointed out that Britain has no written constitution, and therefore judicial irremoveability is in no way entrenched. In theory the statutory safeguards of judicial independence could easily be repealed, though it would require a major revolution in social and political attitudes towards the judiciary for such a change ever to be seriously contemplated.

Judges and Politics Although judicial appointments are made by a government minister, it would nowadays be regarded as highly improper if the party political affiliations of an appointee were found to have played a part in securing his appointment. This is not to say that past or present service in Parliament is a disqualification for an aspirant to a judgeship (at the present time about 90 out of 635 Members of the House of Commons are barristers); indeed such service may be regarded as a positive advantage in broadening the judge's experience. But party loyalty as such no longer plays an overt part in the appointment process.

This was by no means always the case. Up to the 1920s it was accepted practice for Lord Chancellors to exercise judicial patronage to reward the party faithful. Professor Harold Laski (a scholarly, but hardly neutral observer, since he was a vigorous activist in the Labour Party), produced evidence in the 1930s which showed that of 139 appointments to the higher judiciary between 1832 and 1906, 80 judges were Members of Parliament at the time of their appointment, and 63 of those

80 were appointed when their own party was in power. Lord Halsbury who was Conservative Lord Chancellor from 1886 to 1892, and again from 1895 to 1905, acquired some notoriety for the partisan character of his judicial appointments, several of which proved to be highly unsatisfactory. One judge who fell into this category was Mr Justice Grantham, whom we have already encountered. In his book, *Tipping the Scales,* Henry Cecil writes that:

'Mr Justice Grantham ... together with Mr Justice Darling, Mr Justice Ridley and Mr Justice Lawrance, made up a quartet of some of the worst judges that this country has suffered from in this century. None of them should have been appointed ...'

He also reminds us that in the days when judicial appointments were a manifest part of the game of party politics the press was much more outspoken about judges than it is today. Of the appointment of Mr Justice Ridley the *Law Journal* said:

'The appointment can be defended on no ground whatsoever. It would be easy to name fifty members of the Bar with a better claim.'

It is not altogether fair to judge yesterday's actions by today's standards. Once the pendulum of a 'spoils' system has started to swing it would have taken a remarkable Lord Chancellor to cease the prevailing practice unilaterally to the detriment of his own party. Politicians were understandably concerned with maintaining at least an equilibrium between parties. In 1911 Robson, the Attorney-General, wrote to the Liberal Prime Minister, Asquith, asking for the appointment of more Lords of Appeal from the ranks of the Liberal Party. He pointed out that the judicial House of Lords,

'would have to play a great part in disputes that are legal in form but political in fact, and it would be idle to deny the resolute bias of the Judges – there and elsewhere. That bias will probably operate more than ever in cases that touch on labour, educational, constitutional and, for the future I might perhaps add, revenue questions.'

Gradually, it came to be accepted that professional skills do not necessarily flow from political loyalties, and by the time we get to Lord Sankey's Lord Chancellorship in 1929 we have reached the era of the professional and non-political judge, certainly at the top end of the judicial hierarchy.

Conflict with Trade Unions This did not mean that, overnight, the judges became immune from allegations of partisanship. In particular, the trade union movement and the Labour Party have frequently alleged that judges are consistently biased against the working man in cases involving trade union rights or disputes between employers and employees. As recently as May 1977, Mr Michael Foot, Leader of the House of Commons and Deputy Leader of the Labour Party, made such an allegation following a controversial decision by the Court of Appeal in a trade union dispute: his views were later endorsed by the Prime Minister, who was careful to say (one suspects disingenuously) that such criticism applied only to old cases and not to recent decisions.

The biggest controversy on this subject in recent years concerned the now defunct National Industrial Relations Court (NIRC), set up under the Industrial Relations Act 1971, which was the Conservative government's optimistic attempt to solve chronic labour disputes by erecting an elaborate framework of civil law. The Court was abolished by the next Labour government in 1974.

The Court was given the same status as the High Court, but conducted its business informally, attempting to work through conciliation rather than by strict application of legal rules and procedures. Although many of the cases that came before it – dealing, for example, with the unfair dismissal of a workman by his employer – were wholly uncontroversial, its very existence was seen by opponents of the 1971 Act as a provocative attempt to involve the judiciary in an area where partisan feeling inevitably runs high. Bitterness reached a peak with a number of cases heard in 1972 and 1973. In one case three London dockers were committed to prison for contempt of court by acting in defiance of an order forbidding them to picket a container depot employing unregistered labour: they were later released by the Court of Appeal. Another case culminated in the fining of a major union for contempt, and in the seizure of some of the union's assets when it refused to pay the fine. It was this case, and Sir John Donaldson's robust public utterances in defence of the Court's actions, which led to the moves in Parliament, already mentioned, to have him removed from office.

But the failure of the NIRC was not due to the failure of a judge, it stemmed from the inherent weakness of a piece of legislation which was not underpinned by the necessary consent of the powerful groups affected by it. The wider issue, whether the courts in general have dealt fairly with the disputes of workers and trade unions is hard to resolve conclusively. It is only fair to say, however, that many of the judges themselves are acutely aware of the difficulty of holding the scales of justice evenly. As long ago as 1923 a distinguished judge, Lord Justice Scrutton, put it like this:

'The habits you are trained in, the people with whom you mix, lead to your having a certain class of ideas of such a nature, that, when you have to deal with other ideas, you do not give as sound and accurate a judgement as you would wish. This is one of the great difficulties at present with Labour. Labour says: "where are your impartial judges? They all move in the same circle as the employers, and they are all educated and nursed in the same ideas as the employers. How can a Labour man or a trade unionist get impartial justice?" It is very difficult sometimes to be sure that you have put yourself in a thoroughly impartial position between two disputants, one of your own and one not of your class.'

Trade union law is one area where the judges are drawn inevitably into disputes which have a strongly political flavour. There are, of course, others. In the last two or three years, for example, the courts have been called upon to adjudicate in disputes about the extent of the central government's powers to issue binding instructions to elected local authorities in respect of schemes for secondary schooling; whether a private citizen has the right to go to the courts to seek to prevent an intended breach of the criminal law in circumstances where he himself is not individually affected by that breach; and whether a minister can repair a loophole in the law (which in this case permitted the legitimate evasion of an impending increase in television licence fees) without going through the proper procedures in Parliament.

In many contexts judicial decisions have significant political implications, however much judges claim to the contrary. A recent study by Professor J A G Griffith, *The Politics of the Judiciary*, refutes the proposition that judges are politically 'neutral'. He absolves them of 'a conscious and deliberate attempt to pursue their own interests or those of their class', but suggests that the most senior judges have 'a strikingly homogeneous collection of attitudes, beliefs and principles, which to them represents that public interest', and that ultimately the judicial process is always directed at conserving the *status quo*.

Constitutional questions The myth of separation between law and politics is still maintained. One manifestation of this is that, unlike other European countries, Britain does not have a comprehensive system of administrative law which closely regulates the conduct of public officials. There is no specialised administrative court. Above all, Britain does not possess a written constitution or a Bill of Rights. The judges have only a small part to play in determining constitutional questions, and no part at all in determining the constitutional validity of Acts of Parliament. Even where it can be shown that a piece of legislation has been enacted by defective procedure the courts cannot declare it invalid.

However, Britain has been going through a period of major constitutional upheaval, particularly in relation to the debate about devolving governmental functions from London to Edinburgh and Cardiff (which some see as the first step on the road to federalism) and to Britain's membership of the European Common Market, which has already made it necessary for the courts to widen their horizons. It has suddenly become fashionable to argue in favour of enacting a Bill of Rights. Britain will soon have to face up to a drastic reappraisal of the role of the judiciary, and it seems probable that future generations of judges will no longer be able to claim that their work is all about good clean law and nothing to do with bad dirty politics.

The Ivory Tower In 1936 Lord Chief Justice Hewart told the assembled throng at the Lord Mayor's Banquet that 'His Majesty's Judges are satisfied with the almost universal admiration in which they are held.' This breathtaking smugness was probably no more justified then than it would be today. The 'universe' of ordinary citizens may feel some degree of abstract reverence for the law, but few people know any more about the judges than they do about, for example, the civil service or the workings of their own elected local councils. One, admittedly crude, test would be to ask a random sample of people to name a senior judge. Many replies would be a total blank.

The remoteness and anonymity of the judges is to a

The Lord Chancellor, Lord Hailsham, and his train
bearer head the procession of judges from Westminster
Abbey to the House of Lords for the Lord
Chancellor's Breakfast

large extent deliberately cultivated. It was once said (by a judge) that 'he is the best judge whose name is known to the fewest readers of the *Daily Mail*.' This is a variation on the comment by Francis Bacon that 'a popular judge is a deformed thing and plaudits are fitter for players than magistrates.' Some judges have neglected this maxim and played unashamedly to the gallery. A notorious example was one of Lord Halsbury's appointees (see above), Mr Justice Darling, who always fancied himself as a wit. Cyril Harvey in his book, *The Advocate's Devil*, describes Darling as 'another real shocker':

'He would lie back in his chair staring at the ceiling with the back of his head cupped in his hands paying scant attention to any argument but waiting until some footling little joke occurred to his mind. When this happened he would make the joke, the court would echo for about thirty seconds with sycophantic laughter, and, then the process would start over again.'

It is probably fair to say that grossly self-indulgent conduct of the kind evinced by Darling would not long be tolerated, though even today one can sometimes detect a note of headline-seeking in the utterances that are made from the Bench.

The explanation for the aloofness and social remoteness of judges is not hard to find. They will have lived most of their adult lives in the cloistered and introverted environs of the Temple and the Inns of Court, and most of them will have had no occasion to become public figures. When they become judges they enter an even more exclusive world. They will, of course, have their own circle of friends; but there are pressures upon judges not to be seen doing even slightly compromising things. It would be almost unheard of for a judge to be found downing a pint of beer with his cronies in his local public house. In his book, *The New Anatomy of Britain*, the journalist Anthony Sampson considered it a fact worth recording that Lord Wilberforce, the senior Lord of Appeal in Ordinary (and descendant of the famous anti-slavery campaigner) had been seen reading the racing newspaper, *Sporting Life*, in a cafe near the Law Courts.

The price to be paid for keeping judges in an ivory tower slightly above and apart from their fellow citizens is that such judges tend to have too limited a view of the real world. Coupled with the exclusive social and educational backgrounds from which so many of them are recruited and with the inward-looking character of their previous professional experience, this blinkered outlook reinforces the suspicion in many people's minds that judges are simply incapable of understanding ordinary people and their problems. This suspicion underlies the complaints by trade unionists and Labour politicians, outlined in the previous section, and receives some support in the passage by Lord Justice Scrutton, already quoted.

As society has changed the law has had to accommodate pressures not just from working-class people but also from self-aware groups such as black people, liberated women, homosexuals and young people. It has not always made the adjustment successfully, and judges must take some share of the blame.

A good illustration of this is provided in a number of recent cases involving charges of rape. In one case the House of Lords held that in some circumstances the fact that an assailant believes a woman to be consenting to sexual intercourse may provide an adequate defence to the charge, even if the belief is wholly unreasonable. In another case the Court of Appeal drastically reduced an already fairly lenient sentence passed upon a brutal rapist, on the grounds that he was a serving soldier who, it was believed (wrongly as it turned out), would be allowed back into his regiment, which was about to do a tour of duty in Northern Ireland. This is no place to discuss the niceties of a complicated area of criminal law; but it is certainly true that these and other decisions, all by male judges (there are now some women on the Bench, but very few) exposed the courts to fierce criticism from those, who regard rape not merely as an abhorrent species of physical assault but also as an extreme manifestation of a deeply engrained male contempt for women. The law has been slow to recognise the changing social attitudes on this subject and some judges have, to say the least, handled rape cases with great insensitivity.

As with most things, the images that members of the general public have about lawyers and the courts are generated, not by the day-to-day routine of the judicial process or by the things that are handled well and efficiently, but by a few cases which get into the newspaper headlines. Rape cases are just one example. Then there are instances where judges cannot resist uttering stuffy and old-fashioned moral homilies when passing sentence; and cases (some very recent) where they have admonished female witnesses (and in one case a newspaper reporter) for wearing trouser suits in court. Many judges are anxious to keep abreast of the times and to overcome the tendency for the law to lag behind social change; but their efforts are set-back by a few who cannot resist displaying their old-fashioned prejudices and their awareness of their own importance to public view.

Lord Denning, Master of the Rolls It was suggested at the beginning of this section that few people, selected at random, would be able to name a member of the judiciary. Even in the days of capital punishment, when the newspapers were full of ghoulish detail about murder trials, the man in the street would probably know more about the accused, the victim and perhaps the counsel for prosecution and defence than about the presiding judge. Nowadays, with very few exceptions, even murder trials receive very scanty newspaper coverage.

In recent years, however, some judges have made modest breaches in the wall of anonymity that surrounds the profession. (The same slight tendency is observable in another traditionally anonymous sector of public employment, the civil service.) One who has

done so more than most is the Master of the Rolls, Lord Denning, who presides over the civil side of the Court of Appeal. Some brief remarks about this controversial and atypical judge provides a suitable note of contrast on which to end this chapter.

Lord Denning's career began in a brilliant but, for a judge, fairly conventional way. After taking a double first class honours degree (in mathematics and jurisprudence) at Oxford, he was called to the Bar in 1923, and became King's Counsel in 1938. Six years later, when he was 45, he was appointed a High Court judge, and was promoted to the Court of Appeal four years after that. As a Lord Justice of Appeal he became renowned for his robustly individualistic judgments and, in particular, for his willingness to repair defects (as he saw them) in statute law, without following the safer and more conventional course of waiting for Parliament to amend its own handiwork. His willingness to adopt this creative role earned him more than one rebuke from more senior judges in the House of Lords.

In 1958 he himself was made a Lord of Appeal in Ordinary; but it was an open secret that he was frustrated by the work of the House of Lords. The House normally consists of five judges, while the Court of Appeal is usually composed of only three, and on many occasions Lord Denning's efforts to steer the law onto new paths were outvoted by crushing four-to-one majorities. When the Mastership of the Rolls was offered to him in 1962 he jumped at the chance to take charge of the civil Court of Appeal. In this capacity he quickly seized the opportunity to make his impact upon the development of the law. On one famous occasion he committed the heresy of suggesting that in some circumstances the Court of Appeal could reverse precedents set by the House of Lords: and a formidable Bench of no fewer than seven Lords of Appeal had to be convened to put the Master of the Rolls firmly in his place. In 1977 he earned a lot of coverage in the media by his handling of a case in which the Attorney-General found himself having to justify his long-established right to grant or withold permission for legal actions ('relator' proceedings) to be brought in his name in order to safeguard the interests of the general public. The Denning Report on the Profumo Affair in 1963 and the publication of his book, *The Discipline of Law*, in 1979 earned him a place in the best seller lists.

Many lawyers, while acknowledging Lord Denning's brilliance, are exasperated by his idiosyncratic approach. They argue, with some justification, that judges like Lord Denning make it impossible to determine with certainty at any given time precisely what the law really is. But there is a counter-argument. Sometimes the legal machinery runs too smoothly for its own good and needs to have a bit of grit thrown into it. Even when Lord Denning gets it wrong he often exposes the other side of an argument which would otherwise go entirely by default. Lord Denning is the nearest approach to a folk-judge, in a system where the judicial process is remote from popular consciousness and where most judges are clever and honest but often dull and pompous purveyors of convention.

3 THE COURTS

Civil and Criminal Courts

James Morton

Early forms of trial One of my favourite pictures in an illustrated history book I had as a child was of a man, his eyes bulging at the sockets, carrying a steaming ball in both hands across a short strip of land. I forget the exact words of the caption but it was to the effect that after his dash his hands were bound in linen strips which, a few days later, were taken off. If the skin had festered he was guilty, if the skin was healing he was innocent. This was trial by ordeal. It was one of the earlier forms of criminal trial in England.

There were other forms of ordeal. The accused could be fed with a piece of bread and cheese into which had been added something like a feather. If he choked – too bad, he was guilty. If he succeeded in swallowing it, he was innocent at the mere cost of an upset stomach. This variation was called 'corsnaed' or 'cursed morsel'. The success or failure of this particular trial was to a certain extent in the hands of the feeder who, at a price, could influence the size of the morsel to be swallowed. Another device was the floating on the water. The accused was bound and laid on top of the water. If he sank, he was not guilty. If he floated he was rejected by the matter and consequently was guilty.

Hitherto, things had been simpler. The accuser had to recite an oath of loyalty. If he made a mistake – end of his case. If he got through without stammering, the defendant had to do the same thing. If he failed – end of defendant. As things progressed, defendants were allowed to enlist oath helpers – who curiously enough numbered twelve (presumably for the twelve apostles). They seem to have been an early form of barrister.

The Normans were robust. They liked a good battle, and that is exactly what trial by combat was. The combatants could employ someone else to fight on their behalf. Winning amounted to proof of innocence or good title to the land, whichever was at issue. William II was particularly opposed of it since fifty men successfully defied trial by ordeal when accused of killing his deer. He forbade trial by ordeal and in 1216 it was condemned by the Church.

The Jury System Trial by ordeal and by combat worked at this time for both criminal and civil law. The next development is seen in the beginning of the jury system. There had been juries of presentment at assizes, who were the complainants and the witnesses, and these were mixed with others who were asked whether the accused or prisoner (since by this time he was almost always the latter as well as the former) was guilty or not. Because of the composition of the jury and their fears of the consequences if they acquitted the defendant the chances of a 'result' in favour of the defendant were minimal.

But out of little acorns great oak trees grow, even though it was the 19th century before juries as we know them came to exist. Even into the 16th century they could be approached by anyone with an interest in the case and could take into account what he told them privately.

In the old days it was a problem to persuade defendants that they would get a fair trial, and so they had to be compelled to submit to justice – if necessary, and such was very often the case, physically.

The Statute of Westminster in 1275 provided that prisoners – of bad reputation – who were accused of a felony had to agree to trial by jury. Those who did not were subjected to strong and hard imprisonment. Techniques had improved by the 16th century, and by then the persuasion consisted of stretching the prisoner on the floor and loading weights on his chest. He either eventually submitted to jury trial with its more or less inevitable conclusion, or died. In fact there were positive advantages in resisting this *peine forte et dure*. If he died under the weights he died an innocent, or at least unconvicted, man and his family inherited his estate. If he was convicted by a jury his property was forfeit to the Crown.

This lasted the better part of 500 years until, at the end of the 18th century, a prisoner who refused to plead was deemed to be guilty anyway. In 1828 there was a change so that a refusal to plead was taken to be a plea of not guilty and the trial proceeded whether he liked it or not. He could call witnesses or make a plea. However, it was not until the very end of Queen Victoria's reign that he could give evidence. Indeed everything turns a full circle, because now there are those who would like to see a defendant compelled to give evidence.

Development of Civil Courts On the civil side, things were progressing along similar lines. Henry II established a jury of twelve knights from the locality to give a verdict on the recovery of land. This was by no means popular and as with every aspect of English law there were exceptions. Trial by battle continued to decide

Right: A jury room in the Central Criminal Court, Old Bailey

Below: The plaque in the Old Bailey which commemorates the "Right of Juries"

civil cases and although it fell slowly into disuse it was not until 1818 when a party tried to insist on trial by battle that it was realised it was still technically an option open to litigants. It was swiftly abolished.

In the 12th century juries were asked to decide the whole question – law and fact. Indeed it was the juries themselves who came to make a distinction between the two. They would give a series of answers on the facts and leave the judges to decide the law. There came to be rudimentary written pleadings and a hundred years later it was firmly established that juries were assessors of the facts and judges made decisions. However, in 1854 the Common Law Procedure Act provided for trial of civil actions by a judge alone subject to the consent of the parties.

The Judicature Acts 1873–75 continued the trend away from juries in civil trials and now, apart from libel trials, the jury is wholly abolished in civil cases.

CRIMINAL COURTS

To the spectator there is no doubt that the criminal courts present the most entertainment. That said, it must be recognized that with the abolition of the death penalty the criminal courts no longer attract the ghoulish spectator. Gone are the days before legal aid when the defendant had to sell his life story to the Sunday newspapers to pay for his defence. Gone are the days when the public gallery was packed to see the latest monster sentenced to death. Gone are the days when a trial took a week at the maximum. Now there are so many courts sitting each day, with defendants legally aided and with trials – even the simplest – taking days to complete, it is not surprising that, like football crowds, attendance at criminal trials is on the decline. We must look therefore to the magistrates' courts, the root or cradle of justice to start the proceedings.

Magistrates' Courts With very rare exceptions, every criminal case must start in the magistrates' court, whether it is riding a bicycle after dark without lights or a case of murder. And even with the rise in violent crime there are a good deal more of the former than the latter.

Magistrates' courts were an extension of the Anglo-Saxon moot court, and then the manorial court. But in 1285 'good and lawful men' were commissioned to keep the King's peace. Originally they were to keep a check on the local sheriff but they gradually expanded their functions and authority.

Today magistrates are divided into two classes, lay justices and stipendiary magistrates.

Lay justices are by far the older and date back to the 'good and lawful men'. Nowadays they are appointed through recommendation by the Lord Chancellor. Their qualifications are residential, being of good character and having the ability to devote one day each fortnight to sitting on the bench. Legal acumen is not a requirement. They are unpaid but can obtain certain expenses if, for example, they are away from their homes for over five hours.

The process of selection is by interview but once appointed it needs real misconduct, as opposed to inep-

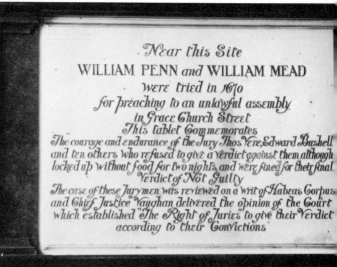

Near this Site WILLIAM PENN and WILLIAM MEAD were tried in 1670 for preaching to an unlawful assembly in Grace Church Street This tablet commemorates The courage and endurance of the Jury Thos Vere, Edward Bushell and ten others who refused to give a verdict against them although locked up without food for two nights and were fined for their final Verdict of Not Guilty The case of these Jurymen was reviewed on a Writ of Habeas Corpus and Chief Justice Vaughan delivered the opinion of the Court which established "The Right of Juries" to give their Verdict according to their Convictions

titude, to have a magistrate removed, although some are not reappointed after their three year term. Up until the 1950s, the vast majority were drawn from the squirearchy or the middle class – but today the bench represents a more real cross-section of the public.

The courts themselves vary from the tiny – held perhaps one a fortnight in a church hall – to the extremely busy, purpose-built courthouse with five or more individual courts.

At least two magistrates must sit at a time except to hear cases to be committed for trial, or remand hearings. These are what they say they are – cases which are remanded to another date.

Magistrates have a qualified clerk – a barrister or

solicitor of at least five years' standing. He is, in theory, the clerk to each court and supervises the justices, directing them as to the law. In practice, in a busy courthouse a number of courts have a solicitor's articled clerk, or even typist, as their clerk. It may seem amateurish but it works quite well.

Stipendiary magistrates as we know them originated with Henry Fielding, author of *Tom Jones*. In 1748 he was given a salary as an alternative to receiving reward money and part of the booty of the criminals whom he had committed.

He was followed by his brother, blind Sir John Fielding – there is an engraving of him at work at Bow Street and, among others, the great Italian adventurer, Jacques Casanova, mentions appearing in front of him on a charge of disorderly conduct. That episode was the beginning of the end of Casanova's career – he had been duped by a London whore – but Henry and John Fielding began a tradition of stipendiary magistrates – 'stipes' as they are known because they are paid a stipend.

The stipendiary magistrate was appointed in various courts throughout London and in such cities as Hull, Manchester, Birmingham. Sadly in the 1950s there was a turn against them and lay justices filled their places when they retired or died. It was thought – a thought possibly promoted by lay justices – that they were too

stern and harked back to harsh pre-war days. Happily there is now a partial revival, at least in London where they are held in real affection and esteem by the flotsam and jetsam who appear before them.

Certainly for the spectator a stipendiary's court is the place for a quick visit. The magistrates at Bow Street and Marlborough Street will have a morning's list of up to fifty cases each. In fairness, however, the lay justices sitting at Tottenham Court on a Friday will have list that is not far short of that total.

The stipendiary's list will contain perhaps a dozen drunks, ranging from the down-and-outs who sleep rough in the West End to the partygoer who couldn't find a cab and decided to sleep it off.

After that there will be a few prostitutes – strictly the lower end of the trade, for prostitution is not an offence. Their offence is soliciting men. Then there will be the street traders, the men selling ice cream or umbrellas in Oxford Street. There is something like a fixed penalty for these offenders except that the girls are always invited to see a probation officer.

After that it is down to the serious stuff, at Bow Street, Hendon, Tottenham, Greenwich, or wherever magistrates, lay or stipendiary, sit. Every criminal case starts with these the day after the man has been charged

– if he has been in custody – or at a later date if he has been on bail.

The first case may be a remand for a murder, the next a shoplifting charge, the third a rape, the fourth breaking into an office and stealing £10. To sit there as each case remorselessly follows the previous one is like being in the pages of the *News of the World*. After the remands – often taking no more than a minute – come the cases where the defendants plead guilty and are dealt with. A middle aged foreign shoplifter who has pillaged Marks and Spencer is fined the maximum £1,000. A young student living on the breadline who steals some cheese from a supermarket is remanded for probation reports. A young man denies having hit a policeman.

After each case lay justices will consult each other and often retire, taking the time out to have a cup of coffee. The court visibly relaxes. Police chat to one another; a solicitor, who can appear and conduct cases before magistrates, discusses the list with the clerk of the court. The defendant leans over the dock to chat to his friends. It is all very informal. By contrast, the stipendiary does not retire. His is the only decision. The court never lets up until one o'clock.

Committal to the Crown Court Apart from hearing cases, the justices must also rule on whether there is enough evidence to commit defendants for trial on charges which must be dealt with before a jury at the Crown Court. Such cases include murder, rape, arson and housebreaking. In addition both police and defendant have the right to have certain cases tried at the Crown Court so it is quite possible for a jury to hear a case in which the defendant is charged with stealing a packet of biscuits. It may seem trivial but it is not. A person's whole life may depend on the decision.

Nowadays there are two kinds of committal to the Crown Court. The first is where the defendant is represented and agrees that there is evidence against him. In this case the papers setting out the prosecution's version of the case are handed to the magistrate. In effect he rubber stamps his agreement and in a matter of minutes the case is on its way to the Crown Court.

If the defendant does not agree then the papers must be read in open court and the witnesses called. The idea behind this is to see whether or not there *is a prima facie* case to be sent 'up the road', as the expression goes. At the end of the prosecution's case, the magistrate considers whether or not it is such that a reasonable jury could convict. The test is 'could', not whether he thinks they might or they might not.

Bail In addition the magistrates' court must consider whether or not the defendant should have bail in any case and this is often the most bitterly disputed part of the whole proceedings. If bail is refused, or if a defendant is convicted and sentenced and he does not agree with the verdict, then he has a right of appeal to the Crown Court. If, when magistrates have heard a case and the defendant's record of convictions, they think they have not enough power to sentence – a maximum of six months in each case or twelve months in all – they may commit him to the Crown Court for sentence.

After the serious crime come the driving and matrimonial cases – all part of the work of a magistrates' court. Indeed motoring cases account for the major part of their work. These will be heard exclusively in the afternoon by a stipendiary magistrate and throughout the day by lay justices.

Extradition Cases For the Metropolitan Magistrates, as stipendiaries in London are known, the pinnacle is to be invited to sit at either Bow Street or Marlborough Street. Those who sit at the former take the hearings of the extradition cases.

These are cases where foreign governments ask the British courts to send a defendant back to them to be dealt with for a crime alleged to have been committed on their soil. For example, if a Spaniard is alleged to have robbed a bank in Barcelona, then the Spanish Government will ask for his extradition. The test as to whether an extradition order should be made is whether there would be a *prima facie* case on which to commit it to the Crown Court if it were an English case.

An appeal in an extradition case goes not to the Crown Court but to the Divisional Court.

The Crown Courts

Quarter Sessions Before 1972 there existed both Quarter Sessions and the Assizes. These were rather splendid, the Assizes particularly so. Now with officialdom in the guise of expedition engulfing us all they have been merged into one enormous body, the Crown Courts. The Crown Courts have three tiers. The first corresponds roughly to the old Assize, the other two to the old Quarter Sessions. It was in 1972 that solicitors as well as barristers were allowed to sit as judges in the lower tier cases. They can now become Judges in their own right, largely as a result of the sudden growth of crime throughout the country, which created a demand for an increase in the number of judges.

In 1388 the ordinance which formulated the power and duties of the justice of the peace also ordered those in each county to meet four times a year. That was the start of the old Quarter Sessions of the Peace. In addition to justices there was appointed a legally qualified chairman, a recorder – a solicitor or, more usually, a barrister of five years standing. Gradually over the years boroughs established their own Quarter Sessions with no justices but a paid recorder.

Only barristers had a right of audience before these Quarter Sessions, with the exception of some far flung places such as Bodmin and Doncaster who, for reasons of distance or general quaintness, permitted solicitors to appear.

Assizes The Norman kings instituted the assize; they sent round their officials to see what was happening in each locality. They could, and eagerly did, hear juries of presentment happily firing them if they got the oath wrong and equally happily finding against the defendant if his side stammered the oath. In that respect they were totally impartial.

The arrival of the king's officials was not welcomed by the inhabitants of the locality. They would do everything they could to delay a visit. In fact on one occasion the people in Cornwall fled to the woods.

Henry II, that greatly underrated monarch, improved the position enormously. He provided what he called a Grand Assize – assize merely meant sitting. If a litigant, dispossessed of his land, wished to avoid trial by battle he could elect to appear before a Grand Assize at the King's Court. The Petty Assize dealt with claims regarding land where the claimant was not in possession.

By 1300 the assize judges dealt not only with civil claims but also with criminal cases. They had three functions

1 To hear civil actions;
2 The commission of gaol delivery which diverted them to try people in custody; and
3 The commission of *oyez* and *terminer* under which they heard cases sent by examining magistrates in the lower court whether the defendants were in custody or not.

Towns – usually only county towns and large county boroughs—were visited two or three times a year. The opening day of the assize was a day of some pageantry. The judges walked from their lodgings to church accompanied by trumpets. Once in court a long commission of the duties was read. The judges carried nosegays – originally to protect them from the smell of the populace. The prisoner stood at a bar in the well of the court. If there were no prisoners for a judge to try at a particular assize he was presented with a pair of white gloves.

But things have changed, progress and crime have eventually defeated the Assize and the Quarter Sessions. Only the Central Criminal Court has partially escaped.

There was more and more crime to be handled. Assizes took longer and longer to complete. To get them heard at all cases had to be shifted from, say,

Below: The Castle, Oakham, formerly the Assize Court of Rutland. A tradition dating back to the reign of Queen Elizabeth I decrees that all members of the Royal Family or the Peerage should present symbolic horseshoes on the occasion of their first visit to Rutland

Bottom: Norwich Guildhall built in 1407, restored in the 19th century. Used as a Magistrates' Court and Assize Court, it contains the ancient Court of Record

The procession before an Assize Service at St. Woolos Cathedral, Newport, Gwent. The Under Sherriff leads the Town Clerk, The Mayor, his Chaplain, the High Sherriff, the clerks, the judges and their marshal

Lewes to Norwich at terrible inconvenience and expense. Intermediate Quarter Sessions were appointed to clear up the backlog. Eventually the whole thing became a running sore and so in 1972 we saw the end of the Assize and Quarter Sessions as such and the introduction of the Crown Court.

The only practical differences are that a piece of tradition died, a few names were changed and the administration of the courts passed into the hands of the Civil Service.

Central Criminal Court Since the Central Criminal Court, or Old Bailey as it is known, fulfils all the functions of the Crown Courts it is easiest to see how it works because the same applies to all the other Crown Courts throughout England and Wales.

It takes all Class 1 cases – murder, rape, arson, from any examining magistrates in the London Area. It is an appeal court from decisions at the Guildhall Justice Room or the Mansion House Court Room, which are the two magistrates' courts in the City, and it also sentences defendants committed from those courts.

The Old Bailey stands on the site of the old Newgate prison. Newgate was the newest of the City gates and housed the worst of London's criminals. Originally the Commission of Gaol Delivery was held in Newgate Prison but for sanitary reasons a sessions house was built

alongside the prison. But this was by no means proof against disease and in 1750 gaol fever carried off the mayor, an under sheriff, two judges and an alderman.

If things went wrong for the defendant – which they usually did – he walked back to the prison or was literally carried off to Tyburn which was the site of gallows at present day Marble Arch. In 1784 the gallows at Tyburn were dismantled and hangings took place outside the Old Bailey. Public hanging continued until 1868.

Court of Appeal (Criminal Division) The only hope of an appeal before 1904 depended on the prosecution's agreement. If agreement was forthcoming the appellant could bring what was called a writ of error. The case of Adolf Beck, twice imprisoned as a swindler on identification evidence, was largely instrumental in bringing about the establishment of the Court of Criminal Appeal. At his second trial it was discovered that not only had there been a mistake of fact but also of law. The writ of error was abolished, as was a half-way house called the Court of Common Cases Reserved, by the Criminal Appeal Act 1907.

The Court of Criminal Appeal lasted until it merged with the Court of Appeal in October 1966. The procedure is simple. The prisoner applies after his conviction for leave to appeal. The application is made in writing to a single judge. If he gives leave then the case is heard by three, or in very serious cases five, judges. A majority decision prevails. If the single judge refuses leave to appeal, the prisoner's application can be renewed before three judges. He has no-one to argue his case for him unless he can pay for a barrister privately and he stands the risk of losing remission on his sentence.

In exceptional cases further appeal lies to the House of Lords.

Procedure A criminal trial in England and Wales takes place in front of a jury of twelve men and women. Nowadays anyone on the electoral list can be a juror, subject to certain exceptions. The jury's verdict must be unanimous unless the judge tells them they may have a majority verdict. This must be at least 10–2 in favour of an acquittal or a conviction.

Before the jury is sworn the defendant is asked whether he pleads guilty or not guilty. If he pleads guilty then the jury never appears and the case is dealt with by the judge alone. The prosecutor – always a barrister – outlines the facts and then a police officer is called to give details of the defendant's character – exactly as in a magistrates' court. Any reports available from probation officers are read and then the defendant, if he is represented, and nowadays he almost invariably is, has his turn. The barrister appointed to defend him or selected by him explains why the accused should not be sent to prison or why, if he must be sent, such a sentence should be a short one.

Formerly the defendant was asked whether he had anything to say before sentence was passed – in addition to what his barrister had said. This led to either a general *mea culpa*, a tribute to British justice, or a load of foul language. It was abolished a few years ago.

The defendant is then sentenced and the public gallery is rewarded with the spectacle of a brave man taking his punishment or with a brief struggle between prisoner and warders (now called dock officers).

If the defendant pleads not guilty then the jury is sworn. The prosecuting counsel outlines the facts of the case to the jury and calls his evidence. Each witness may be cross-examined by the defending counsel. The process is slow: the record for the length of a criminal trial, over 130 days, has recently been set in a murder trial.

Evidence of witnesses which is undisputed can be read to the jury. It has exactly the same force as if that person had given evidence in person but saves a witness travelling twenty miles merely to say, 'I took that photograph'.

Once the prosecution has completed its case the defence may submit that there is no case to answer, just as was possible in the magistrates' court. A refusal by justices to uphold a submission of no case to answer does not preclude a fresh submission in the Crown Court. Not only is this a completely new hearing but the Crown Court is senior and not bound by anything done or not done at magisterial level.

If that submission is overruled then the defendant may or may not decide to give evidence and call witnesses. If he decides to give evidence then he too will be open

Bottom: The interior of No. 1 Court, Central Criminal Court, Old Bailey as it appears today. The jury box is at the far end of the court under the clock with the dock on the right. The witness box is on the left with the microphone

Below: The Justice Hall in Old Bailey. Built after the Great Fire of 1666, the Justice Hall stood on the west side of the street and was open to the fresh air. It was in use for about 100 years

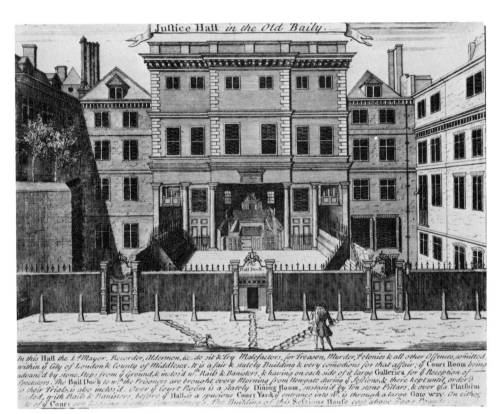

to cross-examination. He can, if he wishes, make an unsworn statement from the dock.

After that the prosecution will address the jury, as will the defence, and the judge will sum up. It all seems very simple and in reality it is. However things can go wrong: judges can make mistakes in summing up, juries do things round the wrong way. Judges sometimes give excessive sentences. It is therefore necessary to have recourse to the Court of Appeal.

THE CIVIL COURTS

The High Court of Justice

The High Court, which together with the Crown Court and Court of Appeal constitutes the Supreme Court of Judicature, underwent a substantial reform as a result of the Judicature Acts 1873–75. The Acts created a new Supreme Court to which was transferred the jurisdictions of all the old superior courts of common law and equity other than the Chancery Courts of the Counties Palatine of Lancaster and Durham.

The new High Court consisted of five divisions, and in 1880 three common law divisions were merged into one Queen's Bench Division. In 1970 the Administration of Justice Act abolished the Probate, Divorce and Admiralty Division and set up the Family Division. Although all three, the Queen's Bench, Chancery and Family Divisions, are supposed to have equal competence, in fact each exercises its own jurisdiction. There are instances, however, where the jurisdictions overlap and it is possible to choose in which Division to start an action.

The rules of procedure of the Supreme Court are encompassed in a book running to two volumes familiarly called *The White Book*. It weighs over fourteen pounds and is of course a bible for every lawyer, covering almost every possible point of procedure which litigants or their solicitors can devise.

Queen's Bench Division The major part of the Queen's Bench Division's work is that of a court of first instance dealing with civil matters. Its jurisdiction over commercial cases is exercised by the Commercial Court, one of the lists of the Queen's Bench Division, and its admiralty jurisdiction, inherited from the old Probate, Divorce and Admiralty Division after the reorganisation of the High Court by the Administration of Justice Act 1970, is handled by the Admiralty Court. The Admiralty Court judges are specially nominated by the Lord Chancellor and may sit with lay assessors.

The criminal jurisdiction of the High Court belongs exclusively to the Queen's Bench Division, whose Divisional Court hears appeals by way of 'case stated' from the magistrates and the Crown Court. The function of the Divisional Court is discussed in more detail below.

Every Queen's Bench Division action commences with a writ. This either claims a specific sum or general damages. A claim for breach of contract can quantify the claim, eg goods sold and delivered but not paid for– £1,000. On the other hand a claim for a broken leg is not so easily quantifiable. The amount of damages awarded will depend on whether the leg healed perfectly and if it did not on such things as the age of the person injured, whether the person was a man or woman, if they played games and so on.

Every writ has to be served on the defendant personally or, if he deliberately avoids being served, then an order can be obtained for substituted service. Once the defendant is served with a writ he must enter an appearance to the writ within fourteen days otherwise judgment may be signed against him. It is still open for him to apply to the court for leave to enter an appearance, but even if leave is given he will almost certainly be ordered to pay some costs, and may well find that he is obliged to pay part of the money claimed into court as security.

If the claim is for a liquidated amount and there is really no dispute that it is owing, such as where the defendant is merely delaying the evil day of payment, then the plaintiff may apply for summary judgment under a procedure known as Order 14. This is a summons supported by an affidavit saying that the goods were sold and delivered and no complaint has ever been made about them. The summons is heard by a master, a solicitor or barrister of seven years' standing, who directs the conduct of a case up to its trial.

If an appearance is entered then the defendant must also enter a defence within another fourteen days or he is again liable to have judgment signed against him. If he fails to enter a defence then the damages will be assessed on a special hearing before the master, or if the claim is for debt then the plaintiff can put the bailiffs in immediately.

Once a defence is entered the plaintiff can ask for further and better particulars of the defence and in his turn the defendant may ask for particulars of the claim. Lists of documents to be produced at the trial are exchanged and the matter proceeds to a summons for directions. This is really half-time in the action. Both parties appear again before the master who gives directions as to the place of the trial together with orders in respect of how many doctors or technical witnesses may be called.

A date is fixed for the action, counsel is instructed – only he may appear in the High Court – and later rather than sooner the case is heard. A party may appeal to the Court of Appeal.

All very simple, you may think, and indeed in theory it is, but the perils of running a High Court action are well illustrated in the maxim 'Never go to law even if you are a hundred times in the right', and the old gipsy curse 'May you have a law suit you cannot lose'.

It is almost certain that one party has no particular desire to have the case heard. He may have a dilatory firm of solicitors. If one side wants to delay matters there are numerous procedural matters they may call in aid to help them. The expense is crippling. No High Court action in the Queen's Bench Division which goes to trial can cost each side less than £1,000. A fair estimate of the length of time between issue of a writ to judgment is not less than eighteen months – and that may be on the short side.

The Divisional Court In a curious way the Divisional Court is perhaps the most important court of first instance in the country. It consists of two judges of the Queen's Bench Division, including normally the Lord Chief Justice, and has a wide variety of functions.

Its function is not only to consider cases stated and sent by magistrates for a ruling on the law but also to preserve the traditional freedoms of England and Wales. Over the years the various writs of *habeas corpus, certiorari, mandamus* and prohibition all found their way to the shelter of the Divisional Court's gown.

The writ of *habeas corpus* – literally 'let us have the body' – is historically the oldest. It was used in times when the courts felt that someone – usually a political prisoner – was being detained unlawfully. They would order the issue of a writ of *habeas corpus* so they might determine whether the man was in fact being lawfully detained. The writ is still used on occasions where it is felt that the police are holding a suspect for an unwarranted time, but in fact it is a clumsy and long-winded process to use nowadays. The Court, generally speaking, will give the police twenty-four hours to respond to the writ and by that time the solicitor will usually find that his client has been charged and is appearing in the local magistrates' court.

More important today are the three remaining writs of *mandamus,* prohibition and *certiorari*.

The writ of prohibition is what it says it is. It prohibits an inferior court from exceeding its jurisdiction. The writ of *mandamus* is a command to a court or public authority to do something it had previously declined to do, and the writ of *certiorari* is where the lower court or tribunal has already exceeded its authority and the Divisional Court orders that court to deliver to them the record of its proceedings in order to quash it.

Such proceedings are by way of an application made by the aggrieved party in the first instance. He issues a notice of motion supported by an affidavit and appears before the Divisional Court at 10.30 in the morning – or at other times in cases of urgency. The proceedings are usually heard in the Lord Chief Justice's court in the Royal Courts of Justice in the Strand and on any one morning there may be half a dozen such applications.

If leave is given the writ is issued and the other party is prevented from carrying on with its determined policy until after the whole thing has been thrashed out by the Divisional Court.

Appeals lie from the Divisional Court, as they do from the High Court of Justice and the county court, to the Court of Appeal.

Chancery Division The Chancery Division deals with matters such as land, trusts, partnerships and related matters. Broadly it works in the same way as a Queen's Bench action but the machinations are infinitely more complicated. All the evidence to be used must be on affidavit, that is a sworn statement setting out the facts. At the trial the deposer to the affidavit is cross-examined. 'No affidavit, no witness' is a simple rule. In *Bleak House* Dickens cited the case of *Jarndyce v Jarndyce*, a Chancery action which dragged on for years ruining its protagonists. Things have improved but actions still take an unconscionably long time to come to trial, possibly because the affidavits must be settled by counsel who because there are relatively few of them specialising in Chancery are able to work at their own pace.

Patents The Patents Act 1977 created the Patents Court as part of the Chancery Division to hear appeals from the Comptroller of Patents. Like the Employment Appeal Tribunal (see below) judges of the Patents Court sit with lay advisers, in this case scientific advisers. The Patents Court differs from other parts of the High Court in that barristers, solicitors and patent agents all have the right of audience whereas elsewhere only barristers are entitled to represent the parties. In certain circumstances an appeal may lie to the Court of Appeal.

The Chancery Division may also sit as the Court of Protection to hear appeals under the Mental Health Act 1959 concerning the management of property and the affairs of mental patients.

Family Division A P Herbert called the Probate Divorce and Admiralty Division the one which dealt with 'wills, wives and wrecks'. And so it was. The third division of the High Court has always been the most accessible.

Until the law relaxed its hold on the sanctity of marriage the divorce case was, along with the murder case and the libel suit, the one which held most attraction to the public. Photographed petitioners in pretty hats filled the newspapers as they revealed the sins of their husbands. Now that is long gone except for the very rare contested case. Today a divorce can be a Do-It-Yourself affair and is almost a rubber stamp procedure.

However there has been a shift in business. Once wards of court were the responsibility of the Chancery Division but this has now been transferred to the less constrained atmosphere of the Family Division. Injunctions can be obtained in a matter of hours ordering husbands – or wives – to return children, and similar injunctions can be obtained preventing violent husbands beating their wives. This is now the real business of the Family Division, along with cases concerning the care and custody of children and the division of matrimonial property.

Employment Appeal Tribunal Although it is part of the High Court the Employment Appeal Tribunal is independent of the three Divisions. It was set up by the Employment Protection Act 1975 and hears appeals from industrial tribunals on employment matters – unfair dismissal, redundancy payments, sex or racial discrimination in employment and so on. Its judges, drawn from the ranks of the High Court or Court of Appeal, sit with two appointed members, laymen with special knowledge or experience of industrial relations either as trade union or employers' representatives.

The Employment Appeal Tribunal bears a striking resemblance to the National Industrial Relations Court which was set up under the controversial Industrial Relations Act 1971, an Act which was almost immediately repealed by the new Labour Government when it came to power in 1974.

Court of Appeal The Court of Appeal was another creation of the Judicature Act 1873, to which English justice owes so much. Before that appeals lay to the House of Lords, the Privy Council or the Court of Appeal in Chancery. Procedurally it was a muddle and could even result in a judge hearing an appeal from his own decision.

The composition of the Court of Appeal is interesting. It consists of the Lord Chancellor, any ex-Lord Chancellor or Lord of Appeal in Ordinary, the Lord Chief Justice, the Master of the Rolls and the Lords Justices of Appeal. A quorum is an uneven number of judges (but not less than three).

Not only does the Court hear appeals but it can, if it so wishes, give leave to appeal against its own decisions. Such appeal is to the House of Lords.

So far as the High Court is concerned the appeal may be on a point of law or fact, but an appeal from the county court may only concern a point of law.

County Court The county court is in fact a relatively modern innovation but harks back to the old Anglo-Saxon 'Shire Moot'. The court as we know it was created in 1846 to provide a way of settling minor disputes quickly.

However, today an action in the county court is almost as expensive and complicated as one in the High Court. The limit of a claim in the county court is £2,000 except where both parties agree to a higher limit. The rules are basically the same as in the High Court. The summons takes the place of the writ, but in general the steps are the same. The cost however has escalated, as has the delay in having an action heard. It is probably not worth bringing an action which may be contested if the claim is for less than £100 – unless you do it yourself!

The county court has however a great bulk of its work in claims under the Rent Acts and disputes between landlord and tenant. To this extent its usefulness has increased over the last few years. The major cases in the county court are presided over by a county court judge – a barrister of seven years' standing – and the minor cases and all the intermediate paperwork are dealt with by a registrar who must be a solicitor also of seven years' standing.

Small Claims Court Because over the years litigation in both the High and county courts has become so protracted and expensive other alternatives have been found to provide quick, clean and cheap justice. Arbitration is one such way and is mainly used by companies. At the other end of the spectrum are the small claims courts.

These courts, instituted in 1974, are aimed at providing uncomplicated hearings for litigants, who are in the main complaining about faulty goods, holidays which do not match up with advertisements and the like. The maximum permitted claim in the London Small Claims Court is £350 but the average level of case is in the £60 to £70 range. In its first year the court handled 775 enquiries and actually adjudicated in fifteen hearings. Representation by qualified lawyers is prohibited and paperwork is kept to a minimum. Hopefully this will continue but as people become more sophisticated and

the cost of running these courts escalates beyond reason and control we shall no doubt see 'minimal claims courts.'

Coroner's Court One of the most fascinating of all the courts is that of the coroner if only because it combines the accusatorial system which prevails throughout British justice with the inquisitorial system used in Europe. Furthermore, the rules of evidence change, and coroners have more or less absolute power in their domain.

The office of coroner is in fact an old one dating back to the 12th century. The title derives from the Latin form of 'crown'. Their duties were to guard the king's revenue, keep a record of crimes committed in their district and to act as a sort of sweeper up. It was their duty to deal with treasure trove, wrecks and those royal fish, the whale and the sturgeon.

It must be remembered that in the 12th century England was an occupied country – occupied by the Normans. Now one of the most legitimate sports available to the inhabitants of occupied countries is that of sabotage and destruction of the occupiers. The crime rate,

looked at from the Norman point of view, grew alarmingly. The natural hostility of the people made tracing criminals difficult. An English version of the Italian *Omerta* applied. Reprisals had to be taken. For every Norman killed a fine was levied on the locals. If it could not be determined whether the dead man was English or Norman he was deemed to be Norman. It was the coroner's duty to sort out the facts.

He was also a negotiator. If a suspect reached the safety of a church, under the rules of sanctuary the king's men could not enter. The suspect was effectively besieged and it was the coroner's job to ascertain whether he wanted to starve, stand trial or have a safe conduct to the nearest port. If he chose the latter all his goods were forfeit to the crown.

With the rise of the justice of the peace the role of the coroner diminished but he still retains the duty of investigating treasure trove and death in unusual or suspicious circumstances, providing he has been informed that there is to be no criminal prosecution. In London he can also investigate the outbreak of fires.

The coroner may sit alone or in graver cases summon a jury of between seven and eleven members. A verdict can be taken on a majority.

Coroners, who are barristers, doctors or solicitors of five years' standing, can be removed by the Lord Chancellor; in theory the chief coroner is the Lord Chief Justice although it is some years since he or one of his predecessors chose to exercise that function.

That brings us back almost full circle to the days of the Norman kings and their faltering and often harsh measures in introducing justice. There are, of course, other courts, such as the courts martial which deal with serving soldiers, but the major gap has been for prisoners who whilst serving sentences are accused of offences against prison officers and prison discipline. Until the *Hull Prison Visitors case* in 1978 there were only the most rudimentary enquiries with the odds stacked against the prisoners. Sentences, the equivalent of twelve months' imprisonment, could be handed out without representation or appeal. As a result of the *Hull Prison Visitors* case the Home Office will have to make available a full and independent appeals procedure.

Below: George Edmund Street RA, architect of the Royal Courts of Justice. This statue stands in a niche on the right of the Great Hall as one enters from the Strand

Bottom: Edwin Wilkins Field, Secretary of the Royal Commission for the Concentration of the Law Courts. It was his inspiration and tenacity which led to the building of the Royal Courts of Justice

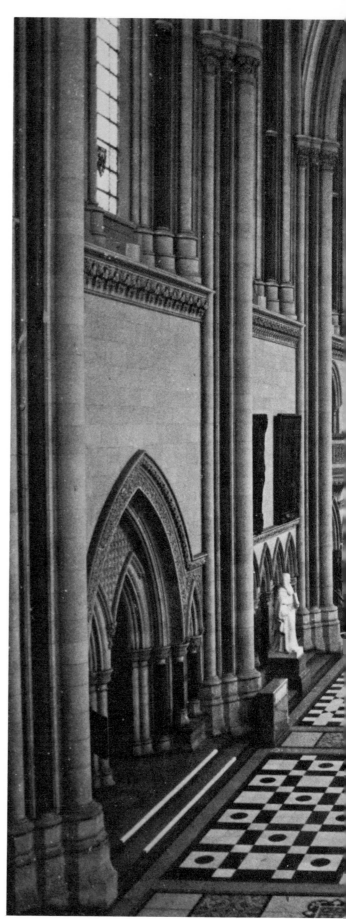

The Great Hall of the Royal Courts of Justice, looking
towards the main entrance. The vaulting is 80 feet
high and the hall itself is 238 feet long. The tessellated
pavement, designed by Street, runs the whole length

THE COURTS

The House of Lords and the Judicial Committee of the Privy Council

Francis Cowper

Queen's Counsel make their way into the House of Lords following the service at Westminster Abbey at the beginning of the legal year

explicit what had long been accepted—the exclusive jurisdiction of the House of Lords to hear appeals from the courts; but it was not till Stuart times that the power was used with any frequency. After the Union of the English and Scottish Parliaments in 1707 appeals from the Court of Session in Edinburgh were brought to the Lords. As long as Ireland remained part of the United Kingdom so were Irish appeals. Since the partition of Ireland in the present century only those from Northern Ireland remain.

One curiosity of the law is that the right to hear appeals resides in the whole body of the peerage and the convention that only peers learned in the law shall in practice exercise it emerged slowly and late. As late as 1806 it was scarcely regarded as anomalous for the Prince of Wales to pack the House of Lords with his friends in order to secure an appellate decision favourable to Mrs Fitzherbert in a case relating to the guardianship of a child. But in the next forty years attitudes imperceptibly changed and in 1844 in an appeal relating to Daniel O'Connell, the Irish Liberator, a case highly charged with political emotions, the lords learned in the law successfully dissuaded several unlearned lords from participating in the decision.

But meanwhile other problems had arisen. In an increasingly complex society appeals were multiplying and there were not sufficient learned peers to cope with them. Arrears piled up and often the Lord Chancellor had to sit with a couple of silent, acquiescent unlearned peers to make up a quorum. It was a commonplace for Scottish appeals to be disposed of by a tribunal none of the members of which was acquainted with Scottish law. So low had the prestige of the House of Lords as a judicial body fallen that, when the Supreme Court of Judicature Act 1873 reorganised the whole English legal system, it very nearly lost its appellate jurisdiction. But it was saved in the nick of time by the Appellate Jurisdiction Act 1876 which put the practice of final appeals on its modern footing.

Lords of Appeal in Ordinary Hitherto the House had had to rely on the Lord Chancellor of the day, former Lord Chancellors and any peers who happened to have held high judicial office. (It has become the almost invariable practice to confer a peerage on the Lord Chief Justice.) Henceforth these were supplemented by a new sort of peer, the Lords of Appeal in Ordinary. These, the first life peers, were eminent lawyers appointed to the House of Lords to fulfil its judicial functions, though they had all the privileges of other peers and could also participate in debates. The first two appointments were an English judge, who became Lord Blackburn, and the Scottish Lord Advocate (the equivalent of the English Attorney-General) who became Lord Gordon.

Still no legislative provision was made confining the hearing of appeals to peers learned in the law, even when in 1883 the second Lord Denman, the eccentric and not particularly distinguished barrister son of Lord Chief Justice Denman, insisted on participating in a hearing, the Lord Chancellor of the day elected to leave the law as it still stands. There are now ten Lords of Appeal in Ordinary of whom two are always Scots.

The House of Lords In the dawn of our history there emerge from cloudy beginnings two distinct and coexisting governing bodies: the *Commune Consilium Regni,* the assembly of the magnates of Church and State counselling the king, and the *Curia Regis*, its core and essence, the king's own court. From these embryos emerged the agencies of government as we now know them, parliamentary, judicial, fiscal, pursuing their own separate developments often in unpredictable directions.

Out of the *Commune Consilium* Parliament grew; first the House of Lords, then the representative House of Commons tacked on to it as a sort of appendage. It is something of an historical accident that the House of Lords, alongside its legislative functions, came to be recognised as the final court of appeal, first for England and then for the United Kingdom. The emergence of the Privy Council as the final court of Appeal for Britain's overseas territories followed a wholly different line of development.

It was in 1485 that a declaration of the judges made

Opposite top: The annual Quit Rents Ceremony held in the Royal Courts of Justice. The Queen's Remembrancer accepts token rents of a hatchet, a bill hook, a horseshoe and a bag of nails from the City Solicitor in respect of a farm in Shropshire and "The Forge" in the Strand which the City rented from the Crown

Opposite bottom: The Lord Mayor of London, at the start of his term of office, arrives in his golden coach at the Royal Courts of Justice to be sworn in before the Lord Chief Justice. Escorting him are the Pikemen of the Honourable Artillery Company

Appeals to the House of Lords Till 1945 the hearing of appeals always took place in the House of Lords itself. During the war, when the House of Commons Chamber was destroyed and its members moved to the House of Lords Chamber, the Lords occupied the King's Robing Room as a temporary Chamber. In the post-war reconstruction work was initiated installing a new heating system just beneath its windows. The noise of pile driving was incompatible with the hearing of appeals and, as a purely temporary measure, it was decided to transfer the hearing of the arguments to a committee room, only the actual decision being delivered in the Chamber. But this procedure of delegation to an appellate committee proved so convenient that ever afterwards it remained normal, though occasionally an appeal is still heard in the Chamber.

Formerly, it was almost invariable for the Lord Chancellor of the day to preside at the hearing of appeals; now the pressure of his other duties usually prevents this and it is the senior Lord of Appeal who presides. The Appellate Committee sits in a lofty committee room overlooking the Thames, the walls irrelevantly but pleasantly adorned with tapestries designed by Boucher for Madame de Pompadour. The Lords sit, without robes, at a wide horseshoe table. Usually five participate. Counsel, robed, occupy tables facing them. There is no raised dais. The hearing of an appeal is usually completed within a week, though difficult cases may take over a fortnight. The decision is promulgated in the House of Lords' Chamber in a month or so, the procedure following that of a debate. Motions for the consideration of the report of the Appellate Committee, for allowing or dismissing the appeal, for the award of costs, are proposed and voted on. The speeches of the Lords participating are not read aloud but are available in print. When the Lord Chancellor presides he wears in the Chamber a black gown and a full bottomed wig.

There are four sessions in the legal year and the business before the House of Lords varies considerably from session to session. In some there may be twenty cases or more and in order to despatch the work two Appellate Committees may sit simultaneously.

Some Lord Chancellors make a point of participating frequently in the hearing of appeals, Lord Hailsham, for example. By contrast Lord Jowitt and Lord Gardiner scarcely sat at all. It is notable that the Scottish Lords of Appeal have often made particularly distinguished contributions to the development of the law by the House of Lords, for instance Lord Dunedin and Lord Reid.

The Privy Council The Judicial Committee of the Privy Council is sometimes regarded as a mere mirror image of the House of Lords. It is, indeed, to a large extent manned by the Lords of Appeal, but not wholly. Its origins, history, development and jurisdiction are wholly different, while the background of its cases, drawn from the ends of the earth, often have an exotic glamour rarely matched in the familiar disputes normally brought before the House of Lords. Yet the setting of the Judicial Committee in the Treasury Building in Whitehall has nothing to match the Victorian gothic glories of the House of Lords' Chamber, all gilt and scarlet, carved heraldic beasts and armorial windows, and high in the walls statues of the Magna Carta barons.

Like the Appellate Committee of the House of Lords, the learned Privy Councillors sit at a great semi-circular table in a spacious and dignified room to hear the arguments of counsel but it never emerges into any more gorgeous surroundings to proclaim its decisions which are quietly couched in the formula that it 'humbly advises Her Majesty' to such and such a course. The basis of the decision is formulated by one of the members of the Board and an Order in Council is subsequently made embodying the advice given. A century ago there was a division of opinion in the highest legal circles as to whether the Committee was, properly speaking, a judicial tribunal at all or just an advisory board. The better opinion prevailed that it was indeed a court of justice in the full sense.

The foundation of the jurisdiction of the Committee lies in the prerogative right of the Sovereign as the fountain of justice to entertain appeals from all courts in her dominions. On English soil properly so called, and within the United Kingdom, there was a settled system of justice and of appeal. But what of those variegated territories beyond the narrow seas: the Channel Islands, for instance, which had been part of the Duchy of Normandy, or Gibraltar, or those coloured lands in the sunrise and the sunset and the blazing tropics, the East and West Indies, North America, Africa, Hong Kong, all with their own infinitely complex laws and ways of life? As it was said in an 18th century appeal from the Isle of Man: 'The King in Council must needs have a jurisdiction in such a case to prevent a failure of justice'.

It was in the late 17th century that the Committee of the Privy Council for Trade and the Plantations which had hitherto heard appeals from British colonial possessions handed over its duties to a special Appeal Committee. Its constitution and functions were set on its modern basis by the Judicial Committee Act 1833. Its position has been further modified by Acts of 1895 and 1908. Not only the Lords of Appeal in Ordinary may sit on the Committee. The Lords Justices of the Court of Appeal, being Privy Councillors, are also qualified, as well as several distinguished judges from overseas.

No other court has ever administered such a wide variety of law. Before it have met Christian theology and the rites of pagan idols, the disputes of Hindus and Moslems, Maoris and Zulus, Chinese and Singalese, white men and black. Questions may turn on the most intricate points of parliamentary draftsmanship or the most primitive tribal customs.

With the dissolution of the British Empire since the last war the jurisdiction of the Judicial Committee has progressively shrunk. Canada, India, Pakistan, Cyprus, Ghana, Nigeria, Uganda, Malta and other territories have withdrawn from its sphere. But a glance at the Law Reports still shows appeals from New Zealand, New South Wales, the West Indies, Hong Kong and Fiji. In these and other lands its influence is still acknowledged and men from afar still come to draw from the secluded fountain of justice in Whitehall.

The Sovereign's Procession at the State Opening of Parliament passes down the Royal Gallery in the House of Lords. Immediately in front of the Queen the Lord Great Chamberlain and the Earl Marshal walk backwards.

Opposite: The State Opening of Parliament. The Lord Chancellor takes the Queen's Speech from his purse and, kneeling, hands it to her

A sitting of the Judicial Committee of the Privy Council being held in the Council Chamber in Whitehall designed by Sir John Soane, subsequently enlarged by Barry

THE COURTS

Some Ancient and Obsolete Courts

Michael Leyland Nash

The Courts Act 1971 meant the end of the old Assizes and Quarter Sessions, the former having lasted exactly 800 years, since their inception in 1171. It also meant the end of those quaintly named courts cherished by law students and historians, the Bristol Tolzey Court, the Liverpool Court of Passage, the Salford Hundred Court and the Norwich Guildhall Court. They seemed to survive the centuries against all the odds, but shared the common characteristic that their existence has been sustained by cities of independent spirit, determined to preserve their privileges; the insistence on judgment locally for local citizens is paramount.

We may therefore inquire as to what purpose these courts served over such a long period (in the case of the Norwich court, 777 years) and include also some other courts, such as the Court Leet, the Court of Pie Poudre, the Verderers' Court and the lowest of the ecclesiastical courts, the Archdeacon's Court, affectionately known as the Bawdy Court.

Bristol Tolzey Court The Bristol Tolzey Court derived its curious name from the place where the tolls were collected. It was a local tribunal for civil causes. Originally the court of the bailiffs of the Hundred of Bristol, it subsequently became merged in the Court of the Lord Steward of the King's Household. Richard II revived its separate jurisdiction in 1395 by charter. It sat under the authority of a charter of Queen Anne, dated July 24, 1710. Its jurisdiction included mixed and personal actions to any amount provided that the cause of action arose within the city. The recorder was an ex-officio judge.

Liverpool Court of Passage The Liverpool Court of Passage was an inferior court of record, possessing a very ancient jurisdiction over causes of action arising within the borough of Liverpool. Up to 1835 it was also called the Borough Court of Liverpool. It was formerly held before the mayor and bailiffs of the borough; but section 2 of the Court of Passage Act 1834 provided that the court should not sit without a legal assessor, while section 8 provided that the attendance of the mayor and bailiffs was unnecessary. The Liverpool Corporation Act 1921 provided that the presiding judge must be a barrister of not less than seven years' standing. The court had jurisdiction in personal actions to any amount where the defendant resided or carried on business within the jurisdiction or, by leave of the court, when any part of the cause of action arose therein; but no action under £20 could be commenced in the court if the county court had jurisdiction. The court had jurisdiction in Admiralty similar to and co-extensive with that of the Liverpool county court.

We cannot now be sure of the origin of this ancient court, as the early records were burnt in a fire in 1795, but Howard Channon in his book, *Portrait of Liverpool*, published in 1970, gives some fascinating information about it. It probably got its name from *passagium*, the term used for the destination of ships sailing in convoy (as a protection against piracy) in the Middle Ages. It seems to have been earlier than the Mayor's Court, a 'piepowder court' or 'court of the dusty feet' (not a very complimentary observation on the litigants) which dealt with claims by people visiting the port. Incidentally, the Bristol Court of Pied Poudre (to give it its Norman French name) which was held before the recorder, was the only such court to survive into modern times.

Several ports had courts of passage, but only Liverpool's survived into the twentieth century. Its business was broadly the same as the county court, but there was no limit on the damages which the presiding judge could award; and it was the only inferior court in which proceedings could be taken against the Crown. It kept up with the times, and anticipated the Family Law Reform Act 1969 (which lowered the age of majority to 18) by reducing the age at which it surrendered funds held in trust for minors. Apart from the presiding judge and the registrar, the court's most important officer was the Sergeant-at-Mace and Marshal. The working relationship between the Sergeant-at-Mace and the judge formed one of the most important aspects of these courts.

In Liverpool the Sergeant had, over the centuries, the power to arrest a ship, nailing or, in modern times, tying the writ to the mast. He has also the power to arrest aircraft and has done so. The emblem of Sergeant-at-Mace was for long a silver oar; and it seems that strictly speaking he should have always carried it when arresting a ship. In the early nineteenth century there was an occasion when, having crossed the Mersey to make an arrest on the Birkenhead shore, the Sergeant was obliged to return to his office to fetch the oar because the sight of it was insisted upon: the Sergeant-at-Mace is responsible for the city regalia (of which the oar forms a part). It is interesting to note that there is, for example, a silver oar in the civic regalia of Southampton, whose mayor bears the title Admiral of the Port, although its Admiralty jurisdiction disappeared long before Liverpool's.

The last registrar of the Liverpool Court of Passage, Colonel Charles John Cocks, by virtue of his being registrar, could lay legal claim to the following offices, which came to him rather by default than decree. The titles in some cases almost defy credibility, for they are: Moss Reever and Burliman, Registrar of Leather Sealers, Scavenger, Alefounder or Taster, and Fryer of Seized Shoes. As Moss Reever and Burliman he would protect the Queen's Liege People from being aggrieved by any fishing and Digging of Holes. As Scavenger he would save them from the annoyance of wayners' carts without fear or dread, profitt or disprofitt. As Alefounder he would have to be satisfied that both the products of Liverpool brewers and bakers were good and wholesome; and as Fryer of Seized Leather he would indifferently and straitly examine that Shoes seized were sufficient and serviceable, according to the best of his Skill and Judgement, so help him God!

It is in the above resumé that we can see the strengths and the weaknesses of these ancient city courts. They guaranteed local consideration for citizens, and they had other virtues which will be considered later; but they suffered from the fatal flaw of overlapping jurisdiction with the local county court, and were therefore in

The Pye Powder Court, Cloth Fair, West Smithfield,
held in a public house, the Hand and Shears. The judge
"is determining a cause between two histrionic
complainants, respecting some injury sustained in the
neighbouring fair of St Bartholomew"

PYE POWDER COURT, CLOTH FAIR, WEST SMITHFIELD.

This Court is held at a Public House, known by the Sign of the Hand and Shears, the corner of Middle Street and King Street, as exhibited in the Vignette. The scene above, is descriptive of the Court held in the dining room, where the judge, attended by his secretary, is determining a cause between two histrionic complain-ants, respecting some Injury sustained in the neighbouring fair of St Bartholomew, by one of the parties.

London, Published Feb. 11, 1811, by R. Wilkinson, N.º 58, Cornhill.   109

danger of becoming redundant, unless they could make out a very good case for their retention.

Norwich Guildhall Court The Norwich Guildhall Court may be examined in closer detail to serve as an example of the history and jurisdiction of such courts.

The rules and practice of the Guildhall Court of the City of Norwich were outlined in a publication by James Goodwin, solicitor and attorney of that court, in 1822. The court dated from a charter granted by Richard I in 1194. That charter was granted to the citizens in consideration of 200 marks, and paying into the exchange the fee farm rent of £108 a year. The charter declared that none should be forced to answer any plea out of Norwich, but as to all debts there lent, and all securities there made, the plea or actions relating to them should be tried at Norwich. Goodwin goes on to outline its jurisdiction:

'This court holds pleas between subject and subject, of all personal actions arising out of the general or common law of the land, for redress of civil injuries arising or committed within the city, and county of the city, whether founded upon contracts or torts, let the subject matter be of what amount in value, or to what extent it may, as actions of debt, detinue, covenant, assumpsit; and of actions of trespass *vi et armis*, as assault and battery, or trespass considered with reference to the person; and of actions of trespass with respect to personal property; and of ejectment or trespass with reference to real property.
It holds pleas of all actions of trespass on the case, as Slander, or case considered with reference to the person, of Trover or Case considered with reference to personal property, and trespass on the case properly called, which includes injuries to real property . . .
The Court of Pleas before the mayor and sheriffs, by writ of right patent, holds pleas of land, or of all real actions for the recovery of lands and tenements situated within the city and liberties. This writ issues out of Chancery, and is directed to the mayor and sheriffs, whereby the lands or tenements demanded only are recovered . . .

This may sound like a roll-call of procedural legal history, but its significance can be illustrated at once by reference to what happened to the court especially since those rules were written in 1822. First, the rules of the court could be, and were, changed.

The practice in this court, was very considerable before the passing of an Act in the year 1700, for establishing a court of conscience, to enable persons to recover small debts under 40 shillings, in a more summary way, and until the 19 George III c 70, 1779 enacted that no persons should be held to bail in any inferior court of law for sums not amounting to £10.

After the act of 1700 the practice in the court declined, and some years afterwards the regular attendance of the under-sheriff at the Guildhall, on court days, was discontinued. It was the Debtor's Act 1869 which greatly revived the jurisdiction of the Guildhall Court in the nineteenth century. In the last years of its life, the Norwich Guildhall Court dealt mainly with civil debts arising from Corporation tenancies and in 1971, its last year, it handled over 1,000 cases.

The earlier court records, dating between 1588 and 1794 are interesting. One sees in these references to 'John Doe' and 'Richard Roe', fictitious names used in the old action of ejectment, an action to try the title to land. This old action, which was very elaborate in procedure, was abolished in 1852. John Doe was the name generally given to the fictitious plaintiff in the action of ejectment; Richard Roe was a fictitious personage who often appeared in actions at law prior to 1852 sometimes as one of the pledgers for due prosecution of an action and sometimes as the casual ejector in an action of ejectment.

Thus in 1816 we read of an action 'in this bailiwick area where the sheriff has jurisdiction . . . Enter and take Edward Deep late of the parish of St Andrew in the said city of Norwich confectioner and John Doe so that you have their bodies before our justices assigned for the conservation of the peace of our said city and county and to hear and determine divers Felonies Trespasses and other offences in the County of the said city committed . . .'

Court Leet The court leet was, and in a few cases still is, a court of record appointed to be held once a year within a particular hundred, lordship or manor, before the steward of the leet, being the king's court granted by charter to the lords of those hundreds or manors. Its original intent was to view the frankpledges, that is, the freeman within the liberty, who, according to the institution of Alfred, were all mutually pledged for the good behaviour of each other. By the Law of Property Act 1922, section 128, Schedule 12 the jurisdiction of courts leet in certain matters, for example relating to works for the protection or benefit of any manor, and registering any liability (under the Land Charges Act 1972) was transferred to the High Court.

The court leet fell into disuse after the enactment of the Summary Jurisdiction Act 1848, but it was kept alive by the Sheriffs Act 1887, s 40. A few have been held in recent times, for example at Laxton in Nottinghamshire, at Southampton, and at St Clements Danes Vestry Hall for the Manor and Liberty of the Savoy. In Southampton it is still, in the 1970s, held once every year, usually in the first week in October, and an extract of the proceedings of just one year will go to show the nature of the cases heard there. It is used as a forum for citizens to air their complaints, and, as such, is looked upon as the prerogative of the citizens. In 1973, Mr E A Chalk, representing Southampton Commons and Parks Protection Society, made a plea for a firm restriction on model power boats events on the ornamental lake.

Mrs R M Stonehouse, a retired City alderman, on behalf of a friend who lives in Woolston, asked that attention be drawn to the footpath said to be in a dangerous condition. Mr Stanley Vincent asked for more support from the City Council for groups such as Age Concern and the Southampton Pre-Retirement Society. Thus it can be seen that many citizens consider the court leet as perhaps the only time in the year that they can really find publicity for their grievances.

Ecclesiastical Courts The ecclesiastical courts lost most of their jurisdiction in the nineteenth century when first matrimonial matters and then probate were transferred to the High Court by the Act of 1857. What remained was largely removed by the Ecclesiastical Jurisdiction

The Court of Arches in the crypt of St Mary-Le-Bow Church, Cheapside. The verger, Mr Wiegand, keeps a day-book dating back several centuries recording all visitors to the Court and to the Church

Opposite top: The Verderers' Court of the New Forest. The Official Verderer reads an address to his nine fellow Verderers, the Senior Agister, and two Agisters

Opposite bottom: The Liverpool Court of Passage. The Presiding Judge, Richard Heddow Forrest sits beside the Lord Mayor of Liverpool, Charles Cowlin

Measure of 1963. Today there remains only the Court of Arches, the Chancery Court of York and the consistory courts. The consistory courts are the ecclesiastical courts of each diocese, and are mostly concerned with church property and the discipline of the clergy.

The Court of Arches is the appeal court of the Archbishop of Canterbury. It is so called because the cases were first heard at St Mary le Bow in London. The Latin name of the church is *Sancta Maria de Arcubus,* because the steeple is raised upon pillars built archwise, thus giving it the name of St Mary of the Arches. Subsequently this court was held in the hall belonging to the College of Civilians (ie those lawyers studying the civil law, of which ecclesiastical or canon law formed a part). That hall was in turn popularly known as Doctors' Commons. By the Public Worship Act 1874 a special judge was appointed from the Admiralty Division of the High Court for ecclesiastical jurisdiction. Procedurally, admiralty law and ecclesiastical law had much common ground. The original (or peculiar) jurisdiction of the Court of Arches was finally abolished by the Ecclesiasti-

cal Jurisdiction Measure of 1963, but its appellate jurisdiction remains, and there is, also, an appeal from the court to the Judicial Committee of the Privy Council.

The Chancery Court of York is the equivalent court of the Court of Arches in the Archdiocese of York. It consists of five judges including the Dean of the Court of Arches, and again there is an appeal to the Judicial Committee.

In the consistory courts there is a single judge styled the chancellor of the diocese. But before the abolition of its jurisdiction in 1963, the court with the most interesting history (indeed, sociologically the most important of the church courts) was the lowest in the grade. This was the archdeacon's court, commonly known as the Bawdy Court. Over five centuries, from about 1300 to 1800, the archdeacon had considerable power over the laity to try and enforce moral standards. These were of course based on the Christian ethic and the rules of the church, and it is instructive to note, as Paul Hair does in his compilation of extracts from these courts (published in 1972) that 'the church courts, acting against

irresponsible and anti-social behaviour, were supported by the general discipline and responsibility of the masses. If not, how could the courts have survived for so many centuries?'

With the grant of toleration to the Dissenters in the late 1680s, there began an irreversible decline in the church courts. Acts of 1690 and 1712 removed the obligation on magistrates to enforce church discipline, and eventually, in 1787, the legislature intervened to remove the staple offence of ante-nuptial fornication. Before then, the number and range of moral offences dealt with was considerable, and an illuminating commentary on both the changefulness and the changelessness of human nature over this period. Offences tried included adultery, bastardy, abortion, overlaying, offences against the Sabbath, Sunday drinking, scolding and offences committed in church and in the churchyard.

The Verderers' Courts 'The laws imposed by the Norman kings and their successors for the regulation of the forests are a forgotten chapter in the evolution of English law' wrote Professor Keeton in 1966 in a treatise on the common law. It is of special interest therefore to discover the history behind a residual survival of the Forest Laws in the courts of the New Forest and the Forest of Dean. It is perhaps difficult to grasp now, when the Chief Agister appears in his green livery with black leather gaiters and gold buttons, bearing the Crown and Stirrup symbol of the New Forest, and when the proceedings of the Verderers' Court are conducted in an urbane and humane manner, that the forest laws of the middle ages could have exercised such power and engendered such fear.

The forest laws were particularly important for two reasons: they operated outside the usual scope of judicial authority and control (like the ecclesiastical and maritime courts) and the fines that were collected from forest courts formed an important part of the royal revenue. For these twin reasons they tended to be arbitrary and oppressive and their history is often not a pretty one.

The forest laws owed their origin in this country to the Norman kings, who had inherited them from their Carolingian predecessors in France, where they formed part of those laws known as the *Capitulations*. Holdsworth calls them the 'Frankish Forest ban', introduced by William I. William the Conqueror afforested huge tracts of land in England after the Conquest for his own pleasure in the pursuit of game, and set up the forest courts run by the regarders, the verderers, the foresters and the agisters. They were instituted to protect the royal interest in game, and for the punishment of all injuries done to the deer or venison, to the vert or greensward, and to the covert in which such deer were lodged.

Forests proliferated. The royal forests and the courts they brought with them still numbered 69 in the time of Henry VIII, and the forest laws were to last, albeit eventually in residual form, for 800 years.

The special forest courts exacted fierce punishments.

Trials took place in the Swainmote, held three times a year, where freeholders within the forest did suit, and of which the verderers were the judges, on charges presented by the verderers in the Woodmote, held every 40 days. Judgment, however, only took place in the justice-seat, or eyre of the forest, held by one of the two chief justices every three years. The court of regard, or survey of dogs, was held every third year.

Each forest group had its own warden, under whom were foresters and gamekeepers, woodwards and agisters, these last named being responsible for overseeing the cattle and swine pastured within the forests.

In each shire four knights were elected by the county court as verderers and twelve as regarders, charged with the regular enquiry into all encroachments on the royal rights. In every forest a court of attachment was held, usually every six weeks, to deal with minor offences against the forest law. Important cases were dealt with by itinerant justices of the forest, who held an eyre in every forest once every few years. Amercement was the usual form of punishment when the forest law was administered in a more humane manner, from the twelfth or thirteenth century onwards.

Amercement was similar to a fine, but differed in that the amount was left to the discretion of the court, whereas a fine was usually fixed and certain. It was a two-edged sword, for whereas it could be used in a merciful way according to circumstances it could also be used in an arbitrary and heavy-handed way. The maladministration of the forest law was amongst the main indictments against King John at the time of Magna Carta in 1215. The Great Charter contained three clauses dealing with the burden of forest law:

1 The king promised to give up the new forests he had created;
2 Men dwelling outside the forest were exempted from arbitrary summons to the forest court;
3 Inquiries were to be held in every county into abuses in forest administration.

These clauses were expanded in 1217 into a separate charter of the forest or *Carta de Foresta*. This generally mitigated the severity of the forest laws and was eventually confirmed by the Statute of Marlborough in 1267. To oversee the limits of the forests – that they did not grow outside their agreed boundaries – 'perambulations', rather like beating the bounds, but with a restrictive rather than a confirmatory purpose – began to be held in the thirteenth century.

By the end of the sixteenth century the forest laws had fallen into decline. The ordinary forest courts could do little except present criminals at the eyre. It was at the eyre that they were punished; so that it may be said that the whole execution of the forest laws depended on the regular holding of the eyre. By the end of the sixteenth century eyres were rarely held. The desuetude of the eyre meant in effect the collapse of the whole system. After the Restoration in 1660 little more is heard of the forest laws, except that a statute of 1667–68 relating to the Forest of Dean declared the forest laws there to be beneficial, and in a statute of 1697–98 relating to the

New Forest, they were expressly saved. The last eyre to be held in the New Forest was in 1670, and the last forest eyre of all was held by the Earl of Holland at the end of the seventeenth century.

In 1817 the offices of Warden, Chief Justice and Justice in Eyre of the royal forests, the last remnants of the forest law machinery, were abolished; in 1829 the powers of these officials were vested in the first Commissioners of His Majesty's woods, forests and land revenues. Extensive powers over existing forestal officers and even disputes as to forest boundaries were vested in the Commission. The jurisdiction of the Court of Attachment was regulated; and the verderers, in the Court of Attachment, were given a jurisdiction to enquire into unlawful enclosures and into the conduct of their subordinates.

In 1832 the powers of the Commission were handed over to the Commission of Woods, Forests, Land Revenues, Works and Buildings, and yet again in 1851 the Commission of Woods, Forests and Land Revenues was separated from that of works and buildings – the greater part of the control over forests being assigned to the former board. The control of the board is now subject (or was until a short time ago) to numerous local Acts which have been passed to deal with particular forests.

These local Acts refer particularly to the Forest of Dean and the New Forest, and to a lesser extent to Windsor Forest and to Epping Forest. Indeed, owing to progressive disafforestation by statute or otherwise, these were the only surviving forests subject to the forest law.

Only in the Forest of Dean and the New Forest did any active administration of the forest law survive.

In the Forest of Dean there is an enactment requiring the election of verderers, but the mode of election is regulated by custom. This is preserved by the Wild Creatures and Forest Laws Act 1971. Substantially, all the law that still operated at the time of its enachment was preserved by that statute.

In the New Forest, the constitution of the verderers is now governed by statute. They are required to hold courts for the dispatch of administrative and judicial business under the New Forest Act 1877, and they may abate inclosures etc, and fine offenders. The verderers consist of the official verderer, five elective verderers and four appointed verderers. The election of verderers is governed by the New Forest Acts 1877–1949.

The ancient forest courts still have a limited jurisdiction. The court of Swainmote sits for the dispatch of judicial business in the New Forest (New Forest Act 1949) and can convict for breach of bye-laws affecting the forest (Forestry Act 1967). The court consists of the official verderer, together with such four of the other verderers as may be nominated by the Lord Chancellor, of whom not less than three are to be elective verderers.

The power to fix the number of animals which may be pastured in the New Forest by virtue of a right of common is governed by the New Forest Act 1949 – these rights of common make a fascinating recital – the commoners claimed during a running legal battle in the last century that they pre-dated both the forest and forest law and comprise (i) common of pasture for commonable animals; (ii) common of mast, a right to depasture pigs to collect acorns and beechnuts (known as mast); (iii) common of turbary (cutting turf for burning); (iv) common of pasture for sheep; (v) common of marl (right to take clay marl for use on the commoner's holding); (vi) estovers: right to take wood, always extremely unpopular with the Forestry Commission and mostly concerning free fuel wood.

The Wild Creatures and Forest Laws Act 1971 abolished any franchises of forest, free chase, park or free warren, and forest law is now abrogated except insofar as it refers to the appointment and functions of verderers.

Even now, this is not quite the end of the matter, and the remaining forest law and its courts may be subject to yet further refinements if recent recommendations of the Law Commission become law. In its publication *The Jurisdiction of Certain Ancient Courts* (February 1976) the Commission states that 'We have no desire to oppose the wishes of those who, solely on historical grounds and so as not to sever links with the past, desire to retain their courts ... there is, however, a practical difficulty ... we cite authorities which show that, until the jurisdiction of a moribund court is taken away by statute, the jurisdiction is capable of being revived, however long the period for which the jurisdiction has been in desuetude. We doubt whether the court authorities of an obsolescent court would welcome an order of *mandamus* requiring the court to be held. Moreover, proceedings before such courts may consume time, and may entail trouble, expense and uncertainty, which could hardly be justified if an alternative remedy is available by the familiar proceedings of an ordinary court'.

This seems to forebode nothing good for such as the forest courts, but then in paragraph 23 the words of timely wisdom are tempered with the following: 'The principle we have endeavoured to follow is that jurisdictions which are not obsolete should be preserved. Accordingly the draft clause is not intended to affect the following courts, and in each case the authority concerned has accepted that it would not do so.'

The courts then are listed and include the Dean Forest Verderers' Court and the New Forest Verderers' Court, known as the Court of Swainmote and Attachment. Thus a very small residue of the original forest law and the jurisdiction of the forest courts remains in a useful and beneficent form. It is as though the authorities which swept away the chief ancient courts by the Courts Act 1971 have paused a moment, perhaps had second thoughts, and it is a happy reflection that they have decided to leave a number of courts, which by their living continuity, represent so many different strands of our legal history. It is right that pre-eminent among these should be two courts administering the forest law, which Baron Pollock, when hearing the famous Sawing Engines case in 1894, and having to examine the laws in detail, declared in their complexities to be 'delicious', should be preserved.

Two views of Westminster by Wenceslas Hollar 1647.
Top: Parliament House, Westminster Hall and
Westminster Abbey from the River Thames. The
jetty was the landing place of lawyers who had come
to the Courts by river from the Temple. Bottom: New
Palace Yard with Westminster Hall and the Clock
House

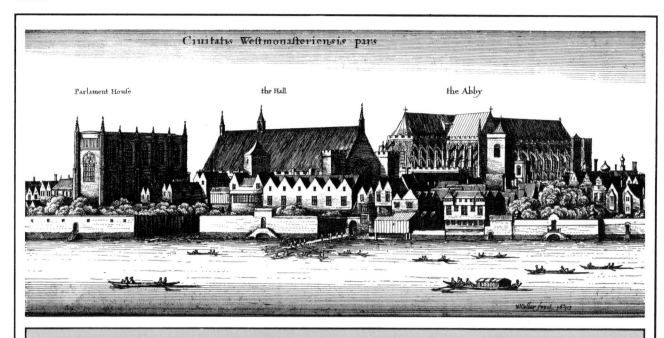

4 THE LAW AND THE EXECUTIVE

Law Officers of the Crown

Gavin Drewry

Sir Patrick Hastings, who was Attorney-General in Ramsay MacDonald's minority Labour Government in 1924, writes as follows in his autobiography:

My day began at seven o'clock in the morning and I rarely got to bed before five the next morning. The day was spent in one long rush between the Law Courts, government departments and the House of Commons. The night, or rather the early morning, was needed in order to get ready for the next day. Nothing that I began was I ever allowed to finish; and nothing was ever finished until something else was begun. Being an Attorney-General, as it was in those days, is my idea of hell.

Sir Patrick's brief spell as principal law officer of the Crown was particularly hectic and unhappy, and it ended with his involvement in the disastrous *Campbell* case (discussed below) which brought down the Government on a vote of censure. But his experience does serve to highlight two important features of the law officers' work. First, as Hastings' words indicate, the duties of office are many, varied and onerous. Secondly, the law officers operate in the no-man's-land between law and politics: they are subject to frequent political pressure and to the rigours of ministerial answerability to Parliament for most of their actions, but they are expected at the same time to exercise what Lord Birkenhead among others, has called a 'judicial mind', and to interpret the public interest independently of any considerations of party advantage or loyalty to ministerial colleagues. This requires almost super-human qualities of judgment and sensitivity.

Position of the Law Officers There are four law officers in the United Kingdom: the Attorney-General and the Solicitor-General, who operate in the context of the English legal system, and the Lord Advocate and the Solicitor-General for Scotland, who perform similar functions with regard to the quite separate and distinctive Scottish legal system. The present account deals only with the English law officers. Until 1872 there was, in addition, a King's Advocate-General, who advised the Government on matters of international, maritime and ecclesiastical law.

In his learned work, *The Law Officers of the Crown,* Professor Edwards traces these offices back to the 13th century, but says that the title, Attorney-General of England, first appeared in 1461, and that of Solicitor-General of England in 1515. He sums up the modern character of the offices as follows:

As the traditional first representative of the Sovereign in the courts ... the control of prosecutions is vested in the holder of the office of Attorney-General. Supporting the Attorney-General in all his multifarious responsibilities is the Solicitor-General who, in effect, may be regarded as the Attorney's deputy. Moreover, the modern law officer is by no means confined to conducting court cases as leading counsel for the Crown. Like the Lord Chancellor and the Home Secretary, the Attorney-General and the Solicitor-General are ministers of the Crown with departmental responsibilities derived from their legal qualifications. As chief legal advisers to the executive their services are constantly in demand by government officials.

Thus in general terms, the law officers are subject to the familiar rules of individual and collective ministerial responsibility though, as we shall see, many of their functions must be exercised independently of any pressure from ministerial colleagues. Since the late 1920s no law officer has held Cabinet rank, but they may be required to attend the Cabinet to tender legal advice and they belong to important Cabinet committees. They are active members of the Legislation Committee, which examines the drafts of Bills before they are introduced into Parliament, which is an aspect of their more general functions in supervising the preparation of legislation.

Law Officers as Politicians The law officers are recruited from the ranks of leading barristers (though they must be members of one House of Parliament – normally the Commons). Indeed, since 1814, the Attorney-General has been titular head of the English Bar. The notion of luring a successful Queen's Counsel away from lucrative private practice to advise the Government in a full-time, salaried capacity is a comparatively modern one. Just over a hundred years ago, Sir William Harcourt commented that law officers were accustomed to pack away the public business of the country into those nooks and corners of time of which a large or moderate private practice may leave undisposed. Controversy arose a few years later when the Conservative Attorney-General, Sir Richard Webster, represented *The Times* both in libel proceedings and before a subsequent Commission of Inquiry, arising out of false allegations made against the Irish MP, Charles Parnell. A Treasury Minute, promulgated when the Liberals returned to power in 1892, initiated the slow process by which the law officers relinquished private practice and became fully-fledged ministers.

A year later, another Treasury Minute authorised

accommodation and clerical assistance to be made available to the law officers at the Royal Courts of Justice. Up to this point, they had been forced to transact State business in their private chambers, with the aid only of the most primitive record-keeping facilities. Now there is a Law Officer's Department, whose civil service head is a high ranking Legal Secretary.

Powers and Functions Given the diversity of the law officers' work, departmental support is essential, though more than is the case with other ministers. They have to take many decisions in person rather than delegating them down the line. The Attorney-General acts as guardian of the public interest. He can, as will be shown later, initiate civil proceedings in the High Court, for example to restrain a public body from exceeding the limits of its powers or to prevent a prospective breach of the criminal law. He often appears as an independent officer of State before official tribunals of inquiry (though he did not appear before the tribunal set up in 1978 to investigate alleged financial malpractices by the Crown Agents). In respect of criminal trials, he can choose the location of a trial on indictment. He is the only person who can enter a *nolle prosequi* to stop the trial of an indictable offence once proceedings have started. He himself can commence criminal proceedings, and he can instruct the Director of Public Prosecutions to take over a prosecution commenced by a private individual, and kill the proceedings by offering no evidence, if he considers that the public interest would best be served by taking such action. In all these matters the Attorney-General has an unfettered discretion, though his actions may be questioned in Parliament and are sometimes challenged (usually unsuccessfully) in the courts.

Attorney-General's Consent In addition to the powers and functions already mentioned, which have evolved through Crown prerogative and constitutional conventions, there are many Acts of Parliament which require the consent of the Attorney-General (or of someone else) before certain offences can be prosecuted. These restrictions upon the bringing of prosecutions have grown up in a haphazard way. In the words of Professor Edwards:

In all, some eighty offences exist at the present time in which no proceedings may be instituted without the consent of the Attorney-General either acting alone or, alternatively, with the consent of the Solicitor-General, ... the Director of Public Prosecutions, or some other person or persons. Examination of these multifarious statutory provisions fails to reveal any identifiable theme underlying the limitations.

Some prominent items from the ragbag of offences for which consent is needed include prosecutions under the Official Secrets Acts and the Obscene Publications Acts, allegations of corruption by public officials, and hijacking. The Franks Report on section 2 of the Official Secrets Act 1911, published in 1972, summarises some Home Office evidence explaining these restrictions:

These are to secure consistency of practice or to prevent abuse, where an offence is drafted in wide terms or is open to misuse; to enable account to be taken of mitigating factors which can-

not easily be defined by statute; to provide central control over the use of the criminal law in sensitive areas such as race relations or censorship; and finally to ensure that decisions on prosecution take account of important considerations of public policy or of a political or international character.

In this, as in other facets of his work, the Attorney-General is required to exercise his own judgment, independently of party and ministerial loyalties, though he is not expected to act in ignorance of current issues of public policy, and this means being on speaking terms with his colleagues. In 1970 there was some controversy over the decision of the Attorney-General, taken after consultations with the Foreign Secretary, to prosecute journalists under the Officials Secrets Acts in connection with the leakage and publication of a confidential memorandum relating to the Nigerian civil war, though there is no evidence that the Attorney's independence was compromised by his seeking advice from other ministers; more spectacular illustrations of this issue are given in a later section of this chapter. It is always difficult for a law officer to maintain the appearance of impartiality in a matter which has a high political content, a difficulty exacerbated in this instance by the widespread disapproval of the laws under which the prosecutions were brought. The Franks Committee's proposal that the filter in this area should be the Director of Public Prosecutions rather than the Attorney-General would be a slight improvement upon present practice, though as will be seen in the next section, the Director works in very close association with the law officers.

The Director of Public Prosecutions The closest approximation in England to a State Public Prosecutor, though the approximation is a feeble one, is the Director of Public Prosecutions (DPP), whose office dates back to 1879. The Director is a civil servant, appointed by the Home Secretary from the ranks of barristers or solicitors of ten years' standing; he now has a staff of about 55 barristers and solicitors, plus an administrative staff of civil servants. He acts under the direction of the Attorney-General, who promulgates statutory instruments which define his functions and powers.

These functions fall broadly into three categories. First, he may, when asked to do so, tender advice to police forces and government departments about issues of prosecution policy. Secondly, he considers a wide range of cases, supposedly of special difficulty, which the police are obliged to report to him (these include allegations of criminal offences committed by police officers) and advises accordingly. Thirdly, he arranges the prosecution of particularly serious cases (including all murder cases), cases referred to him by government departments, and all other cases which appear to him to be of peculiar importance or difficulty.

Although the proportion of indictable offences actually prosecuted by the DPP is very small, he exercises considerable influence over the development of prosecution policy through his advisory and co-ordinating functions. His role interlinks with that of the law officers to an extent that fully justifies his inclusion in this chapter.

Like the Attorney, to whom he answers and with

whom he consults, the Director is by no means insulated from political criticism. In recent years, for example, he has had to unravel the legal tangle of the Poulson corruption scandal, to decide upon the prosecution of the former Liberal leader, Jeremy Thorpe, and to consider whether prosecutions should be brought against any of the actors in the case of Rhodesian sanctions-busting by British oil companies. But ultimately the Attorney-General answers in Parliament for the DPP's actions, or inactions.

The Law Officers' Claims to Judicial Office Until quite recently it was generally believed that the law officers had strong preferential claims to be appointed to certain high judicial offices if any such posts fell vacant during their periods of office. In particular, it was recognised that the Attorney-General had a strong claim upon the office of Lord Chief Justice. This convention was established in the long era, which ended in or about the 1920s, when appointments to senior judgeships in general were part of a political spoils system.

Of particular interest in this context is an unedifying story which concerns the elevation of Lord Hewart to the Lord Chief Justiceship in 1922; the outline that follows is derived largely from Robert Jackson's biography of Hewart, *The Chief*.

Sir Gordon Hewart was Attorney-General in Lloyd George's coalition administration in the early 1920s: his post was at that time included in the Cabinet. The serving Lord Chief Justice, Lord Reading, had strong ambitions to exchange his judicial post for a diplomatic one. Hewart wanted the senior judgeship, which he felt was his right by well-established convention, if it fell vacant. Lloyd George had it in mind to appoint Reading to the post of Viceroy of India but, as he explained to Hewart, he did not want to lose his Attorney whom he regarded

as an indispensible member of his ministerial team. The Prime Minister then proposed a devious scheme to overcome the difficulty: Reading would be made Viceroy, but the Chief Justiceship would be filled on a strictly temporary basis by a senior judge, who would undertake in advance to resign when Hewart was ready to leave political life. It was made clear that Reading's coveted appointment as Viceroy depended upon Hewart's agreement to these arrangements, and Hewart eventually acquiesced, albeit with misgivings that he might ultimately be cheated. Mr Justice A T Lawrence was appointed as Lord Chief Justice, with the title of Lord Trevethin. In Robert Jackson's words:

Lloyd George kept his original bargain. Trevethin, abandoned without ceremony, read of his own resignation in the *The Times,* and at the age of fifty-two Hewart achieved his life's ambition as he stepped into the Law's most honourable permanent judicial post.

Hewart served as Lord Chief Justice until 1940. He was succeeded by Lord Caldecote who had served two terms as Attorney-General, but was Lord Chancellor at the time of his appointment. His successor, Lord Goddard, was a career judge, then serving as a Lord of Appeal, and the next two incumbents, Lord Parker and Lord Widgery, were also appointed from the ranks of senior judges rather than from politics. Previous service as a law officer is certainly no disqualification to eventual judicial advancement: Lord Dilhorne, for example, served first as Attorney-General and later as Lord Chancellor before his appointment as Lord of Appeal in Ordinary in 1969. But no law officer today would lay any claim to automatic appointment to a senior judgeship.

Independence of Judgment In July 1924, the Communist newspaper, *Worker's Weekly,* carried an article addressed to serving members of the armed forces, exhorting them not to turn their guns on their fellow workers, to smash capitalism, and to turn their weapons on their oppressors. After rather perfunctory discussions with the DPP the Attorney-General, Sir Patrick Hastings, gave his consent to the prosecution of J R Campbell, the acting editor, under the Incitement to Mutiny Act 1797. It soon became clear that Hastings had not apprised himself of the likely political consequences of his actions (many Labour backbenchers held views which were not very different from those expressed by Campbell) and that, for a variety of reasons which had not been taken into account, the prosecution would probably be an embarrassing failure, likely to provide a feast of left-wing propaganda. Thereupon, after consultations with the Prime Minister and with the Cabinet, the over-hasty and clumsy decision to prosecute was, with equal clumsiness, reversed.

There followed a motion of censure in the Commons in the course of which the Attorney-General, denying that he had allowed himself to be influenced improperly by pressure from his colleagues explained that although he was aware of the Cabinet's views, the decision to withdraw the prosecution had been his alone. The Prime Minister, Ramsay MacDonald supported Hast-

ings' view about the propriety of his actions: 'Surely every law officer who is undertaking a prosecution in the interests of the state must possess himself of guidance on this question, whether if a prosecution is instituted, the effect of the prosecution will be harmful or beneficial to the state in whose interests it has been undertaken.' The House was clearly unconvinced that it had been told the whole story, a view that was reinforced by MacDonald's unwillingness to set up an investigatory select committee: the Government was defeated by 364 votes to 191, and that was the end of Britain's first taste of Labour administration.

Subsequent accounts of these events have underlined Hastings' honest ineptitude and MacDonald's disingenuousness. The next Prime Minister, Stanley Baldwin, revealed to the Commons that he had rescinded a hitherto undisclosed Cabinet instruction, issued at the time of the Campbell affair, expressly directing that no political prosecutions (a dangerously ambiguous phrase) should be directed by the Attorney-General without Cabinet permission.

In 1951 the position was re-stated in the Commons by Sir Hartley Shawcross, Attorney-General in the first post-war Labour administration:

I think the true doctrine is that it is the duty of an Attorney-General, in deciding whether or not to authorise the prosecution, to acquaint himself with all the relevant facts, including, for instance, the effect which the prosecution, successful or unsuccessful as the case may be, would have upon public morale and order, and with any other considerations affecting public policy. In order to inform himself, he may, although I do not think he is obliged to, consult with any of his colleagues in the Government; and indeed, as Lord Simon once said, he would in some cases be a fool if he did not. On the other hand, the assistance of his colleagues is confined to informing him of particular considerations which might affect his own decision, and does not consist, and must not consist, in telling him what that decision ought to be.

This almost certainly accords with today's conventional wisdom on the subject, and would doubtless have been echoed (albeit with differences of nuance) by Sir Patrick Hastings and most other law officers of his era.

Accountability and Control The law officers' functions in respect of criminal prosecutions derive from their role as guardians of the public interest, standing as gate-keepers to the courts in difficult areas of public policy. This has its parallel on the civil side of their work where the Attorney has discretion to sue, either on his own account or on behalf of a 'relator' (a private citizen or body lacking the necessary legal standing to bring an action of this kind to safeguard the public interest).

One recent civil case in which the Attorney-General achieved public prominence, and one which underlines the contentious nature of any attempt to define public interest, was the unsuccessful quest for an injunction to prevent publication of the *Crossman Diaries* in 1975. An account of the proceedings, by Hugo Young, illuminates the role of the law officers and their relationships with ministerial colleagues and with civil servants.

It seemed firmly established by precedents consistently confirmed since the turn of the century that the exercise of the Attorney-General's discretion in civil and criminal proceedings is a matter for Parliament and not for the courts. But is this good enough in modern circumstances where Attorneys-General may be reluctant, on public policy grounds, to enforce the law against powerful bodies like trade unions which make up the modern corporate state, and against agencies which are offshoots of Government itself?

This question has recently been asked in connection with relator proceedings. Private citizens cannot sue to protect the *general* public interest unless they themselves can show that they have some special stake in the outcome of such an action; however, they can apply to the Attorney-General to bring an action either in their names or on his own behalf as custodian of the public interest.

McWhirter v IBA In 1973, Mr Ross McWhirter, a private citizen, requested the Attorney-General to take action to prevent the Independent Broadcasting Authority from screening a film about Andy Warhol. Newspaper reports of a preview of the film suggested that it contained offensive matter, and McWhirter claimed that the IBA was in breach of its statutory duty to satisfy itself that programmes do not include material which is offensive to public feeling. The Attorney said he would consider a relator application. But in view of the imminence of the broadcast, and of the fact that making such an application requires considerable time for preparation, McWhirter went directly to the courts: by a two to one majority the Court of Appeal granted an interim injunction.

A few days later, the Attorney-General having now consented to relator proceedings, the issue of McWhirter's right to sue was argued more fully, with the Attorney himself in attendance. The same majority of the Court of Appeal affirmed that, in the words of Lord Denning, 'in the last resort, if the Attorney-General refuses leave in a proper case, or improperly or unreasonably delays in giving leave, or his machinery works too slowly, then a member of the public who has a sufficient interest can himself apply to the court itself.' This was said *obiter* (ie it went wider than the grounds required to reach the decision in the instant case) but it provided a clue to the way in which the Court might approach similar cases in the future. In the result, their Lordships unanimously decided to lift the injunction on the grounds that the IBA had now fulfilled its statutory duty by viewing the film in order to reach its decision about showing it.

Gouriet v Union of Post Office Workers Lord Denning was to recall his own words in another important case that arose in 1977. Mr John Gouriet, a private citizen representing a right-wing pressure group, tried to persuade the Attorney-General to take action against the Union of Post Office Workers, which had called upon its members to impose a ban on postal and telephone communications between Britain and South Africa in protest against the latter's apartheid policies. Mr Gouriet alleged that this would constitute the statutory criminal offence of wilfully delaying postal packets; but the Attorney said that, having considered all the circumstances including the public interest '... I have come to the conclusion that I should not give my consent.' Despite this decision the Court of Appeal granted an interim injunction (with which the union complied); and the case was fully argued a few days later, with the Attorney added as defendant.

At this hearing the Attorney-General was subjected to an extraordinary interrogation from the Bench. He stoutly maintained the traditional view that he was answerable only to Parliament, that he was obliged to act independently of any pressure from his ministerial colleagues, and that the Court was not entitled to enquire about, let alone set aside, his reasons:

... the court cannot question the Attorney-General's reasons for acting or refusing to act. It cannot question his reasons directly or indirectly or deduce what those reasons were. I say with the utmost repect to your Lordships but also with the utmost firmness that the courts must not assume the mantle of Parliament.

The majority of the Court of Appeal agreed that the Attorney's decision was not susceptible to review by the Court, but held that where there is no discernible reason why a breach of the criminal law should not be restrained then citizens might be allowed to seek an interim injunction or a declaration. Lord Denning said, in a dissenting judgment, that the Attorney's refusal of consent could be reviewed indirectly, particularly where there is a prospective breach of the criminal law, and that the courts could grant a full injunction where appropriate. He held that the Attorney's actions amounted to a dangerous claim to a power to set aside the law, and was 'a direct challenge to the rule of law'.

The decision was reversed unanimously by the House of Lords; Lord Denning and his colleagues were, in the mannered language of judicial review, firmly rebuked. Thus the Attorney-General's discretion was restored to its former inviolate state. It is sad to see a small but promising constitutional revolution nipped in the bud, but there can be little doubt that, on the authorities, the House of Lords had little room to manoeuvre, even if it had wished to do so.

This country has opted (by default, in not canvassing any alternatives) for a ministerial and party-political Attorney-General as custodian of wide areas of public interest. He is obliged to apply a 'judicial mind', but not in open court or with any reasons given. If he is ever corrupt, inept or partisan we can never know; even if we could find out, the only sanctions (save in the extreme case of his indulgence in criminal corruption) are haphazard political ones. This is a worrying state of affairs. But on the other hand, how far are the courts competent to adjudge the public interest in these areas? It is the absence of any meaningful facility to scrutinise the exercising of important areas of a necessarily wide ministerial discretion, rather than the principle of that discretion which should cause concern. This is at least as much a matter of 'open government' as it is of 'the rule of law'. Meanwhile we would do well to recall R M Jackson's words that, 'it is quite as necessary to provide against being ruled by judges as it is to guard against being judged by ministers.'

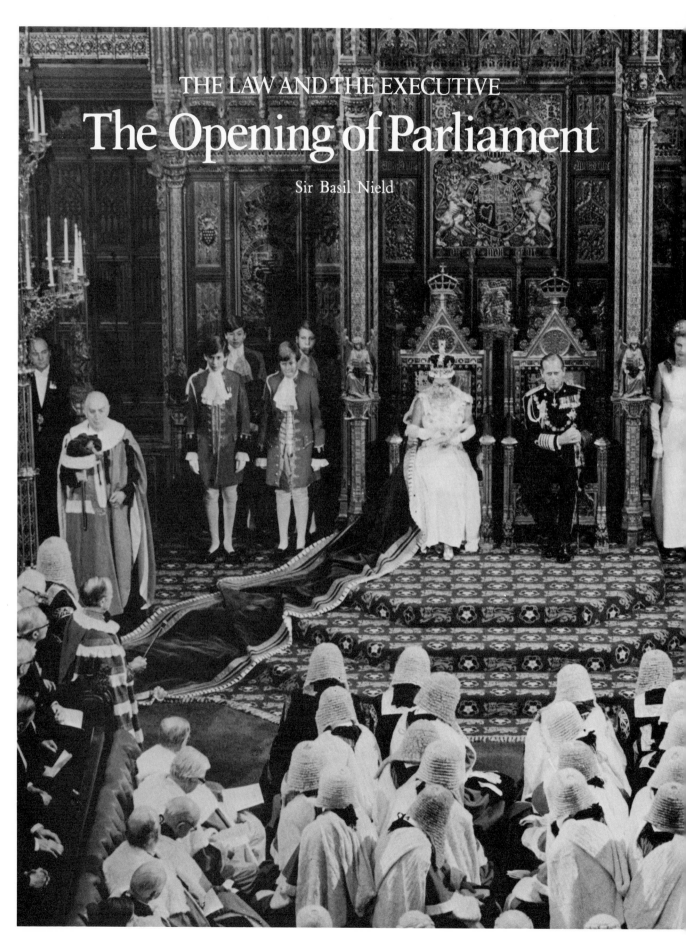

THE LAW AND THE EXECUTIVE
The Opening of Parliament
Sir Basil Nield

"Mr Speaker, the Queen commands this honourable House to attend Her Majesty immediately in the House of Peers."

This is the message delivered by the Gentleman Usher of the Black Rod – requiring the loyal and dutiful Commons to attend the Sovereign at the State Opening of Parliament.

The Meeting of the Three Estates It is on this occasion that the three estates of the realm – the Lords Spiritual (the archbishops and senior bishops of the Church of England), the Lords Temporal and the members of the House of Commons – meet together to hear the Queen's Speech, outlining the Government's plans for the forthcoming parliamentary session. It is not only a meeting of Lords and Commons, it also brings together the legislators and senior members of the judiciary – those who enact law and those who interpret it.

The Ceremonial From many parts of London and beyond there converge upon the House of Lords carriages and motor cars carrying members of the diplomatic corps, bishops, peers and peeresses as well as distinguished visitors. Members of the Royal Family arrive later in their separate carriages and take their places in the Chamber of the House of Lords beside the dukes upon the front bench to the right as one faces the dais. Then, under guard from the Tower, comes the Crown of England, the Imperial State Crown, the symbol of sovereignty and royal authority conveyed in its own coach.

At the appointed hour the Queen and the Duke of Edinburgh leave Buckingham Palace in the State Coach. Her Majesty and His Royal Highness are accompanied by a Sovereign's Escort of the Household Cavalry – each cavalryman with his plumed helmet glinting, his breast plate gleaming and his top boots shining – the black horses seemingly aware of the magnificence of the great procession. Down the Mall, under the Admiralty Arch, along Whitehall, into Parliament Square – the route throughout lined by the Brigade of Guards until the State Coach reaches the Victoria Gate of the Palace of Westminster. Here the Queen and the Prince are received by the Lord Great Chamberlain and the Earl Marshal. These great officers of State must walk backwards before the Queen. To do so in full ceremonial robes is something of a feat and it is made no easier if you are unlucky enough to have only one leg. This was the case when Lord Ancaster was Lord Great Chamberlain, he having lost a leg in battle. He made the journey successfully and bravely.

The Queen makes her way to the Royal Robing Room. It is interesting to remember that the House of Lords sat in this room during the 1939 War when, in 1941, the Chamber of the House of Commons was destroyed and the Lords allowed the Commons to use the Chamber of the House of Lords.

Crowned and robed, the Sovereign proceeds slowly with the Duke down the Royal Gallery where visitors watch, with deep interest and regard, this strangely moving scene.

The Irish State Coach, bringing the Queen, arrives at the House of Lords accompanied by the Household Cavalry

At the head of the procession as it passes between the lines of Beefeaters are the four pursuivants – Rouge Croix, Blue Mantle, Rouge Dragon and Portcullis wearing their tabards. The Lord High Chancellor carries the Purse, a distinguished personage holds aloft the Sword of State and another carries the Cap of Maintenance. Admiral of the Fleet Earl Mountbatten, Field Marshal Viscount Montgomery of Alamein, Marshal of the Royal Air Force Lord Tedder and Field Marshal Sir Gerald Templer have, I think, been among those who have undertaken one or other of these duties.

Immediately in front of the Queen are the Lord Great Chamberlain and the hereditary Earl Marshal of England, the Duke of Norfolk.

In the meantime the great concourse in the House of Peers awaits the arrival of Her Majesty. The two thrones stand empty – the one rather higher than the other. This was arranged, it is said, by Queen Victoria who, while having every possible dignity, was of no great height. To the right facing the throne are the royal personages and present are the dukes, marquesses, earls, viscounts and barons – all robed in scarlet and ermine. To the left are the archbishops and bishops in their purple and lawn, and behind them the members of the Diplomatic Corps—ambassadors and others from many countries—their uniforms resplendent with gold lace and ablaze with decorations. On the Woolsack facing the throne are the judges also in scarlet and ermine, their full-bottomed wigs looking from behind like so many beehives, their number including always the Lord Chief Justice of England, the Master of the Rolls and the President of the Family Division.

The Woolsack, a square couch stuffed with wool, is a reminder of England's staple trade and is said to have been placed in the House of Lords in the time of Edward III (1327–1377). It is the seat of the Lord Chancellor when the House is sitting but is fictionally outside the precincts of the House so that when the Lord Chancellor wishes to address his fellow peers he steps aside and so 'enters' the House.

Politics and the Law This brings to mind the problem which concerns many members of the legal profession – can they follow that profession with success and at the same time engage in active political life and furthermore can a politician – ceasing of course to be a politician – properly undertake judicial office? Many of us pursued both the law and politics and it was the view of the late Lord Reid – whose judicial stature was unequalled – that an ex-politician might bring advantage to judicial office. As Mr Marcel Berlins wrote in *The Times*:

his [Lord Reid's] strong political views made no difference whatever to his conduct as a judge and Lord Reid sees no conflict in a 'political animal' which he admits he was, becoming a judge.

It may well be thought that lawyers – and perhaps particularly members of the Bar – are not outstandingly effective in the House of Commons. The chief reason for this I think, is that in court a jury, captive in their box, must – and a judge always should – listen with attention to counsel's arguments and submissions. In the House of Commons however no-one listens unless he wishes to do so – many members walk in and out during the speeches and many engage in conversation in the Chamber. There are of course brilliant exceptions such as F E Smith who won such acclaim with his maiden speech that a successful parliamentary career was assured. F E Smith had a powerful personality and carried all before him both in the law and in politics. Mr. Justice Bigham when he was made a peer, and required to choose a title, he and F E Smith having both been Liverpool juniors, is quoted as saying: 'I will be Mersey – I must leave the Atlantic for F E'. In the end F E Smith, as we know, became Earl of Birkenhead, the town where his family business was.

In spite of the lawyers' difficulties in the Commons, their presence is, it is thought, of great importance and in Committee – especially of course upon legal subjects

– their aid is of much value. Also be it remembered that rich prizes may come their way when the offices of Attorney-General, Solicitor-General and, indeed, Lord Chancellor come to be filled. These however are temporary prizes lasting only for the lifetime of a Parliament, but ex-law officers of the Crown can command very high fees and an ex-Lord Chancellor will usually become a Lord of Appeal in Ordinary. The position of a Lord Chancellor as head of the judiciary on the one hand and a spokesman for the Government of the day on the other is wholly anomalous but the system has worked well for a long time.

In the House of Lords I feel that lawyers of both branches of the profession play a particularly useful part. The records show that very many amendments proposed in the Lords are gladly accepted in the Commons.

Thus far – and before Black Rod's summons is obeyed – two of the three estates of the Realm are present – the Lords Spiritual and the Lords Temporal: the Lords Spiritual consisting of the archbishops and, by right, the Bishops of London, Durham, and Winchester; twenty-one other bishops are chosen by seniority; the Lords Temporal consisting of all peers of the Realm who have been summoned to Parliament – and not by any means all peers have been so summoned.

Life Peerages The history of the creation of life peers and their emergence into a position of special moment is of interest. Life peers are nothing new. Indeed it is recorded that some life peerages were created between the reigns of Richard II (1377–1399) and Henry VI (1399–1413). Further than this, women life peers are

Sir Basil Nield as Treasurer of Inner Temple, presides at dinner on Grand Night. On his right is Lord Peart, then Leader of the House of Lords, and on his left is the Duke of Northumberland, Lord Steward of the Queen's Household

nothing new. Between the reign of Charles II (1649–1682) and George II (1727–1760) several ladies received life peerages. In the late 19th century the Lords themselves challenged the power of the Sovereign to appoint life peers with the right to sit and vote in Parliament. It arose because Queen Victoria was advised to appoint Sir James Parke, an eminent judge, to be a life peer so as to add to the judicial strength of the House. The Queen purported to appoint the judge as Lord Wensleydale with the right to sit and vote. The Lords, jealous of their hereditary position, objected. The difficulty was in the end overcome by the Queen creating the judge an hereditary peer. It was, however, clear that some means of improving the appellate jurisdiction of the House of Lords was needed and in 1876 three Lords of Appeal in Ordinary were constituted by statue with the right to sit and vote "so long as they continued in office."

Peeresses An agreeable feature of this aspect of the constitution of the Upper House is the creation to be life peeresses of women with good claims on their own account and those who are the widows of men who have given signal public service to the State.

While this congregation of notabilities awaits the arrival of the Queen, there is much conversation – some of it buzzing beneath the beehives – and not all of it on the gravest level. On one occasion when I was fortunate enough to have a place upon the Woolsack, I noticed much laughter among some of the senior officers of the House. Upon enquiry it turned out that they were conducting a ballot to decide which was the best tiara among the peeresses. I cannot remember – and would not say if I could – which duchess was the winner with enormous emeralds and which marchioness the runner-up with large ice-blue diamonds. When I say 'I would not remember' I have in mind the excellent advice to parliamentary candidates who think of judging baby shows – don't.

It has been a matter of controversy whether the wives of peers, who have no other status in their own right, are entitled to be present at the Opening of Parliament in the body of the House. Whether 'Women's Lib' comes into this I do not know, but here is the story. The House of Lords resolved in 1738, when there was to be a particularly important debate, that no lady should be admitted because on previous occasions they had made too much noise. The ladies responded by demanding admission at the door of the House of Lords. The Lord Chancellor refused them admission. Lady Mary Wortley Montagu records:

The Duchess of Queensberry as head of the squadron pished at the ill-breeding of the lawyer and continued the siege for many hours with violent thumps, kicks and raps against the door.

Then a stratagem by the ladies of dead silence for half an hour led the Lord Chancellor to believe that they had gone. The door was accordingly opened and the ladies all rushed in and promptly occupied the front rows of the gallery. At least since then at the State Opening they have decorated the crimson morocco of the benches in the Chamber of the Lords to the delight of everyone.

But the Sovereign's procession through the Royal Gallery approaches. In the Chamber, with a proper sense of theatre, the lights are lowered, the conversation ceases. There is silence. The lights are raised and through the open archway comes the Queen. The great assembly rises, the Queen takes her place upon the throne, her long purple and ermine mantle and train carefully spread by her pages. Her Majesty then speaks – and it will be noticed that no other voice is heard during the whole of the ceremony: 'My Lords, pray be seated'.

Black Rod It is at this moment that the Gentleman Usher of the Black Rod advances to the Commons to deliver the Royal message. Let me say a word about his office. It originated soon after the foundation of the Order of the Garter and from 1361 ushers were approved to bear the rod in the processions at St. George's Chapel, Windsor. In 1522 it was provided that the usher

should also have the care and custody and pre-eminence of keeping all our secret chambers . . . as well in the High Court of Parliament as in any other places.

Among his Parliamentary duties are to be in constant attendance on the House of Lords and to carry the King's Sovereign's commands to the Commons to attend in the House of Lords.

The House of Commons As Black Rod comes to the House of Commons lobby he reaches the Churchill Arch – the arch which has been preserved in its battle-scarred state since the destruction of the Chamber of the House of Commons by enemy air action on May 10, 1941. I remember returning to the Commons for a short time in 1943 long before victory in the War was by any means certain and listening to a debate as to 'how and where' – not 'when' let it be noticed – the new Chamber should be built. This was on October 28, 1943. In the end Winston Churchill – a House of Commons man indeed – recommended that we should rebuild on the same site in similar manner and he ended his speech:

We owe a great debt to the House of Lords for having placed at our disposal this spacious, splendid hall. We do not wish to outstay our welcome. We have been greatly convenienced by our sojourn on these red benches and under this gilded, ornamental statue bedecked roof. I express my gratitude and appreciation of what we have received and enjoyed, but

> mid pleasures and palaces
> Tho' we may roam
> Be it ever so humble
> There's no place like home.

As Black Rod reaches the door of the Chamber it is slammed in his face. This apparently discourteous gesture dates back to the year 1642 when Charles I tried to arrest five members in the House, Hampden, Pym, Holler, Hasilrig and Strode. Since then no reigning monarch has ever been permitted to enter the House of Commons. It is said, and I hope it is so, that King George VI was allowed to take a look at the rebuilt Chamber in 1950 before it was put into use.

Black Rod knocks thrice and is admitted, delivering the message which I have already quoted. In response to the message Mr Speaker in black and gold – Black Rod walking beside him – leads the faithful Commons from their Chamber. Behind him comes the Prime Minister with the Leader of the Opposition, side by side in temporary and perhaps uneasy amity. Two and two come the Ministers and Shadow Ministers and the back benchers – along the long corridor, part of Sir Charles Barry's grand design leading through the great Victorian gothic, gold and coloured glass of the Central Lobby from the Lower to the Upper House: and so they reach the Bar of the House of Lords.

The Commons make obeisance to:

Queen Elizabeth II by the Grace of God of the United Kingdom of Great Britain and Northern Ireland and of the British Commonwealth beyond the Seas, Queen, Defender of the Faith, over all persons supreme.

The three estates of the Realm are now present.

The Queen's Speech All are now anxiously concerned to hear the contents of the Queen's Speech – the Gracious Speech – for no part of which is Her Majesty responsible but which sets out the Government's legislative programme for the new Session of Parliament. As Bagehot points out:

The Queen is only at the head of the dignified part of the Constitution. The Prime Minister is at the head of the efficient part. The Crown is, according to the saying, the 'fountain of honour'; but the Treasury is the spring of business.

The Speech is carried by the Lord High Chancellor of Great Britain resplendent in black and gold gown and with a train and full-bottomed wig. He mounts the steps of the throne, kneels and takes the Speech from the Purse and hands it to the Queen. Then comes a most anxious moment for he must descend the steps of the Throne backwards and try to avoid any entanglement with his train. I remember one Lord Chancellor plainly

a little tremulous at the ordeal and grateful indeed to that master of ceremonial, the late Duke of Norfolk, whose hand placed beneath the Lord Chancellor's left elbow guided him discreetly to his rightful place in the close cluster of nobles and notables at the foot of the throne. It is said that the word 'marshal' in this connection derives from mearh, meaning horse and sceale, meaning groom – that is horse groom. This sounds a rather humble office but it was one of the six great offices which were all offices in the Royal Household: Chancellor, Steward, Constable, Marshal, Chamberlain and Butler.

Since 1672 the office of Earl Marshal has been hereditary in the family of Howard and the holder is head of the College of Heralds and judge in the Courts of Chivalry.

During the present reign the Gracious Speech is read in calm, clear tones ending with the words: 'May the blessing of Almighty God rest upon your labours.'

The Queen rises, descends the steps of the Throne, bows to either side and on the arm of Prince Philip leaves to proceed once more to the Royal Robing Room, down the Royal Stairway, past the Gentlemen-at-Arms and Yeomen of the Guard to the State Coach and out into the November sunshine. The knowledgeable and reasonably nimble members of the Commons can hasten from the Lords to the pavement outside Palace Yard and so have a view of the procession as it draws away.

The Lord Great Chamberlain For much of this spectacular ceremony the Lord Great Chamberlain as well as the Earl Marshal is responsible. A 'Master Chamberlain' officiated as a member of the Royal Household from the time of William I. In 1641 the holder of the office was required to see that the Orders of the House were correctly exhibited. Since the Restoration he has had general supervision of the use and preservation of the Palace of Westminster. The right to hold the office has been vigorously contested over the years but it would seem that this right rests with the Marquesses of Cholmondeley, the Earls of Ancaster and the Earls Carrington.

The Queen has gone – the red benches of the House of Lords empty – the Commons, returned to the green benches of their own Chamber, begin their debate upon the Gracious Speech.

Another chapter has begun in the long history of Parliament which goes back for a thousand years. It is remarkable to think that even before the Norman Conquest the wise men of the Council met where the Houses of Parliament now stand – Edward the Confessor it was who started to build a palace there in 1042. Those earlier wise men may well have watched from their meeting house the great Abbey Church of Westminster, begun in 1050, rising stone upon stone on the desolate marshland beside the Thames wide waterway. The stillness of reflection upon the wonders of the past is broken by the clashing out from Big Ben's great clock of its timely supplication:

> Lord through this hour
> Be Thou our guide
> That by Thy power
> No foot shall slide.

5 LAW REPORTING

The Official Reports

R N G Harrison

Although to the lawyer it is a commonplace, it may be a matter of surprise to the non-lawyer that the sources of English law are to be found not merely in the statutes enacted by Parliament but also in the recorded decisions of the judges. Those records are known to the legal profession as 'law reports' or, more simply, 'reports'. 'A report', said Coke, who was Chief Justice under James I, and himself the author of one of the most celebrated series of reports, 'signifyeth a public relation or bringing again to memory of cases judicially argued, debated, resolved, or adjudged in any of the King's Courts of justice, together with such causes and reasons as were delivered by the judges.'

It is one of the cardinal principles of justice that like cases should be decided alike. If two cases which do not differ in any material particular are decided differently, it is reasonable to infer that in one of those cases the losing party has suffered an injustice. It is understandable, therefore, that from the earliest times a demand has existed among the legal profession for information about the judgments which have been delivered in the course of litigation. This demand was, in the early days, satisfied in part by word of mouth and in part by manuscript notes taken by barristers present at the hearing, passed from hand to hand and perhaps copied. The invention of printing presented an obvious opportunity to publishers but it was not until the late sixteenth century that reports began to be printed and published in any systematic way. Until that time the reports which did appear, for the most part in manuscript, were anonymous; indeed not only their authorship but their exact purpose is a matter of debate. For want of a better term, they are referred to by legal historians as the 'Year Books' because they are cited by reference to year and folio.

The Nominate Reports It appears that by the sixteenth century it had become the practice for lawyers to keep their own manuscript notes of decided cases and, by the middle of the century, enterprising booksellers had realised that there might be a profit to be made by printing and publishing such documents under the name of a well-known lawyer.

In any event, what is certain is that the mid-sixteenth century witnessed the appearance of the first of the series known as the 'nominate', or named, reports, ie reports which appeared under the names of their authors, as reporters. The nominate reports continued for over three centuries. The earliest are those of Spelman (who died in 1545) and Dyer (who died in 1582). During the next two hundred years, until the appearance of Burrow's reports in 1765, over 100 different series were published. By modern, and indeed contemporary, standards most of these reports were unsatisfactory; they were often inaccurate, sporadic and dilatory.

Bulstrode, writing in 1657 in the 'epistle dedicatory' to his own series, refers to 'these late and flying reports, most of them being *incerti temporis* and of late published, not by the authors themselves (who were well known to be profoundly learned), nor yet by them during their lives fitted and prepared for the press, but after their deaths, thus published by others, yet not known by whom, having not named themselves, and these reports not without many gross mistakings in them, whereby they do cherish rather than extinguish law suits'. In the same year Sir Harbottle Grimston, in his preface to Croke's Reports, complained, 'A multitude of flying reports (whose authors were as uncertain as the times when taken, and the causes and reasons of the judgements as obscure, as by whom judged) have of late surreptitiously crept forth.'

In contrast, the reports of Plowden, Coke (1572–1616) and Sanders enjoyed a high reputation. Coke's reports in particular set a standard for future reporters; such was their reputation that they came to be referred to simply as 'The Reports'.

The last forty years of the eighteenth century witnessed a marked increase in the general standard of reporting. Burrow's reports in five volumes (1756–72) and Douglas's reports of decisions of the Court of King's Bench in four volumes (1778–85) introduced the 'headnote', a brief analytical summary of the decision written by the reporter, and a systematic arrangement of the reports, while Durnford and East's *Term Reports* (King's Bench 1785–1800) were the first to aim at a speedy and regular publication.

Advent of 'Authorised' Reports It was at about this time that it became the practice for the judges to take it upon themselves to examine the draft reports of their judgments before publication and a custom arose whereby a single reporter was given an exclusive privilege to such assistance. Such reports became known as the 'authorised' or 'regular' reports.

Independence of Law Reports It is a remarkable feature of English law reporting that, with one brief exception, the state has played no part in, and made no financial contribution to, the publication of law reports. At one time an erroneous belief prevailed that the Year Books from Edward III to Henry VII had been the work of four official reporters paid by the Crown and it was the belief that he was reviving an ancient custom that prompted Chancellor Bacon to persuade James I to appoint two official law reporters at a salary of £100 a year. There is no evidence that the experiment ever bore fruit. Otherwise, from the earliest times until the present day, the law reports, accepted by the courts and the profession as setting forth the common law as declared by the judges, have been the product of private enterprise. The only formal requirement, accepted since time immemorial, is that, before it can be cited in court, a report must be vouched for by a barrister. This rule probably derives from an early rule whereby any barrister present in court who knew of another decision relevant to the case being heard was obliged to draw it to the court's attention.

'Irregular' Reports The informal practice of judges authorising particular reports is the nearest that the law reporting system has come to lending an official *imprimatur* to particular series. The practice did not prevent the continued appearance of other 'irregular' reports which could be, and frequently were, cited to the court. From 1822 the number of reports was multiplied by the appearance of a new type of law report which, because of its prompt and regular appearance, soon achieved considerable popularity. These were the reports which appeared in the pages of the journals for the legal profession which began to make their appearance in the early nineteenth century, the first being the *Law Journal* which started life in 1822. In the preface to the first issue the publishers were at pains to disclaim any intention of competing with the regular reporters. The success of the *Law Journal* was such as to provoke competition; in 1837 the *Jurist* made its appearance followed by the *Law Times* in 1843; the *Weekly Reporter,* which first appeared in 1852, combined with the already established *Solicitor's Journal* in 1858. All these publications contained their own reports of cases, following the pattern set by the *Law Journal*. At first it was the practice to include the law reports with other materials, such as articles and digests of Acts of Parliament, but in 1832 the *Law Journal* started issuing a 'new series' separate from the journal itself and called *Law Journal Reports;* the *Law Times* followed suit with a series called *Law Times Reports*. Both were to continue in existence for over a century.

Although the 'irregular' reports disclaimed any intention of competing with the authorised series, they had, as the Lord Chancellor's Committe on Law Reporting declared in 1940, 'virtues which ensured their popularity. In the first place they were published at regular intervals and they contained reports of cases within measurable time of their decision. This marked a great change from the leisurely methods of the authorised reporters.... In the second place these anonymous publications gave a promise of continuity which their future justified'. As examples of the 'leisurely methods' of the authorised reporters the committee noted that he last issue of *Ellis and Ellis's* reports, published in 1864, contained reports of cases decided in 1860.

The Incorporated Council of Law Reporting A singular characterisic of our Victorian predecessors was their devotion to the cause of improvement and reform in all fields, not least the law. The chief matters of complaint against the law reports were not only the delays in publication of the authorised reports, but also their haphazard coverage of cases, the multiplicity of different series and the separate existence of the irregular reports which contained cases not reported in the authorised series. It was estimated that the annual cost to a practitioner of subscribing to all the authorised series was £30; if in addition he wished to subscribe to the irregular reports a further outlay of £15 was necessary. In 1849 the Society for Promoting Amendment of the Law set up a special committee 'To consider what improvements, if any, may be made in the present system of Reporting'. The committee produced two reports recounting the manifold defects in the existing system but no proposals for reform were forthcoming or acted upon.

In the end it was left to the Bar to take the matter into its own hands. In 1863 a group led by W T S Daniel QC succeeded in persuading the Bar to set up a council, consisting of representatives of each of the Inns of Court and the Incorporated Law Society, the governing body of the solicitors' profession; the council was to undertake the responsibility for publishing a new series, which would be known simply as *The Law Reports* and would replace the existing authorised reports. With varying degrees of reluctance the authorised reporters agreed to discontinue their own series and join the new scheme. So the Incorporated Council of Law Reporting for England and Wales was established and the new series began publication in 1865. Thereupon the nominate reports ceased to exist, the last being volume 31 of *Beavan's* reports which appeared in 1866.

Since their establishment in 1865 *The Law Reports* have continued in an unbroken series. Although sometimes referred to as the 'official' reports, this is to use the word in a somewhat loose sense. The Incorporated Council was a private enterprise, controlled by the legal profession. Although non-profit making, the subscriptions charged for the reports were sufficient to make the enterprise self-supporting financially.

Despite their undoubted success the expectations of the founders of the series were to some extent disappointed. As the Law Reporting Committee noted in 1940, it had been the confident hope that, 'inaugurated with such aims and under such auspices', the Law Reports 'would drive all competitors from the field and thus there would be established a single series of reports, accurate and scientific, reporting all cases that ought to be reported and none that ought not to be reported'. Although the *Jurist* ceased to appear in 1867, the *Law Journal*, the *Law Times* and the *Solicitors' Journal*

continued to flourish, publishing cases which did not appear in the *Law Reports*. Nor could the prestigious backing of the Incorporated Council ensure that reports in the *Law Reports* always achieved the highest standard.

All England Law Reports Furthermore, the old complaint about the delay in publication of cases was again heard. In 1884 a new series, the *Times Law Reports,* containing cases which had first appeared in *The Times* newspaper, began publication on a weekly basis. So matters continued for another fifty years until, in 1936, Butterworths who, since the turn of the century had established a dominating position in the world of legal publishing by producing a number of high quality legal encyclopaedic works, including *Halsbury's Laws of England,* decided to venture into the field of law reporting by producing a weekly series to be known as the *All England Law Reports*. The declared object of the new series was to 'publish weekly reports of all cases of importance within a very limited number of days of the delivery of judgment'; as a result cases appeared in the *All England* within three or four weeks of judgment in contrast with the year to two years which it often took for them to find their way into the *Law Reports*. That in this respect the series met a need was attested by their immediate success. But their welcome was not without discordant notes in some quarters; certain judges in particular were, in the early days, unwilling to allow them to be cited in court.

Lord Chancellor's Law Reporting Committee In 1939 the Lord Chancellor, Viscount Maugham, took the matter in hand by appointing a Law Reporting Committee whose task it was 'to report and advise him in regard to

representations which had been made from several quarters to the effect that the great number of Law Reports which appeared to be increasing was causing difficulty for members of both branches of the profession engaged in the actual work of the Courts by reason of their multiplicity, of the expense occasioned by the necessity for purchasing them and the pressure on space available for the storage of books. . . .'

The committee reported in March 1940. The majority report was inconclusive; the members took the view that no 'large measure of reform of Law Reporting [was] feasible'. They laid stress, however, on the accuracy of the *Law Reports* which was 'assisted by the fact that the Judges themselves read and approve the Reports of their decisions before they are published'. The committee, however, expressed its unanimous opposition to a proposal, made originally in 1864, 'that the right of exclusive citation in the Courts should be given either to the *Law Reports* as at present established or to some single series of reports established under some sort of official control'. The committee did however express the view that, in point of accuracy and completeness, the *Law Reports* were 'in merit pre-eminent and, since they get no public subsidy, it is the obligation of the legal profession to ensure that they are adequately supported', at the same time noting that, in achieving their high standard of accuracy, they were 'assisted by the fact that the Judges themselves read and approve the Reports of their decisions before they are published'.

By 1940, when the committee reported, matters of greater moment had supervened to distract the attention of the legal profession from questions of mere parochial interest and the somewhat tame conclusions of the

committee were hardly calculated to stir up interest from anyone other than those who had a direct concern in the matter. In fact the immediate post-war years saw some rationalisation of the position. The *Law Times* series ceased publication in 1948 and the *Law Journal* in 1949, both series being amalgamated with the *All England*. In 1952 the *Times Law Reports* ceased to appear as a separate series, and in its place the Incorporated Council started a new series of weekly reports in opposition to the *All England* and known simply as *Weekly Law Reports*. The new series also replaced the *Weekly Notes* which the Council had published since 1865 containing summaries of recent cases.

The Current Series Since 1953 the position has, so far as the general series are concerned, remained unchanged. The two weekly series, the *All England* and the *Weekly Law Reports*, contain a broadly similar selection of cases with full judgments and are published within a matter of weeks of the judgments being delivered. These are followed, at a later date, by the *Law Reports* themselves, published at monthly intervals and containing a narrower selection of cases, but distinguished by the fact that, unlike the weekly series, the reports usually contain a full summary of the arguments of counsel, as well as the complete text of the judgment. Partly for this reason, and partly because of their origin and the auspices under which they appear, when a case has been reported in the *Law Reports* that report will generally be cited to the court in preference to others.

In addition to the general series, mention must also be made of the numerous specialist series of reports, that is to say reports confined to a special field of law, such as taxation, criminal law, planning, rating and so on, and containing many reports of cases within that field which do not appear in the general series. Perhaps the most

notable specialist series is *Lloyd's Reports,* published by Lloyd's of London since 1919 and containing reports of commerical cases, in particular cases on insurance and maritime law. The *Reports of Tax Cases,* published by the Inland Revenue Commissioners since 1875, and the *Reports of Patent Cases,* published by the Patent Office since 1884, are perhaps the only series that can properly be described as 'official' reports. The *Justice of the Peace Reports,* containing cases of interest to magistrates' courts, has the distinction of being the longest continuous series still current, having started publication in 1837 as an integral part of the journal known as the *Justice of the Peace and Local Government Review.*

Official Shorthand Writers Perhaps the most profound change that has affected law reports, in particular their accuracy, in recent years, is one that has gone largely unremarked. It appears that in the early part of the present century official shorthand writers were appointed to record and transcribe judgments delivered in the Court of Appeal. It was not, it seems, until the late 1930s that this practice was extended to all the superior courts and not until much later that the judges began, as a matter of practice to check and revise the transcripts before their release rather than checking only the proofs of those cases destined for publication in the *Law Reports.* Unlike his predecessors of the more remote past, the modern law reporter has the inestimable advantage of preparing his report on the basis of an official transcript of the judgement which, more often than not, will already have been checked by the judge. In addition, since the early 1950s it has become the general practice for the judges to check the proofs of their judgments prior to publication in the *All England Law Reports* as well as in the series published by the Incorporated Council, a tradition which as we have seen in the

case of the *Law Reports* goes back to their predecessors, the authorised reports.

Law Reporting Today With such safeguards, it is hardly surprising that, as authentic records of what the judges have said, or on reflection meant to say, the general series of reports have, over the past twenty-five years, been able to achieve a high degree of accuracy.

In those circumstances it may be asked what part does the modern law reporter, relieved of the burden of making an accurate record of the judge's words, still have to play. Both the Incorporated Council and the *All England* maintain teams of barristers whose duty it is to attend the courts and produce reports for publication in the respective series. One of their prime functions is to select the cases which merit reporting. Only cases which establish a new principle of law or which illustrate the application of existing principles to new circumstances in such a way as to amount to a modification of those principles are generally regarded as meriting publication. It is the reporter's role to pick out such cases and order a transcript from the shorthand writer. Once it has arrived he is responsible for ensuring that the report contains all the information that the reader requires for a full understanding of the case. This information, perhaps containing a fuller version of the facts or pleadings in the case than will be found in the judgment, is to be found in the reporter's introduction which precedes the judgment.

In addition a reporter preparing a case for publication in the *Law Reports* will be required to prepare an accurate summary of the arguments of counsel. Nor is the judgment simply reproduced in the form in which it is presented by the shorthand writer. A great deal of work is done both by the reporters and the publishers' editor-

ial staff in verifying and amplifying citations, checking the accuracy of quotations (a process which often necessitates frequent amendment of the transcript), as well as putting right the obvious mistakes which sometimes occur. The reporter may also check the shorthand writer's transcript against the notes which he made in court. Occasionally a representation by the reporter or editor to the judge may lead to a modification of the wording of the judgment. Perhaps the most demanding part of the reporter's task is the preparation of the headnote, expounding succinctly the material facts of the case and the points of law which it decides. This is a task requiring considerable skill. A well-prepared headnote may save a busy practitioner a great deal of time whereas a badly drafted headnote may, at best, force him to spend valuable time reading a judgment to find out whether the case is relevant to his problem and at worst may mislead courts and practitioners, giving currency to erroneous notions for which the case is not, in fact, authority.

Even with modern aids, it can be seen that the task of reporters, and editors, of law reports is an onerous and responsible one. In the nature of things they cannot escape criticism, for example, on the one hand that they report too many cases, on the other that they do not report the right cases. On occasions mistakes do occur. By and large however one may assume that, since the activities of the reporters excite little attention from the profession, they are doing their job well and that the present system of reporting, at least so far as the general series are concerned, is one that meets the practical needs of the profession. Perhaps the big question which now hangs over the future of law reporting is what, if any, impact the prospective advent of computer based techniques for the storage and retrieval of information will have on the role of the reporter.

133

Example of an early 19th century Broadsheet,
illustrated with a woodcut, reporting trials and
sentences at Old Bailey

The Trial and Execution of Chas. Butcher for Sheep Stealing.

Who Suffered in the Front of the OLD BAILEY this Morning.

CHARLES BUTCHER. aged 27. was found guilty of stealing, on the 9th of June, two sheep and three lambs, the property of Richard Woodman, of Shepherd's Bush. Buckridge, an Officer of High-street, Mary-le-bone, having received information, accompanied the prisoner's landlord to a cottage on the Harrow Road, close by the Paddington Canal side, which the prisoner rented ; the cottage was fastened up, and on the back door the officer observed the print of a hand with bloody finger marks, & perceiving a very bad smell come from the house, he forced a window up and got in, and on the mantel-piece were the plucks of 3 lambs and 2 sheep, & on the hearth were the heads ; part of a paunch and a quantity of fat in a cupboard. There was no furniture in the cottage, nor did it appear to have been occupied, and there was a quantity of blood on the floor, as if sheep had been slaughtered there. Buckridge got a warrant against the prisoner, who was apprehended the next morning by Webster the officer

Philip Webster stated that he was an officer and went to the prisoner's cottage, who not being there, he set a person to watch, & in a short time, Butcher came, who peeped round the corner of the house, as if to see if he was noticed : I collared him, and told him to consider himself my prisoner, for I had a warrant against him for felony. He made no answer. I asked him what he had in the cottage ; he answered; nothing at all. I said, "Are you sure you have got nothing at all" he said nothing but some hooks and knives; I said "what then have you done with the heads and pluck that were there?" he said he had tied them up in a basket, and they were outside the house ; we then went in and found two knives some hooks, and a piece of wood, which I believe they use to hang sheep on. Saunders and myself had before that found part of the sheep's guts in the canal, which is about six yards from the cottage.

Two of the skins were afterwards found in the cut of the Paddington canal, & the marks on them and on the heads found in the cottage were sworn to by the prosecutor.

In his defence the prisoner said—"I am a poulterer. I went to St. John's-street, and as I returned through Clerkenwell, passing a butcher's-shop, he asked me to buy—I bought ten heads and plucks—some were lambs' heads and some sheeps'.

John Cope, butcher, of Coppice-row, Clerkenwell, stated that he had sold the prisoner several plucks.

On Sunday the unfortunate man attended the chapel, in company with John Fordham, who is ordered for execution on Monday next, where an impressive discourse was delivered from the 6th of Romans, 23d verse. The unhappy men (Butcher particularly) expressed their great sense of feeling on account of the kind attention which they had received from the Sheriff, the Governor, and the religious friends, which has been unremitting in regard of their welfare.

This morning at the usual hour this wretched man was conducted to the place of execution, which he ascended with feeble step, and every preparation being completed, the drop fell, and he was launched into eternity.

LAW REPORTING

Press Reporting

Frank Goldsworthy

The Watchdogs of Justice The Press bench is just as much a part of any courtroom as the judge's bench, the witness box or the dock.

The practical necessity of hearing both sides dictates that reporters sit on the sidelines, broadside to the exchanges between judges and counsel; in a world of contention they are the neutrals, the silent minority who provide the link between the court and the vast public beyond its doors.

Lord Denning, the Master of the Rolls and a great champion of the open door in the administration of justice, has many times called court reporters the watchdogs of justice.

He once told a party of European legal journalists:

Our law is very largely judge-made but none of that would be of any avail unless there were reporters to report what happened in courts and printers to publish reports of the cases which have a day-to-day sociological effect on the public.

That is why I have always held that every court of justice must be open to every subject of the Queen and that newspaper reporters are the watchdogs of justice.

I think the part played by newspapers in the administration of justice is as significant as that played by lawyers and all of us.

I say to all judges: give the reasons for your decisions. We must give our reasons not only so that if we are wrong a higher court can upset us, but so that the public can learn of the basis on which we reach our decisions.

Lord Denning said that the judges themselves were on trial when they conducted a case. If they did anything wrong it would be noted and published – 'it keeps us in order.'

Newspapers, he always insists, are free to comment and criticise. And he told the foreign reporters, 'If we give decisions – for instance sentences which may be considered harsh or oppressive or savage – that is a comment which people are entitled to make.'

There are in England and Wales 684 magistrates' courts, 320 county courts, 97 Crown Court complexes of which the 23 courtroom Central Criminal Court, better known as the Old Bailey, is the biggest; and there are 59 courtrooms at the Royal Courts of Justice.

While it would be nice to think that the watchdogs of justice are vigilant in each and every court room it would not be true. Newspapers are commercial enterprises with shrinking budgets and limited space. Courts provide a vast source of inexpensive news but to cover them all continuously would make manpower demands out of all proportion to the column inches waiting to be filled.

Yet such is the nature of the reporter, an inquisitive creature with friends among the lawyers and officials, that little of real public interest slips the local or national net.

But how should the public interest be defined?

Certainly for the popular newspapers the guiding rule is that people are interested in people, and particularly in people in conflict.

Court stories lift the lid from other people's lives, exposing their behaviour and emotions with a frankness which cannot be indulged in any other form of news reporting. Taken individually news stories may seem to be personal intrusions; but collectively they present a picture not only of the administration of justice but of the social history of our times.

And they do much more; they interpret for the ordinary reader the way the law itself is changing. For an Act of Parliament is only the blueprint of the law; the final shape, as Lord Denning has said, is moulded by the judges.

When the breathalyser, with all its attendant arrest ritual, was first introduced a steady stream of cases reached the High Court as lawyers probed the wording of the Act, seeking to save their clients' licences.

The Trade Descriptions Act provided another fountain of fees for the lawyers and neat little interpretative stories for the High Court reporters. The Race Relations Act did much the same.

Reporters must be selective in choosing the courts they attend, the cases they listen to; so friendly relations with the Bar, court officials and the police, as well as personal judgment, are essential.

Reporting the case itself is very much the art of omission. An average day's hearing in the High Court will involve the uttering of 36,000 words – half the length of a novel and all duly recorded on tapes or in the official shorthand writers' notebooks.

A half-column story in a national paper consists of about 300 words; the 'heavies' may indulge themselves with twice that length. So the reporter must discard well over 35,000 words and yet include the outline of argument and the highlights as well as the basic facts like names, addresses, ages, occupations and dates.

Put another way, however long the hearing lasts the reporter cannot use more words than are spoken in the first three or four minutes.

The greatest privilege the reporter enjoys is the right to report what is said in court without fear of libel writs – but only if his report is fair and accurate. Accuracy can be achieved by care; fairness needs judgment and integrity and it says much for the standards of skill on the Press Bench that libel claims on grounds of misreporting are very rare indeed.

The reporter must respect a whole array of legally backed taboos.

Reports from juvenile courts must not reveal the identity of the child or young person concerned in the proceedings – and that extends to witnesses as well as defendants. That can mean that not even a school may be named in the newspaper.

As long ago as 1926 Parliament, shocked by detailed

Below: Temple Bar was the scene of a clash in 1768 between the supporters of John Wilkes, the first man to test the freedom of the press, and "loyal" supporters of the court of George III

Bottom: The press coverage of the pre-trial committal proceedings in the Jeremy Thorpe case raised the question of whether such proceedings should be reported at all

Below: The Wig and Pen Club, formerly the Gatekeeper's house of Temple Bar, is now the regular meeting place of lawyers and Fleet Street editors

Bottom: The Press Association room in the Royal Courts of Justice from where reports are despatched all over the world

Evening Standard

43,490   THURSDAY, APRIL 16, 1964   ●●3d.   5

'The game is not worth even the most alluring candle'

ROY JAMES—30 years

DOUGLAS GOODY—30 years

CHARLES WILSON—30 years

THOMAS WISBEY—30 years

RONALD BIGGS—30 years

ROBERT WELCH—30 years

JAMES HUSSEY—30 years

BRIAN FIELD—25 years

LEONARD FIELD—25 years

WILLIAM BOAL—24 years

ROGER CORDREY—20 years

JOHN WHEATER—Three years

SEVEN GET 30 YEARS EACH

the GREAT TRAIN ROBBERY

Sentences total 307 years

Evening Standard Reporter: Aylesbury, Thursday

It was the crime of the century . . . the £2,517,975 raid on a mail train in the 3 a.m. darkness of Buckinghamshire. And today came the reckoning: 307 years in jail for 12 of the men involved.

Sentences on all counts totalled 573 years but because they were concurrent the period of imprisonment was cut by 266 years.

It took Mr. Justice Edmund Davies 32 minutes to pass the sentences at Aylesbury.

A WINK . . . A 'THANK YOU'

Seven of the men found guilty of taking part in the raid and conspiracy were each jailed for 30 years.

They were Ronald Arthur Biggs, Douglas Gordon Goody, Charles Frederick Wilson, Thomas William Wisbey, Robert Welch, James Hussey and Roy John James.

The other sentences ranged from 25 to three years.

The 12 men heard their sentences calmly.

Biggs, a slight smile on his face, winked at his wife as he left the dock. Wisbey drummed his fingers on the dock rail but gave no sign of emotion. Wilson paled . . . and said nothing.

Welch worked his mouth as if he was chewing gum. Then he bowed low.

From Hussey came an almost inaudible "Thank you, your Honour." James held his hands clasped behind his back.

Goody, grim-faced, gave a toss of his head and clenched his fists as he was led away.

'OH, MY POOR BOY'

The only outburst came when Leonard Field, 31, was sentenced to 25 years for conspiracy.

His 73-year-old mother, a grey-haired tiny figure in a black velvet coat with fur collar screamed: "Oh, my poor boy . . ."

As she was led out Field called out: "Never mind, mother. I am still young."

Mr. Justice Edmund Davies told the court that to deal with the charges leniently would be an evil thing. Saying that the crime was the first of its kind in the

● Back Page, Col. Three

WEATHER—Warm.—See Page 17.

❛ This conduct constitutes a menace to society . . . It is nothing less than a sordid crime of violence inspired by vast greed . . .

The consequence of this outrageous crime is that the vast booty of £2,500,000 remains almost entirely unrecovered.

It would be an affront if you were to be at liberty in the near future to enjoy these ill-gotten gains. I propose to secure that such an opportunity will be denied to you for an extremely long time. ❜

MR. JUSTICE EDMUND DAVIES, THE JUDGE AT THE MAIL ROBBERY TRIAL TODAY.

Royal wedding in September

COPENHAGEN, Thursday.—King Constantine of Greece and Princess Anne-Marie of Denmark will marry in Athens on September 18, the Danish court announced today.

'Ferranti company beat Whitehall'

The MPs' "watchdog" committee on public accounts reported today on the Ferranti contract.

The committee find that:

THE COMPANY was able to beat Whitehall's technical cost estimate by "an enormous margin"; and

THE MINISTRY—"one of the most disturbing facts"—had not been able to establish how it happened.

The MPs consider that the firm made an "excessive profit." This was contested by Mr. Sebastian de Ferranti, the chairman and managing director.

Fuller report—Page FIVE

New plans to beat the dopers
PAGE TWENTY

reporting of the more salacious society divorces, imposed restrictions which are still broadly the same today. They allow only the names, addresses and occupations of the parties and witnesses; a concise statement of the charges, defences and counter-charges; submissions on points of law and rulings on them; the observations of the judge in giving judgment. Only the observations of the judge – and very occasionally a tricky new point of law – provide approved material for the court reporter.

When a case goes undefended the judge need only outline the order he is making; judges of circuit or county court status normally deal with about 24 petitions in a single day's sitting. But when the suit is contested the loser may appeal and for the information of the appeal court the judge must review the facts, express his opinion of the parties and witnesses and give reasons for his decision. Such a judgment can last several hours and give the court reporter a mass of interesting copy.

In the days when divorce was based on the proof of a matrimonial offence – adultery, cruelty or desertion – there were many bitter open court battles, each spouse seeking to lay the blame for the break-up of the marriage on the other, chiefly in order to gain advantage in the real contest over children, maintenance and property.

All that has changed. Now decrees are granted only on the grounds of irretrievable breakdown of the marriage *as evidenced by* adultery, unreasonable behaviour, desertion, two years' separation (the other spouse consenting to a decree) or five years' separation.

The two year rule means that nobody need be branded 'the guilty party' and even when another ground is chosen only the proof of 'gross and obvious' misconduct by one spouse or the other is likely to affect the custody and cash issues, which are argued in private behind 'In Chambers' notices.

So open court contests – and reportable judgments – are rare, and usually involve a litigant in person who is too obstinate to take legal advice to submit to a painless two year 'no blame' decree.

Until 1974 applications for injunctions – demands that violent husbands quit their homes or estranged wives keep away from their husbands' offices or funds be kept within the jurisdiction of the court – were heard in open court unless they affected children. Then a change in Family Division practice rules directed that they shall normally be heard in private unless they involved an application for commital for contempt. The ruling applied not only in London and the provincial centres of the High Court but in those county courts with matrimonial jurisdiction. Right across the land a curtain was drawn over part of the social history of our times.

Now, apart from the occasional open court judgement on some new point of law, the only public view of how matrimonial jurisdiction is being exercised is to be found in the Appeal Courts. There the judges have continued to sit in open court even when the disputes centre on children. By an unwritten agreement with the High Court Journalists' Association the judges rely on the good faith and judgment of the reporters not to identify parties if harm to children will result.

It is an interesting comment that just when changes in the law put rows in the home beyond the public gaze the introduction of industrial tribunals empowered to compensate for unfair dismissal has provided a window on the human conflicts in offices, shops and factories.

Of vital importance in the High Court are the law reporters, all practising barristers, most of them women. They combine day-to-day reporting for *The Times* – the only newspaper which can be quoted as evidence of an earlier court ruling – with the compiling of official law reports. As appeal court decisions are binding on other judges they are fully covered in the law reports, which are usually submitted to the judges concerned, before publication in permanent form.

The Criminal Justice Act 1967 severely limited the reporting of commital proceedings before magistrates. It is normally the practice for the defence to reserve its case till the subsequent jury trial and proponents of the change argued that publication of the prosecutions case at the commital stage would prejudice potential jurors.

But if the defendants – or any one of several defendants – asks for the raising of reporting restrictions they do not apply. Unless restrictions are lifted reports are limited to names, addresses, occupations, ages, the offences charged and the court decision. It has even been held to be an offence to say the prisoner appeared in the dock wearing a blue suit!

When judges send juries out of court the reporters rest their pencils; they must not report anything that is being kept from the jury.

However, the law takes a realistic view of what can be said to be prejudicial to future trials. When a *Daily Telegraph* contributor expressed pungent views on the definition of sherry at a time when the whole trade was about to be involved in major litigation on just that issue a motion to punish the editor for contempt of court failed. It was held that there must be a real probability of prejudice, not just a theoretical possibility. In this case there was no real danger of a judge, armed with his professional detachment, being influenced by a newspaper article.

The same approach makes it possible for uninhibited publication of 'background' after a criminal trial ends in conviction – even though it is certain to be the subject of appeal.

The issue of probability of individual jurors being affected – or not affected, for so few were likely to read it – underlay the dismissal of a motion against the satirical magazine *Private Eye* on the grounds that forthcoming jury trials would be affected by an attack on the plaintiff.

On the other hand heavy fines were once imposed on a newspaper for prejudicing a murder trial – even though nobody was under arrest when the offending matter appeared. It was an interview with a man who said, 'They are all pointing at me because I've been in jail before.' He was arrested and the paper and its editor were condemned because they should have known it was likely to happen – and the premature disclosure of an accused's criminal past is something the courts will never tolerate.

6 OTHER LEGAL SYSTEMS IN THE UNITED KINGDOM

The Law of Scotland

Lord Kilbrandon

I want to begin by setting out clearly the limitations of this section. It would be impossible on so small a scale to make an intelligible abridgement of a complete system of law, and I do not attempt it. Nor do I intend that the article shall be of any value to a person who wants information for professional purposes. It may rate no higher than a piece of journalism. No references to authorities will be found. Some of its inaccuracies will be inevitable consequences of compression and over-simplification. But one use it may have; I am continually being astonished to find how few non-lawyers outside Scotland know that England and Scotland have separate and distinct systems of law and independent courts of justice – except that they share a supreme civil court of appeal in the House of Lords – so that the courts of one country have no jurisdiction in the other, unless reciprocity has been arranged for by statute. Indeed in England Scottish law is foreign law and *vice versa,* with all that that implies. I do not intend – for reasons of space – to say anything whatever about the historical reasons for this. It will be enough to say that in accordance with the Acts of Union passed respectively by the English and Scottish Parliaments in 1707 it was provided that the supreme courts of Scotland were to remain as constituted at the Union in all time coming, and that no causes from Scotland were to be cognisible in any court in Westminster Hall.

Accordingly this paper will be largely concerned with drawing the attention of its readers to the respects in which the Scottish system of today differs from the English without going into the history and details of legal doctrines, such as would be found in a comparative study of an academic or professional character.

The Courts As a background I will describe the functions of the courts of justice, confining myself to the three principal courts of general jurisdiction, namely, the Court of Session, the High Court of Justiciary and the Sheriff Court. There is also a district court in a form set up by a recent statute, but its jurisdiction is very limited.

Court of Session Her Majesty's College of Justice in Scotland comprises the Court of Session, the supreme civil court, and the members are the judges, known as Senators of the College or Lords of Session, the advocates and solicitors who practice there and certain officials. The court is divided into the Inner House, with largely appellate duties, and the Outer House, responsible for first instance matters; the Inner House sits in two divisions. The court is truly of a collegiate character and may sit if it thinks fit with any number up to the whole court (eighteen) and has done so in difficult cases or where it is desired to reconsider a previous line of authority. The Lord President presides over the whole Court, and over the First Division. The 'second-in-command' is the Lord Justice Clerk, whose title really comes from his office in the criminal court; he who presides in the Second Division of the Inner House.

High Court of Justiciary The supreme criminal court is the High Court of Justiciary. All the senators today sit as judges therein, the Lord President under the title of Lord Justice-General. The judges preside at criminal trials in Edinburgh and in the circuit towns. The Court's appellate jurisdiction is generally exercised by a bench of three, although any number may sit; the whole court sat in 1933 to decide the question whether the vicennial prescription of crime was part of the law of Scotland, as of Rome. A majority decided that it was not. Appeals on stated questions of law come, under the common law, although the form may be regulated by statute, from all inferior courts, and by statute a jurisdiction similar to that of the Criminal Division of the Court of Appeal is exercised. Unlawful interference with the liberty of a subject by anyone will be remedied on application to this court.

Sheriff Court The Sheriff Court is the local court, to be found in all important burghs, and is given boundaries to accord with local government areas. The judges consist of the sheriffs principal who have supervisory, administrative and some appellate jurisdiction over a group of courts, and the sheriffs, who are the judges in those courts. All are qualified lawyers, the majority being members of the Bar, but a substantial number are solicitors. In this court, which is that in which the majority of cases are heard, the civil and criminal business is done by legally trained, professional judges. In civil matters the competence of the court is unlimited so far as the value of the sum at stake is concerned. There are some classes of case, notably, up to now, actions involving status, together with large company windings-up and some actions relating to the status of documents, in which the jurisdiction of the Court of Session is privative. But in, for example, commercial

Parliament Square, Edinburgh, showing the Old
Parliament House, now the Courts of Justice, and the
statue of Charles II

matters of unlimited size and complexity the sheriff shares with the Court of Session the competence at first instance. Here there is a remarkable, though I think little remarked, similarity to some continental systems, notably the German, where the whole of the important first instance work is confided to the local court, the *Landgericht,* leaving to the central and superior courts the appellate work. In criminal matters, the sheriff is not competent to try cases of treason, murder, attempted murder, or rape. But that does not mean that he tries every case of other crimes. His form of punishment is limited, and, as will be seen later, the decision whether a charge of crime which could competently be heard by the sheriff should in fact be heard by him or by the High Court is one for the public prosecutor.

At the time of the Union, an appeal for 'remeid of law' lay from the Court of Session to the Parliament. After the Union, that right was transferred to the House of Lords, which has never sat in Westminster Hall, and so escaped the statutory disqualification. An appeal accordingly lies, without the necessity of leave, from the final judgment of the Court of Session. No appeal lies from decisions of the High Court of Justiciary.

The Legal Profession The Scottish Bar consists of the Faculty of Advocates, in Edinburgh. Members have exclusive right of audience in the Court of Session and High Court. Both general and legal academic qualifications are demanded of entrants, as is also a period of training in a solicitor's office. The head of the Bar is the Dean of Faculty, who is responsible for decisions on etiquette and disciplinary questions. He is elected annually – as are all the Faculty officers – by the members.

The solicitors are members of the Law Society of Scotland. Some are also members of associations of ancient origin such as Writers to the Signet and Solicitors to the Supreme Courts, in Edinburgh, and the Faculties of Procurators in the provincial cities and towns. It is noteworthy that, since the Sheriff Court's jurisdiction is so wide, solicitors have the right to conduct the first instance stage of highly important cases, and to defend in serious criminal charges. Although by the constituent charter of the College of Justice (1532) members of the Society of Writers to the Signet may be appointed judges, I do not know of any instance of this.

Civil Law It is in this branch that any differences are most acute. The historical and philosophical foundations of the system must remain untreated. How far the law of Scotland derives from Rome, and why, as also its similarity to other systems in its original attachment to the 'natural law', are fascinating questions which would require more space and greater expertise than I have at my disposal. I must, as I say, confine myself to noticing a few differences between England and Scotland.

Mercantile Law In the mercantile field, much has been done by UK statutes to remove these differences. According to the report of a Royal Commission set up in 1852, 'If a specific article be sold for a full price and the fault be so latent as not to be observable at the time of the sale, the buyer on discovery of the fault may in Scotland return the article and is not bound to pay the price. There is an implied obligation on the seller to warrant that the article is of marketable quality even against latent defects unknown to himself'.

This doctrine was abolished by statute in 1856, with the declared intention of making the laws of England and Scotland the same: in the course of these 100 years the pendulum has swung far. One distinction in the law of contract which I must merely mention is more interesting to the lawyer than to the layman: consideration is not a requisite of a Scottish contract. Another is that the primary remedy for breach of contract is an order for specific performance, damages being available where the primary remedy is inappropriate. The insistence of

Scots law on the distinction between real and personal obligations, so familiar to the Roman lawyer, has an interesting effect on the procedure for buying a house, which may roughly be as follows. A, a solicitor, advertises his client's house for sale. B, a buyer, inspects the house, and then instructs C, his solicitor, to make an offer, subject to survey and perhaps to certain conditions which will be negotiated between A and C. When these are agreed, and after a procedure which may have taken a very short time, although the preparation of the necessary deeds may take long enough, B acquires an immediate personal right against the vendor, so that he can if necessary go to the court to obtain an order for the delivery of a good title. But if the vendor has sold the house to D in spite of his bargain with B, B has a good action of damages against him for breach of contract, although the real right to the house is in D. So 'gazumping' is a word not known in Scotland.

Real Property The state of a piece of real property, eg proprietorships and real burdens upon it, depends entirely upon the entries relating to it in the public registers. This would be perfectly familiar to, *inter alios*, an Australian or a New Zealander. So no proprietor or mortgagee is in possession of his title-deeds: he may have official copies supplied by the registry.

Family Law In family law, much assimilation between the systems has been effected by statute. As regards marriage, it is only necessary to notice that in no circumstances is parental consent necessary. This is what causes the resort of teenage foreigners to Scotland for matrimonial purposes. The divorce laws are now for practical purposes indistinguishable (adultery and desertion became grounds for divorce in Scotland in 1573). In common with most countries whose law does not derive from England, a person leaving wife and/or children does not have an unlimited power of testamentary disposal of his estate. On his death his estate will be divided into equal parts, three if he has children, two if he has not. One part is *jus relicti* or *relictae* for a spouse, another is *legitim* for the children, the remainder is 'dead's part', which he may bequeath as he pleases. These rights may be varied by an ante-nuptial settlement.

A father must support his child, either by monetary payment or by making a home for him, and this obligation subsists in case of need throughout life. If the father is dead, or indigent, the obligation falls upon the mother, whom failing, upon the grandparents. And these obligations are reciprocal, so that, all more immediate sources failing, a person may find himself bound to support indigent grandparents, just as they may be bound to support him. There is no obligation of support between brother and sister.

A child passes, before reaching majority, through two phases, pupilarity before the age of puberty (12 for females, 14 for males) and minority after. The position of a pupil sufficiently resembles that of a minor in England; that of a minor is very different. He may dispose by will both of his real and his personal property. If he has a guardian, he may contract with the guardian's consent, or without it in the case of contracts for service or apprenticeship, or contracts in the course of a trade he carries on. Not having a guardian, he has full power to contract. But in either case he may, within four years after majority, ask the court to set aside any contract entered into minority which is unfairly or seriously damaging to him or his estate. This power does not extend to a contract entered into by him in the course of carrying on a trade.

Wills As regards wills, it may be worth noting that in Scots law the witnessing of a will by a beneficiary thereunder does not invalidate a legacy to that witness; it is possible that this obscure fact might be useful to the framers of detective fiction.

Delict Since it is not proposed to look at historical development, there is little to be said on the law of torts, or delict as it is known in Scotland. Decisions of the House of Lords, sometimes necessarily corrected by reforming statutes, have tended to bring the law of the two countries into line. But the recent reforms of occupiers' liability have left one quite important difference between the systems. In Scotland, an occupier may be liable in damages to a trespasser if he has not taken that care which was reasonable in all the circumstances. In defamation, there are certain differences. In Scotland, no distinction is made between libel and slander; the written and the spoken defamatory word have the same consequences. It is not necessary that there should have been publication of the defamatory matter to a third party. This is because Scots law, following the Roman *actio iniuriarum,* allows damages for an affront to the personality. The insult is a separate ground of damage from the loss of reputation. The law of Scotland does not countenance the award of punitive damages.

Until recently, most actions on delict were tried by jury. This unsatisfactory method was introduced in 1815 by statute in order to assimilate Scottish to English practice. The practice in now to a great extent departed from in injury cases.

Criminal Law It is not to be expected that the substantive criminal law will differ greatly between two contiguous countries, such as England and Scotland, which share a common legislature. The code of conduct enforced by the State upon the citizen under the sanction of punishment is an emanation of the code of morality in terms of which the citizen expects and demands certain standards of behaviour on the part of his neighbour, and systems of morality vary very little from one 'western' country to another. Of course a lot of crime nowadays, and the kind of crime which circumstances have made us all likely to commit, is far removed from breaches of the ten commandments, although it would be wrong to divorce infringements, for example of the road traffic laws, from breaches of morality. Such offences are for the most part creatures of recent statutes, almost always having a United Kingdom scope. The distinction, for what it is worth, between the grave crime which is almost everywhere and at all times punishable on one hand, and on the other the offence which consists of failing to obey a directive made by the legislature for the better keeping of order, is in one sense easier to observe in Scotland than in England. In Scotland the former class of crime is still, largely, created by and enforced as part of the common law. There are no equivalents to the Offences against the Person Act and the Theft Act. One curious result is that the maximum penalty is the same for the most trifling as for the most heinous theft – imprisonment for life, although there was a time when thefts were classified as capital and non-capital.

The jurisprudential analysis of this conception of crime cannot be closely examined without the disclosure of features which, as may indeed be said of much of the common law, could today occasion some uneasiness. It did not trouble our forebears. Hume, writing at the end of the 18th century, could say, 'Our Supreme Criminal Court have an inherent power to punish every act which is obviously of a criminal nature, though it be such that in time past it has never been the subject of prosecution'. Fifty years ago it was judicially declared that 'all shamelessly indecent conduct is criminal'. There was a time when the role of judge as *custos morum* was generally acceptable, but it is not so now. In sexual questions especially, where there is no public unanimity, it is difficult to see how the judge can, in declaring the law, constitute himself the spokesman for a generally held contemporary opinion, although of course by relying on precedent, as he must do, he is enabled to expound repressive doctrines which were once socially acceptable.

Strangely, it is in this field that some differences between the two countries have been observable. In Scotland, incest was by a statute of 1567 declared a capital crime, although of course the penalty was long ago changed to imprisonment, whereas in England it was not punishable at all until 1908. Again, whereas for England the statutory prohibitions on homosexual conduct between males have been much relaxed, the relevant United Kingdom statute remains, for Scotland, unamended. These details are unimportant, except perhaps as showing that Parliament, in fashioning the criminal law, is bound to pay attention to widely held opinions, so that in the first example what would have been publicly regarded as a defect in the law was duly remedied, and in the second the state of public opinion in one part of Great Britain was seen to be different from that in another. If these are not Parliament's motives, they ought to be.

Two further examples may be given. First, the nature of the crime of murder differs somewhat as between the two countries. The doctrine of constructive malice never formed part of the law of Scotland, and although it has been abolished by a recent statute in England, it is still English law that death resulting from an assault with the intention of inflicting grievous bodily harm is murder. In Scotland, if the intention be not to kill, the assault must, if murder is to be substantiated, be such as to show a wicked recklessness whether death result or not. The use of the word 'wicked' in a definition is open to academic objection as leading to circularity, but it is intelligible to a jury, and, curiously, no such objection is made to the use of the Latin word *reus*. The other example is that in Scotland there is no separate crime of conspiracy, which accordingly cannot be added to as a long-stop on the end of an indictment. The doctrine of accession, however, has full force; no distinction is made between him who is principal, or concerned as 'actor', and him who is accessory, or implicated 'art and part'. Both are guilty of the substantive offence.

The Public Prosecutor There is one fundamental difference between the English and Scottish systems. I do not believe that this arises out of some Scottish idiosyncracy, but that rather the English system exhibits a feature which is not to be found in any other country except some of those – and there are many – whose laws derive originally from English law. In Scotland, almost all criminal prosecutions are initiated and conducted by a public prosecutor, and private prosecutions are confined to those instances in which statutory powers have been conferred, for example on public undertakings and government agencies. From the general and social point of view the important aspect of the system is that the police, who as I understand act in England technically as private prosecutors, have in Scotland no power to prosecute in any capacity at all. When what appears to the police to be criminal conduct comes to their notice, they make a report to the public prosecutor, who decides whether proceedings are to be taken, against whom, on what charge, and in what court. In those proceedings he has the personal conduct of the case for the Crown. Who then is this official?

The Law Officers The formal title of the public prosecutor is Her Majesty's Advocate, generally referred to, in the old-fashioned style, as the Lord Advocate. He is a minister of the Crown, usually a member of the House of Commons, and as such answerable to Parliament for the administration of his office. If he is not a member, questions relating to his office are answered by the Secretary of State for Scotland. He would probably refuse to answer questions calling for facts which would explain why a prosecution was or was not brought; it is easy to see how great injustice could result from such disclosures. But the important point is that the general conduct and policies of his office are, like those of other ministers, subject to the democratic control of Parliament. Sharing his work and responsibility is the other Law Officer of the Crown, the Solicitor General for Scotland. Together they direct the work of the Crown Office, which is the organisation through which the prosecutor's function is performed. It consists of a number of Advocates Depute, counsel to whom the work of the law officers may be delegated, and who are in charge of those actual prosecutions in which the services of counsel are required in Court. The Crown Agent is the solicitor in charge of the office.

Procurators Fiscal The Crown Office is situated in Edinburgh, but throughout the country, at the seats of the courts of local jurisdiction, are stationed the Procurators Fiscal. This official has recently attained United Kingdom publicity through having been made the hero of a popular television series, and indeed he is in a sense the keyman of the system. Every complaint of crime comes from the police first to him. In cases of gravity or difficulty he will consult the Crown Office and take instructions. But in the ordinary run-of-the-mill case – and these form the great majority – he carries the whole responsibility, and is indeed the public prosecutor.

How far are the activities of the procurator subject to the control of the courts? I would say, very little. In many respects the prosecutor is the master of the proceedings. When he has decided to bring an accused person to trial there are three methods of trial available, and he will select the one which is appropriate to the gravity of the charge and the record of the accused. Summary proceedings, before the sheriff sitting alone, account for by far the greater part of the criminal output. Many statutory offences must be tried summarily, but in some cases the prosecutor may decide to proceed by way of a jury trial before the sheriff, in which case severer

penalties are available on a finding of guilty. Or in cases of the most serious character, and on the orders of the Crown Officer, the accused will be tried by jury before the High Court of Justiciary, where maximum penalties may be imposed. The contrast with England is striking. An accused person cannot in any circumstances demand trial by jury. Another feature, and one which has occasioned adverse criticism, is that from a summary conviction there is no appeal to a higher court except in a question of law, upon findings in fact which are made by the officiating sheriff. There is no equivalent to the re-hearing before a superior tribunal as in England.

There are other instances of the authoritative position of the Lord Advocate and his staff which I believe may be characteristic of some systems employing a public prosecutor; one is reminded, perhaps faintly, of the powers of a *Procureur Général* in France or a *Generalstaatsanwalt* in Germany. There are some quasi-judicial features here. For example, just as the prosecutor selects (except in a case where the law may have prescribed either summary or High Court proceedings) the tribunal of trial, so in the course of a jury trial he has some striking powers. The presiding judge cannot at any stage by his own decision bring the trial to a stop and order an acquittal. He can of course when the evidence is over, and the prosecutor has addressed the jury, direct the jury to return a verdict of not guilty on the ground of insufficient evidence, but until that stage the prosecutor is in charge. So, after a verdict of guilty, the court is powerless to pronounce sentence unless a formal motion for sentence is made by the prosecutor, though the prosecutor will never address the court on sentence unless, on request, to refer to precedents. There are legends, which I cannot confirm, of a Lord Advocate in person refraining from moving for sentence when he had reason to suspect that the judge had a very excessive punishment in mind. It is possible to make a bold claim here, and to suggest that there may be powers in a prosecutor which, while acceptable when one is speaking of a public official, would not be acceptable when the prosecutor may be a private individual, especially if he may be a police officer, who was concerned with the detection of the crime and the selection of the accused. We are sometimes, in our entirely necessary anxiety lest innocent people be convicted, tempted to over-look what is almost equivalent to denial of justice, namely, the putting of an innocent person on trial.

In the best British text-book of French law it is suggested that in France the *occasional* acquittal is to be regarded as an assertion of the public's congenital right of putting the establishment in its place. In Scotland, although the arrest and detention of an accused who is to be tried by jury nominally proceeds on a judicial warrant, granted by the sheriff, my impression is that it is granted more or less in reliance on information provided by the procurator fiscal; there is no public hearing of evidence sufficient to establish a *prima facie* case, as in England. But such a hearing, obviously necessary in a climate of private prosecution, may perhaps safely be dispensed with when the action is taken on the responsibility of an official ultimately subject to Parliamentary

control. The sheriff's warrant to commit for trial in custody, not on bail, is noteworthy in this respect, that thereafter time begins to run against the prosecutor. It is provided by a statute of 1701 that if the trial be not finished within 110 days from the warrant, and the prosecutor is unable to point to circumstances beyond his control, the court will order the accused to be liberated in the same way as it would on the application of any other person who could show that he was incarcerated without legal warrant. Such an order is regarded as equivalent to an English order in *habeas corpus,* a writ which does not run in Scotland. From the practical point of view, the difference between England and Scotland as to the time which may elapse between committal and conviction is quite astonishing.

The exercise of the discretionary power of the public prosecutor to refuse to take proceedings upon complaint having been made to him is necessarily subject to the control of the court; it is a tribute to the system that it is more than sixty years since that control was applied. On that occasion a limited company complained that it had been defrauded by a merchant. The Lord Advocate refused to prosecute, giving as a reason that the complaint was truly of the nature of a civil claim; there was however some suspicion that the real reason was that the merchant was a supporter of the political party then in power. The refusal to accord to the citizen, for political reasons, the protection of the criminal law, on the say-so of the public prosecutor, is intolerable in a civilised society; the High Court of Justiciary therefore exercised its undoubted power of authorising the prosecution to proceed at the instance of the company without the concurrence of the Lord Advocate, and a conviction followed. I do not know whether this analogue was referred to in a recent English case.

Evidence There are certain differences in the law of evidence; I will instance one which is of first-rate importance. It is a general rule that a person cannot be convicted of crime upon the uncorroborated evidence of a single witness. It is not a question of the presiding judge warning the jury not to convict on such evidence in particular classes of case. It is for the judge in every case to decide as matter of law whether there is corroboration, and, if he holds there is not, to direct an acquittal. One consequence of this rule is to reduce to some extent, though by no means entirely to avoid, the danger of a conviction which depends on the identification of the accused by strangers. Another is that an accused cannot be convicted upon his extra-judicial admission or confession alone. It must be corroborated; this again reduces, to some extent, the danger of relying on disputed conversations between accused persons and police officers. The 'verbal' is still evidence, but it cannot be sufficient evidence. The only uncorroborated admission which will suffice for a conviction is a plea of guilty.

Indictment and Defences The indictment is a written charge addressed to the accused by 'The Right Honourable AB, Her Majesty's Advocate'. The charges are set out rather more fully than in the corresponding English

The annual procession along the Royal Mile to St Giles' Cathedral and Parliament House to mark the opening of the new session of the Court of Session and the High Court of Justiciary. Scottish Q.C.s, (below) identifiable by their long bands, and (bottom) judges of the High Court of Justiciary

document, and will specify the date and place at which the crime is said to have been committed. There will follow a list of the names and addresses of all the persons whom the prosecutor intends to call as witnesses. It will be the duty of the accused's solicitor to take statements from these witnesses. There will also be a list of all the productions, or exhibits, which are to be proved in the trial. These then become open to inspection by the defence. When the indictment has been served, the accused is required at a preliminary hearing to plead to it. If he pleads guilty, no further proceedings take place, except that he will be brought in a very short time indeed before a judge for sentence. If he pleads not guilty a trial is fixed, and some days before the trial he must supply the prosecutor with a list of his witnesses and exhibits. The prosecutor will take statements from these witnesses. Notice must be given of what are termed 'special defences', ie insanity, alibi, and that the crime was committed by another named person, otherwise these defences cannot be stated at the trial. All these rules are made in order to prevent either party from being taken by surprise at the trial, though it must be observed that their strictness is frequently relaxed on the application of an accused, but not of the prosecutor.

The Criminal Trial It is intended only to note some significant differences from English practice. Legal aid was instituted in a somewhat limited way by an Act of the Scots Parliament of 1424, but is now on the same basis as in England. Counsel have always appeared on both sides as in a civil trial. Perhaps the most striking feature is that counsel do not make opening speeches. It does not seem that inconvenience arises from this; on the other hand there is no danger of counsel telling the jury about evidence which he genuinely expects to be given, but in the event is not. There being no depositions, neither the judge nor the jury has, when the evidence begins, any information whatever except what is in the indictment.

The jury consists of fifteen men and women, though there are proposals to reduce this number. They may deliver their verdict at any time by a simple majority. It is understood that at one time the two verdicts available were, as accurate reasoning would demand, that the charge was proven or that it was not proven. The verdict of 'not guilty' was later introduced, but the verdict of 'not proven' remains. It has the same consequence as a verdict of not guilty, that is that the accused cannot be arraigned again. But the alternative verdicts of acquittal are difficult to justify. If the prosecutor has failed to discharge the burden of making out his case, the presumption of innocence – which is now firmly embedded in international conventions which Britain has affirmed – has not been rebutted, and anything other than a verdict of not guilty seems inadequate. It is, however, maintained by some experienced practitioners that an accused who can achieve nothing better than a not proven would, on the same evidence, be found guilty in England.

There are some special provisions relating to young people. No person under the age of 21 may be sentenced

to a term of imprisonment. Corresponding custodial treatment is provided in young offenders' institutions, which are penal establishments special to the young, admitting no other class of inmate, and thus in a position to regulate the treatment accordingly. The revolutionary scheme for young people introduced by the Social Work (Scotland) Act 1968 cannot be gone into in detail here. The principle which informs the policy is that a child who is charged with an offence, or is in need of care and protection for any reason, is not to be dealt with by a criminal court of any kind, but is to be referred to a small, specially and carefully trained body ('children's hearing') who will make such order as will have the effect of rehabilitating the child, and will after making it continue to see that all possible support is given to be child. If there is any dispute whether the child committed the offence charged, the question is decided by the sheriff, who will, if he finds the child 'guilty', remit back to the hearing for the appropriate treatment to be assessed. It is significant that any appeal on a matter of law from the sheriff goes to the Court of Session, not to the criminal court. A residual power remains in the public prosecutor to take criminal proceedings in special cases. Much research has been published, in several countries, on this system, which has attracted widespread interest as a solution to an intractable problem. The subject is perhaps more related to the social organisation than to the law of Scotland.

The Law
of
Northern
Ireland

Lord MacDermott

Stormont Castle

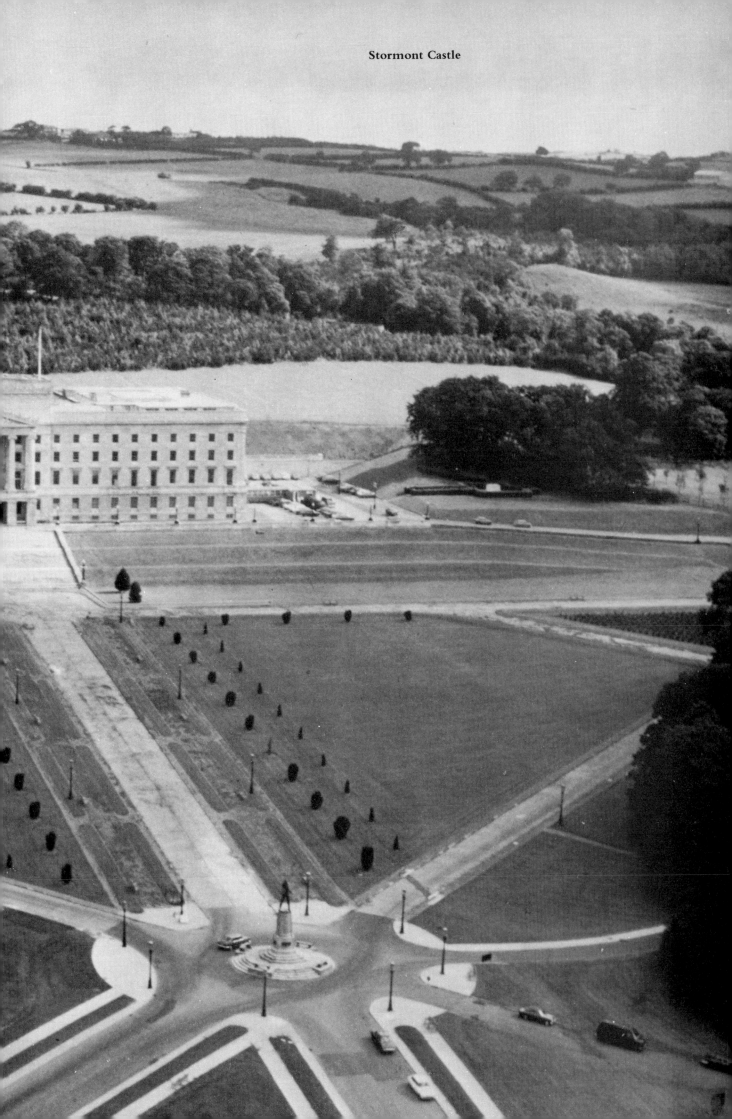

As a political entity Northern Ireland only goes back to 1921 when the Government of Ireland Act of 1920 came into force. That measure, which was passed by the United Kingdom Parliament at Westminster in a determined effort to settle the Irish question, established a Parliament for Northern Ireland at Stormont, Belfast, with substantial but limited legislative powers relating for the most part to internal affairs, and an executive government whose authority was of corresponding scope.

This setting suggests the relevance of comment on the political history of Ireland before 1921. But it is a suggestion to be resisted. No matter how laconic, such a commentary would absorb far too much of the space at my disposal; and, in any event, the political history of Ireland, North and South, remains too confusing, too controversial and too divisive to cast much light on the subject in hand.

After a short description of Northern Ireland I propose to consider first its substantive law in general terms; then to speak of its courts and their organisation; and lastly to look at its legal professions, their education and training.

Factual Background Northern Ireland consists of the parliamentary counties of Antrim, Armagh, Down, Fermanagh, Londonderry and Tyrone, and the parliamentary boroughs of Belfast and Londonderry. Its total land area is some 5,206 square miles or about one-sixth of the land area of all Ireland. It has a sea-board of 259 miles and the land boundary, dividing it from the Republic, is almost as tortuous and quite as long. The farms are much smaller than those in Great Britain and, for reasons which appear later, are nearly all owned in fee simple by the farmers. But agriculture remains a major section of the economy and there can be little doubt that, since 1921, the amenities of country life have improved and farming has become more profitable.

The total population (1971 census) is 1,536,000, about a third of the entire island or half that of New Zealand. The whole area is well endowed with communications and the longest journey any Northern Ireland litigant has to make to get to the Supreme Court in Belfast is under 110 miles. Shipbuilding and engineering and the textile trades account for the larger part of the country's manufacturing activities; and, despite current difficulties and political unrest, the farms and factories continue to produce a substantial external trade.

The population derives from a mixture of native Irish, English and Scots, the two latter stocks being mainly the result of official plantations organised by the English government and, particularly in the case of the Scots in North Antrim and North Down, of private settlements as well. Approximately one-third of the population is Roman Catholic in religion and most of the remaining two-thirds is Protestant. Politics are associated with these groupings but the division is not precise and seems to be more historical than religious. Political differences have from time to time produced deep antagonisms, but never more so than in the period commencing towards the end of 1969 and still continuing – a period of confrontation and terrorism which I shall refer to as 'the emergency'. The result has been a campaign of assassination and the wholesale destruction of valuable property. The armed IRA want the British security forces out, and the armed Protestant para-military extremists call themselves loyalists and also resort to violence. A form of guerilla warfare exists. The great majority, however, long for peace and hopes are mounting. But violence, and organised violence at that, enables a relatively small number, aided by firearms, high explosives, incendiary devices and motor vehicles, to challenge the rule of law. These are facts and they cannot be left out of account in any assessment of the situation which now faces the law and the lawyers of Northern Ireland.

The Law The English came to Ireland in the early 12th
century. Dermot McMurrough, King of Leinster, was
getting beaten in one of the local wars by which Ireland
was then plagued. He sought the aid of Henry II who
allowed him to enlist any Englishmen willing to cross to
Ireland. The Earl of Pembroke responded, married
McMurrough's daughter Eva and was promised the
succession to the throne of Leinster. This promise was
duly fulfilled in 1171 and the Earl (usually known as
'Strongbow') then subjected himself and his Irish Kingdom to the King of England. After this romantic conquest Henry II came to Ireland, received the Earl's subjection in person and seems to have appropriated Dublin, Wexford and the adjacent areas on the East coast as
Royal Demesne. A few years later the rest of Ireland was
brought under English sovereignty when Henry's son
John was made Lord of Ireland. But this extension was
little more than a gesture. For centuries the field of English influence was confined to Dublin and a neighbouring area which was continually changing in size. This
was known as 'the Pale' and within it English law and
English legal institutions took root and developed.

The English conquest of the whole of Ireland took
centuries and finally resulted in the virtual extirpation of
the ancient laws and customs of the native Irish. That
was almost ancient history when the Act of 1920 was
passed. What is now Northern Ireland was then, with
the rest of Ireland, ruled by English law, that is to say
the common law of England, the principles of English
equity and the statutes applicable to Ireland which had
been passed by the English Parliament, the Irish Parliament and the United Kingdom Parliament. I know of
no law then or now current which derived from native
sources. There are occasional traces, in maps or documents, or on the ground, of an earlier dispensation, but
to-day these are only of antiquarian interest. So when
section 61 of the Act of 1920 made provision for the
continuation of all existing laws and authorities in Ireland, the body of law with which the new state of
Northern Ireland was thus endowed was entirely
English.

This, however, does not mean that the laws of these
two jurisdictions are now identical. There are numerous
variations, some of detail and some of substance. But as
it would be quite beyond the range of this article to deal
with these exhaustively, I shall, after noting some recent
changes in the constitutional status of Northern Ireland,
confine myself to considering the two branches of the
law where the differences are now most marked,
namely the land law and the criminal law.

Constitutional Law The Act of 1920 gave Northern Ireland a written constitution, providing, *inter alia,* for the
powers of its Parliament, its judiciary, its executive
government and its public services. It also prohibited
measures interfering with religious equality, the taking
of property without compensation etc.; and it proclaimed in clear terms the continuing supremacy of the
Parliament of the United Kingdom. The Parliament of
Northern Ireland was thus, from the beginning a
subordinate Parliament; but in 1949, just after Eire

(formerly the Irish Free State) had become a Republic,
the United Kingdom Parliament added to Stormont's
powers an important right which is thus expressed in
section 1(2) of the Ireland Act of that year –

It is hereby declared that Northern Ireland remains part of His
Majesty's dominions and of the United Kingdom and it is
hereby affirmed that in no event will Northern Ireland or any
part thereof cease to be part of His Majesty's dominions and of
the United Kingdom without the consent of the Parliament of
Northern Ireland.

But after the emergency had developed, the United
Kingdom Parliament passed the Northern Ireland
(Temporary Provisions) Act 1972 under which the government of Northern Ireland was taken over by the Secretary of State for Northern Ireland, a Minister of the
United Kingdom. This happened in the spring of 1972;
the Parliament of Northern Ireland thereupon ceased to
function: and there began a period of Direct Rule from
Westminster which ended its first phase on December
31, 1973. Meantime, the Northern Ireland Constitution
Act 1973 had been passed providing for the transfer of
certain legislative and executive powers to a 78-member
Northern Ireland Assembly, which had been established
by an earlier statute of the same year.

The Constitution Act of 1973 abolished the Parliament of Northern Ireland as well as the office of its
Governor and repealed section 1(2) of the Act of 1949,
substituting a declaration similar to that just quoted but
with the words 'without the consent of the Parliament
of Northern Ireland' replaced by 'without the consent of
the majority of the people in Northern Ireland voting in
a poll held for the purposes of this section in accordance
with Schedule 1 to this Act.' No poll has been held
under this provision; but a similar poll, under an Act of
1972, had been held for the same purpose on March 8,
1973, and had resulted in a large majority vote in favour
of Northern Ireland remaining in the United Kingdom.

The Constitution Act of 1973 had also provided for a
Northern Ireland Executive or Cabinet to be appointed
in the first instance by the Secretary of State. This was
done on a power-sharing basis, that is to say the members of the Executive were chosen from several of the
minority parties as well as from the majority party. The
Assembly had been elected in June 1973 and the Executive, under its chief Minister, the late Mr Brian Faulkner
(as he then was), took up the reins of government at the
beginning of 1974. The experiment of a power-sharing
administration had, however, engendered much hostility in some quarters and a general strike, organised by a
body known as the 'Ulster Workers' Council', was called in protest. This led to the fall of the new Government. Mr Faulkner and those of his party resigned and
on May 29, 1974, the warrants of the remaining members of the Executive were revoked and the Assembly
was prorogued.

By a further statute – the Northern Ireland Act 1974 –
the Parliament at Westminster provided for the dissolution of the Assembly and the establishment in Northern
Ireland of an elected Convention '... for the purpose of
considering what provision for the government of
Northern Ireland is likely to command the most

widespread acceptance throughout the community there.' The Convention reported in November 1975; but its conclusions were not acceptable. It was dissolved on March 5, 1976 and Direct Rule by the Westminster Government, which has been provided for by the Act of 1974, has continued since. It is not a very convenient form of governance.

The Secretary of State and his Ministers are on the move constantly between England and Belfast; but even jet travel cannot quite off-set the disadvantages of remote control, particularly for a people accustomed for half a century to having those with power on local issues members of their own community and generally at hand. And, so far as Northern Ireland legislation is concerned, the present arrangement whereby such legislation is passed by an Order-in-Council procedure at Westminster is more than inconvenient.

In a Parliament so crowded with other important business it is hard to get time for full discussion; improving amendments mean a new draft Order and the 12 members which Northern Ireland returns to Westminster have not yet been able to procure a really satisfactory system. Some critics take the view that a fuller integration of Northern Ireland and the rest of the United Kingdom would provide a solution. Others see no hope in anything short of a restoration of devolved rule from Stormont. And some again pin their political faith regarding these and other matters on a united Ireland. This is not the place for expressing an opinion on such conflicting courses: but I think two things may now be said without entering the confused arena of Northern Ireland politics. First, anything much better than the present regime depends on making further progress in restoring the rule of law and healing the fears and hatreds that the emergency has served to intensify. And secondly, the rule of law remains vulnerable to terrorism; and the laws against terrorism must be kept adequate and fairly and constantly enforced if the virtues of democratic government are to endure.

The Land Laws Unlike the Irish the Normans had a genius for centralisation and the land law which they brought to Ireland was based on the feudal system which had followed their conquest of England in 1066 and under which all land was held from the Crown. This is still a feature of the land law of both England and Northern Ireland. But many of the tenures and incidents of English feudalism did not survive in Ireland. In particular, the manorial system never became generally established and copyhold remained virtually unknown.

Though the statute of *Quia Emptores* (1290) had been applied to Ireland, it seems to have been Crown policy in making grants of lands confiscated from their Irish owners, to dispense with the provisions of that statute prohibiting sub-infeudation; and this, no doubt coupled with a desire on the part of new grantees to create a revenue out of their grants, goes some way to explain why new kinds of estates began to appear on the Irish scene and to have remained there ever since, such as fee farm grants and leases for lives renewable for ever. Further changes were also occurring in relation to leaseholds and at long last, by section 3 of the Landlord and Tenant Act 1860, it was provided that in Ireland the relation of 'landlord and tenant shall be deemed to be founded on the express or implied contract of the parties, and not upon tenure or service, and a reversion shall not be necessary to such relation. . . .'

This entirely changed the basis of the landlord and tenant relationship but, though it must have resolved a number of conveyancing problems, its practical effects do not seem to have been as marked as those produced by the earlier changes consequent on the introduction of English land law. These had had at least two more noteworthy results. Sales of land were (and still are) frequently carried out by way of long leases (10,000 years is not uncommon) or by fee farm grants subject to a perpetuity rent, so that in many titles one may find a whole series of such assurances intervening between the owner in occupation and the original Crown grantee. These superior interests cause little discomfort provided all concerned pay their dues; but it is a cumbersome system which can bristle with complexities, especially for conveyancers who are not used to it.

The other consequence had much more serious repercussions. In the course of time the general picture came to be one of estates covered by small holdings whose occupying farmers had a very precarious form of tenancy, usually from year to year, from which they could easily be evicted. There were good landlords; but many were absentees who looked to their local agents to enforce their rights and develop their rental revenues. The hardship and distress thus arising were general and what is now Northern Ireland did not escape; but there the build-up of unrest was somewhat less as many tenancies in Ulster became subject to what was known as the Ulster Tenant-right Custom which, though it varied from place to place and was not formally legalised until 1870, generally recognised a tenant's claim to have a fair rent fixed, to be able to sell his interest and to enjoy a certain degree of security.

Happily the last century has seen an end to most of the agrarian problems which caused so much bitterness. By a series of Land Purchase Acts spanning the period 1870–1925 practically every farm holding has become vested in fee simple in the occupying farmer subject to a terminable annuity payable to the Government in recoupment of advances made by it for the purchase of all superior interests. The holdings, as I have indicated, are small, but this serves to emphasise the remarkable social change which land purchase has brought about. Go where you will, the land belongs to those who toil upon it. The absentee landlord has ceased to trouble and, perhaps most important of all, the diligent and progressive farmer has the satisfaction and encouragement of knowing that the fruit of his efforts will be his own.

Another variation between the land laws of Northern Ireland and England is the much greater extent to which a system for the registration of *title* to land is now operated in Northern Ireland. There is a folio and map for each title and, as the Register is conclusive, the process of investigating and completing ordinary transactions is

An historic picture of the Northern Ireland Executive in 1973. From the left: Paddy Devlin, Oliver Napier, the late Brian Faulkner, John Hume, Basil McIvor, two secretaries, John Baxter, Austin Currie, Herbert Kirk, Gerry Fitt, Roy Bradford and Leslie Morrell

relatively simple, cheap and expeditious. The system in Northern Ireland was introduced by the Local Registration of Title (Ireland) Act 1891, which is now being superseded by the Land Registration Act (Northern Ireland) 1970. What distinguishes it is that all agricultural land purchased under the Land Purchase Acts – and to-day that means virtually all the agricultural holdings in Northern Ireland – is registrable compulsorily. Other land may be registered voluntarily; but full advantage of this provision has not yet been taken, particularly in urban areas. The Act of 1891 also provided that land purchased under the Land Purchase Acts, though realty, was to pass on death to the personal representative and to devolve on intestacy as personal estate. Similar provisions now apply to unregistered realty; and primogeniture, dower and tenancy by the curtesy have become things of the past.

In addition to registration of *title* a system for the registration of *assurances,* which is peculiar to Ireland, has been in operation there since 1708. The Registry for Northern Ireland, known as the Registry of Deeds, is situate in Belfast. Registration there affords a measure of security to purchasers and mortgages and is of value in fixing priorities. It is not, however, essential to the validity of most transactions and is unnecessary, of course, where the lands have been registered under the Act of 1891; but instruments passing or creating any substantial interest in other lands are almost invariably registered and searches in the Registry for prejudicial acts are a normal step in most investigations of title.

The Birkenhead legislation which was passed in 1925 for England and Wales did not apply to Northern Ireland; but several of its subject-matters (eg trustees and the administration of estates) have since been dealt with on similar lines by the Parliament at Stormont, and what has not been thus adopted is unlikely to cause any difficulty to English and Irish practitioners which a short course would not remove.

Criminal Law There have always been some divergencies between the two jurisdictions on this branch of the law; but the relevant principles of the common law, both as regards substantive and procedural matters, are very much the same; and since 1920 the enactments passed at Stormont have tended, on the whole, to follow the more important legislative changes made at Westminster respecting crime and criminals. What ranks as important in this context has sometimes been controversial; but by and large the criminal law of the two countries is so similar that it will suffice for present purposes to consider only the more drastic of the statutory divergencies which have been brought into operation to restore law and order during the present emergency. These fall under three heads – detention, trial procedures, and evidence.

Detention This means the statutory detention without trial of persons suspected of being a danger to the State, for the purpose of protecting the public and securing peace and good order. It is a stringent and distasteful power as it deprives those detained of their liberty without recourse to the ordinary processes of law. The power to detain in Northern Ireland was conferred originally on its Minister of Home Affairs by regulations made under the Civil Authorities (Special Powers) Act (Northern Ireland) 1922. That statute was passed to meet the tide of violence which greeted the establishment of Northern Ireland at a critical time when the Royal Irish Constabulary had ceased to exist and the Royal Ulster Constabulary was only in the course of formation. Its powers of detention were employed then and on subsequent occasions to quell outbreaks of violence and were not operated otherwise. After the present emergency had produced a grave degree of violence the United Kingdom Government opposed the use of detention until August 9, 1971 when the powers authorised by the Act of 1922 and the regulations made under

it were again resorted to. This method of preserving law and order has been used in various foreign and Commonwealth countries, and also in the United Kingdom during each of the World Wars. But it has to be remembered that it is an executive and not a judicial process, and that those detained are not under punishment and must be accommodated and treated according to reasonable standards for unconvicted persons.

Unfortunately, detention in August 1971 got off to a very bad start in several respects. Too many were arrested at the outset with the result that some were for a time without proper accommodation; and, more important, a limited number suspected of having knowledge of subversive activities were interrogated by methods which had recourse to techniques of physical and mental interference that are described in the report of the Compton Committee of November 3, 1971 (Cmnd. 4823) and were quite illegal.

Detention was continued during Direct Rule from Westminster under the Northern Ireland Act of 1922 and its regulations, then under the Detention of Terrorists (Northern Ireland) Order 1972 and after that under the Northern Ireland (Emergency Provisions) Act of 1973 and the Northern Ireland (Emergency Provisions) Amendment Act 1975. It was one of the matters considered by the Gardiner Committee on Measures to Deal with Terrorism in Northern Ireland which reported to the Secretary of State in January 1975 (Cmnd 5847). The Committee took the view that detention could not remain as a long-term policy and could only be tolerated in a democratic society in the most extreme circumstances, but added –

We would like to be able to recommend that the time has come to abolish detention; but the present level of violence, the risks of increased violence, and the difficulty of predicting events even a few months ahead make it impossible for us to put forward a precise recommendation on the timing.... We think that this grave decision can only be made by the Government.

In December 1975 the Secretary of State (Mr Merlyn Rees, MP) informed the House of Commons that he had decided not to continue detention. The enabling legislation remains on the statute book, but the detainees were released and the system has not been resorted to since. What the effect of this has been may never be known. It certainly enlarged a substantial number of implacables and it has not ended terrorism. Perhaps in the long-term it may reduce tensions and make normality easier to re-discover. But however that may be, and speaking quite generally, it would I think, be going too far to say that a clear case has been shown for abandoning detention altogether as a means of restoring law and order when other less obnoxious remedies are not effective. In certain circumstances, and if used carefully and with judgment and in time, it can resolve the practical dilemma of terrorism which is how to restore the position without destroying or causing serious injury to the due process of law as well. One of terrorism's most powerful weapons is the intimidation of witnesses to prevent the conviction and punishment of terrorists by making admissible evidence unavailable. So it has frequently happened that when the security forces have reliable information which, though not admissible in evidence shows clearly that a particular person or body has committed a crime, they cannot prosecute successfully in the ordinary courts. Now if, in such case, a detention order is made the common law may suffer in some degree for a time. But if detention is not available, as a matter of policy or because the power to detain has gone, the Queen's Peace and those it exists to protect may suffer grievously instead.

Whether detention is used or not, this danger of the law's requirements obstructing its own ends during an emergency may be reduced by acceptable alterations in its normal procedures in dealing with terrorist activities. This difficult and important subject was referred by the United Kingdom Government in October 1972 to a Committee presided over by Lord Diplock which reported in December of the same year. Its report (Cmnd 5185) contains an informative analysis of the problem, and a series of recommendations which were in large part given statutory force by the Norther Ireland (Emergency Provisions) Act of 1973 (the 'Diplock Act'). This was passed as a temporary measure but has been renewed and amended from time to time since. For reasons of space I must restrict my comments on it to the matters discussed in the next two sub-headings.

Trial procedures These only affect terrorist offences which are set out in the Fourth Schedule – a list of 'scheduled offences', be it observed, that does not include treason, treason felony or seditious conspiracy. The most notable departure of the Diplock Act from normal practice is contained in section 2(1) which reads: 'A trial on indictment of a scheduled offence shall be conducted by the court without a jury.'

This was based, at any rate in part, on the dangers of intimidation. The change places a heavy burden on the judges who have to try scheduled offences, but this departure from the common law has been generally well received. It also saves time, a point of importance when, as now, the criminal lists are unusually long. The Diplock Act had been in operation for a year when the Gardiner Committee reported. Its general conclusions on this radical divergence appear in the following excerpts from paragraphs 29 and 33 of its Report –

'... the right to a fair trial has been respected and maintained and ... the administration of justice has not suffered. We therefore recommend that subsection 2(1) should stand.' And again – 'We recommend that the courts sitting under section 2 ... should continue to be constituted by a judge sitting alone.'

Evidence at criminal trials Under English Law the admissibility of statements (generally confessions) made by accused persons to police and others have become the subject of highly technical rules, which go back to the days when an accused could not give evidence on his own behalf at his trial, and were founded partly on a series of judicial decisions and partly on what are known as the Judges' Rules – which are really rules of guidance for the police rather than rules of law.

The Diplock Committee considered that the technical requirements and practice as to the admissibility of inculpating statements by the accused were hampering the course of justice in Northern Ireland terrorist cases and came to the conclusion that, as respects terrorist crimes, they should be replaced by the test to be found in Article 3 of the European Convention for the Protection of Human Rights and Fundamental Freedoms. These views led to the enactment of section 6 of the Diplock Act. It provides by subsection (1) that in proceedings for a scheduled offence a statement made by the accused may be given in evidence is so far as relevant to any matter in issue and not excluded in pursuance of subsection (2). And that subsection provides that if, in such proceedings, where the prosecution proposes to put in evidence such a statement, prima facie evidence is adduced to show that the accused was subjected to torture or to inhuman or degrading treatment in order to induce him to make the statement, the court shall exclude the statement unless satisfied by the prosecution that it was not so obtained.

This section was considered at some length by the Gardiner Committee, particularly as to whether on its true construction it ousted the judge's common law discretion to exclude a statement by the accused which, though seemingly admissible in law, might operate unfairly against him. The Committee's conclusion was that the judge's discretion had not been ousted, and this had indeed been the view taken by the judges presiding over the trials of scheduled offences in Northern Ireland. That view has since been maintained, and the construction favoured by the Committee appears to have been generally accepted. As thus read section 6 seems to have been procedurally satisfactory and to have proved compatible with the concept of a fair trial.

Seen in the light of the Reports mentioned, the emergency legislation passed at Westminster has been careful to avoid new solutions which would rend the protective fabric of the common law too widely. But it has undoubtedly increased the number of terrorists being made amenable in open court: and it may now be said with some confidence that the great majority of all sections of the community hope that this process will continue until peace and tranquillity are restored. Much, however, is at stake and it will not be enough to achieve what has been described as 'an acceptable level of violence' and stay there. Terrorism can have no acceptable level. The rule of law, and the good life it makes possible, can only flourish when terrorism and the fear it begets and feeds upon are beaten and disappear.

The Courts The court system of Northern Ireland will in its general features be familiar to the English lawyer. Apart from specific statutory tribunals which fall outside the 'ordinary courts of the land', it consists of three tiers. Starting at the bottom these are – the magistrates' courts, the county courts and the Supreme Court.

Magistrates' Courts Before 1935 these were manned for the most part by lay justices of the peace. Then by the Summary Jurisdiction and Criminal Justice Act of that year the judicial powers and duties of the lay justices were taken away, almost in their entirety, and transferred to a number of resident magistrates, or stipendiaries as they would be called in England. These are appointed

by Her Majesty from barristers or solicitors who have practised for not less than six years. At present there are 17 permanent and four deputy or temporary resident magistrates. The permanent class retire at 70 and are removable only, if appointed before January 1, 1974, upon an address from both Houses of Parliament and, if appointed after that date, by the Lord Chancellor.

The law relating to these courts, their jurisdictions, procedures and practice was consolidated and amended by the Magistrates' Courts Act (Northern Ireland) 1964. Their criminal jurisdiction corresponds so closely to that of the corresponding English courts that I need not detail it. They also have a civil jurisdiction which includes various licensing matters, the making of separation and maintenance orders, affiliation proceedings, ejectments where the rent does not exceed £110 per annum and the recovery of small debts not exceeding £100.

These courts function in over fifty Petty Sessions Districts throughout Northern Ireland. They are conducted by a resident magistrate sitting alone except in certain special cases as, for example, in the juvenile courts which are constituted by one resident magistrate and two lay members one of whom must be a woman.

County Courts These are part of the county court system which obtained in Ireland prior to 1921. Like the English county courts they are statutory in origin, but their statutory basis is quite different. The jurisdiction is organised in a series of local divisions or circuits made up of counties or parts of counties. There are at present ten county court judges, five of whom are normally attached to specific divisions, the remainder being available to sit where required. Appointments to the county court bench are made by Her Majesty from members of the Bar of ten years' standing and practising in Northern Ireland. The title of recorder has not the same meaning as in England, being used to signify the county court judges of the County Boroughs of Belfast and Londonderry.

Until 1935 the county courts exercised only a civil jurisdiction. But the county court judges, sitting with lay justices of the peace, constituted courts of Quarter Sessions and had a criminal jurisdiction in that capacity. Then by the Act of 1935, which, as already noted, abolished most of the judicial functions of lay justices, the business of Quarter Sessions was transferred to the county court judges sitting alone.

The next statute I must mention was also passed at Stormont. It is the County Courts Act (Northern Ireland) 1959. It consolidated and amended much of the previous law and reorganised the whole county court system. It provides for the dividing, already referred to, of Northern Ireland into a series of county court divisions with each served by a county court; and enacts that such courts shall be courts of record and have the powers and jurisdictions which the Act specifies. Part III of this statute declares the general civil jurisdiction of the county courts to be exercisable by the judge sitting alone. Part VI provides for the hearing of appeals from magistrates' courts and other tribunals and Part VII provides for appeals from and cases stated by county courts.

The history of the county courts in Northern Ireland shows a gradual increase in the monetary limits of their jurisdiction which marks a response (not always very prompt) to the decline in the value of money; and it also shows a trend towards the adoption of High Court procedures which makes the county court less a poor man's court than it was. Costs are generally awarded according to a scale, and both solicitors and counsel have a right of audience. But there are few interlocutories and few pleadings and it can still be said that without the county courts the burden of civil actions in the High Court would be much heavier and harder to dispose of with despatch.

The principal, and probably the oldest form of litigation in the county court, is for the recovery of money claims due under contract or tort; but other jurisdictions have been added and, though the county court jurisdiction of today does not include bankruptcy or lunacy proceedings or matrimonial causes or disputes as to tolls, fairs, markets or franchises, it extends over much of what is within the ambit of the High Court, but almost invariably subject to monetary limits, such as to take but a few examples: ordinary money claims, which in 1920 were limited to £50, may now be brought up to £1,000. The limit for recovery of rent is also £1,000. Suits for the recovery of land or in which the title to land comes in question are subject, in general, to the annual value of the land not exceeding £75. Orders for the administration of estates or trusts or by way of relief in respect of fraud or mistake or for the construction of documents may be sought if the property in question other than land does not exceed £2,000 in amount or value and, so far as it consists of land, is not more than £75 in annual value.

Decrees made in the exercise of the civil jurisdiction are normally appealable by way of re-hearing, with the witnesses called and examined as at first instance. This is an unusual procedure but it has been in vogue for many years, has proved acceptable and is cheaper and probably better than if a transcript were used.

The Supreme Court Under the 1920 Act the Parliament at Stormont and the Northern Ireland Government were given power respectively to legislate for and to administer the county courts and what are now the magistrates' courts. But, while Stormont was enabled from time to time to confer specific jurisdictions on the Supreme Court, the latter has always constituted a reserved service with its legislative requirements dealt with at Westminster and its administration in the hands of the British Government. This system of dual administration is less obvious since Direct Rule was introduced and it has worked reasonably well; but it means that the court staffs are not fully interchangeable, and that a greater degree of integration is more difficult to achieve.

The Supreme Court of Judicature Act (Ireland) 1877 was based on the English Judicature Act of 1873 and caused a similar revolution in the organisation of the former superior courts, in the concurrent administration of the rules of law and equity and in the framing of a uniform code of procedure. The Supreme Court of

Northern Ireland was established by sections 38 and 40 of the Act of 1920, an operation accomplished by taking the Supreme Court in Dublin, as constituted under the Act of 1877, and cutting it down to fit the needs of a smaller population and a diminished territory. As so established it comprised a High Court and a Court of Appeal and its judges were five in number, the High Court consisting of the Lord Chief Justice as president and two puisne judges, and the Court of Appeal of the Lord Chief Justice as president and two Lords Justices of Appeal. As work got heavier, both before and during the emergency, the judicial strength has been increased.

Under the rules of court the High Court sits in two divisions, Chancery and Queen's Bench, with the latter also dealing with probate, matrimonial and admiralty matters in addition to its ordinary common law lists and its business on the Crown side, such as applications for orders of prohibition, *mandamus* and *certiorari* or writs of *habeas corpus*. There is little admiralty work. The amount of matrimonial business is growing and accident cases arising on the highways and in the factories form the bulk of the common law claims. Most of these accident suits that go to a hearing are dealt with by a judge and a jury of seven. Juries are popular for this class of litigation and can be sought almost as of right. The number of jurors was changed from 12 to 7 in 1962 in an effort to reduce the burden of jury service.

And now, before I say more on the subject of jurisdiction, it will be convenient to mention a matter which still holds a fascination for many – the matter of judicial dress.

The robes worn by county court judges are simple – a black gown with a bench wig and bands. The judicial dress of the judges of the Supreme Court is similar to that worn by their counterparts in England, with a few minor variations. The ceremonial attire for the Chancery judge, for instance, is not scarlet and ermine, but, following what used to be the Dublin practice, a gold and black robe. Hats are not worn or carried and, so far as I can ascertain, the ermine mantle has never been part of the judicial wardrobe. Bands and bench wigs are part of the working dress, but on state occasions the Lord Chief Justice wears scarlet and ermine with a chain of SS, a full-bottomed wig and a lace cravat. The full dress for Lords Justices is a gold and black robe with lace cravat and full-bottomed wig. Another difference that may be noted in passing is that the judges are not provided with personal clerks as in England; each has a tipstaff or personal servant who also acts as a court usher on circuit.

The Chancery business is normally discharged by one of the puisne judges who is assigned for the purpose by the Lord Chief Justice and designated officially as the Chancery judge. His jurisdiction is very similar to that of the Chancery Division in England; and he also takes his turn at the transaction of criminal business, and at helping with the hearing of common law and statutory claims. This variation of his judicial duties applies to the other judges of the Supreme Court as well, and is particularly useful in a small jurisdiction in order to meet the requirements of the work in hand.

The assize circuits are ordinarily manned by two judges of the Supreme Court. They are part of the High Court, and go out each spring and autumn. There is also a winter assize held in January each year, now in one county, now in another. This assize is generally taken by one Supreme Court judge and deals entirely with criminal matters.

The Court of Appeal functions very much in the same way as the Court of Appeal in England. In addition to hearing appeals from the High Court it may also, in certain cases, review decisions of the county courts and magistrates' courts, usually brought before it by way of case stated.

I must now mention two jurisdictions which, so far, are not part of the Supreme Court though intimately connected with it and staffed by its officers. First there is what used to be called the lunacy jurisdiction, partly prerogative and partly statutory in character. The prerogative element stems from the function and duty of the Sovereign as *parens patriae* to succour and protect the weak. In Northern Ireland this function is now delegated, by an instrument signed by the Sovereign and known as the Sign Manual, to the Lord Chief Justice and such other members of the Supreme Court as are named therein. The statutory element in the jurisdiction goes back to an Act of 1871 and confers certain powers on the head of the judiciary as 'the person entrusted as aforesaid' by virtue of the Sign Manual. This strange jurisdiction has become outmoded in several respects, but it works well and can be brought into operation quickly.

The other separate jurisdiction is that of the Court of Criminal Appeal for Northern Ireland. This was first established in 1930 to take the place of the old Court of Crown Cases Reserved, and was later modernised to accord more closely with the corresponding Court in England, by the Criminal Appeal (Northern Ireland) Act of 1968.

An appeal lies from the Court of Appeal, the Court of Criminal Appeal and, in some instances, from the High Court to the House of Lords, subject to obtaining leave to appeal and, in criminal cases, a certificate of general public importance, on lines similar to those now obtaining in England.

The foregoing description of the courts gives a broad picture of them as they were towards the close of 1978 and, in many respects, as they have been for a considerable period. But although the Irish Judicature Act of 1877 in its application to Northern Ireland has stood many of the tests of time, the need for modernisation has been felt increasingly over the years and has led to several investigations and reports. Of these mention should be made of two. The most comprehensive was that of a Committee appointed by the then Lord Chancellor of Great Britain, Lord Gardiner, which reported in December 1969 and made 97 recommendations, including one for a new Judicature Act for Northern Ireland. The other was that of a Committee, presided over by Lord Justice Jones, which reported in 1974 and recommended that a Crown Court for the hearing of all criminal trials on indictment throughout Northern Ireland, should be established on lines similar to those introduced in England and Wales by the Courts Act 1971.

The result of these and other investigations has been the passage into law on June 30, 1978 of the Judicature (Northern Ireland) Act (the 'Act of 1978'). Under s 123(2) it comes into force on such day as the Lord Chancellor may by order appoint and different days may be appointed for different provisions. Some relatively minor provisions are already in force but the main provisions including most of the more important changes are not expected to be brought into operation before the Spring of 1979. The Act of 1978 is a lengthy and comprehensive measure and a detailed summary would be out of place here. But, though the existing system will not be altered in any very fundamental sense, various features of it will undoubtedly be modified or disappear in the near future and a brief outline of some of these, with particular reference to several of its present features which have already been mentioned, will enable the reader to understand the situation as it should develop within the next year. Without being exhaustive I would enumerate the principal changes thus:

(i) The High Court is to consist of the Lord Chief Justice as President and not more than six puisne judges; and the Court of Appeal is to consist of the Lord Chief Justice as president and three Lords Justices of Appeal.

(ii) A Crown Court shall be established to deal with criminal cases on indictment whose jurisdiction shall be exercisable by the Lord Chief Justice as president, any judge of the High Court or the Court of Appeal or any county court judge.

(iii) The jurisdiction of the county courts to try indictable cases shall be abolished.

(iv) All courts of assize shall be abolished.

(v) There shall be three instead of two divisions of the High Court, namely, the Chancery Division, the Queen's Bench Division and the Family Division.

(vi) The jurisdiction in relation to persons under disability shall be vested in the High Court, including the jurisdiction heretofore exercisable under the Sign Manual.

(vii) The Court of Appeal shall exercise all the Jurisdiction of the former Court of Criminal Appeal in Northern Ireland.

(viii) The three tiers of judicature shall all be administered by the Lord Chancellor and his Department and the Lord Chancellor shall have the various powers and discretions vested in him in relation thereto by the Act of 1978.

(ix) There shall be a unified and distinct civil service, the Northern Ireland Court Service, to serve and facilitate the business of the Supreme Court, the county courts, the magistrates' courts and the coroners' courts.

I cannot pass from the courts without mention of the Judgments (Enforcement) Act (Northern Ireland) which was passed at Stormont in 1969 in an effort to improve the enforcement of civil judgments pronounced in all three tiers of the court system. For long the methods of enforcement by the under-sheriffs and their bailiffs had been unsatisfactory, and the Act of 1969 followed upon the Report of a Working Party under the Chairmanship of the Taxing Master of the Supreme Court which was published in 1965. The policy adopted by the Act was to abolish the existing machinery and to start afresh with the powers of enforcement vested in a new body, the Enforcement of Judgments Office, administered by the then Ministry of Home Affairs of Northern Ireland and with its judicial officers designated by the Lord Chief Justice, generally from senior officers of the Supreme Court.

The Office was empowered to make such enforcement orders as might be appropriate in any particular case for applying a debtor's assets in satisfaction of his judgment debt. It has power to make fourteen different kinds of enforcement orders. Of these most are counterparts of the old writs of execution and the several remedies formerly obtainable from the courts (eg attachment of debts) but at least three are entirely new; the most common and effective being the attachment of earnings order.

The Office procedures are based on the principle that enforcement can only be efficient if the means of the debtor are known to the Office. To this end enforcement officers are empowered to interview debtors as to their means and the Office itself can compel the attendance of debtors for examination.

The ancillary powers of the Office include jurisdiction to stay enforcement in appropriate cases and the power to grant a certificate of unenforceability which constitutes an act of bankruptcy.

The Enforcement Office has worked well and has already proved itself much more effective than the system it replaced.

The Legal Professions The law has long been served throughout Ireland by two professions – the solicitors' profession and that of the Bar; and this is still the position in each of the jurisdictions which came into existence on October 1, 1921 under the Act of 1920. Those then entitled to practise as members of either profession in Ireland were accorded liberty to continue doing so and to have a right of audience in the new Supreme Courts of both North and South; but others, qualifying later, had to comply with the separate requirements laid down by the law of each of the new jurisdictions.

On its establishment the Supreme Court of Northern Ireland had to be accommodated in the County Courthouse, Crumlin Road, Belfast, while permanent premises were built for it on a more central site between May Street and Chichester Street, just west of the River Lagan. In 1933 the Supreme Court moved to a fine Portland stone structure of four storeys which had been erected on this site. The ground floor is occupied by the five main courts, consultation rooms, some of the court offices, the Bar Library and its robing rooms – all opening off a central hall of distinguished proportions. The first floor accommodates most of the remaining court offices and also the library and offices of the Incorporated Law Society. The second and third floors are occupied by the offices of the Director of Public Prosecutions and of the Attorney-General and also by various offices of executive departments. This conjoint user of the site by both the judicial and executive branches of government was not the original intention and came about because of the economic pressures then prevailing. But it was not a popular change of plan and, for many years after, the rule was that the interior doors connecting these two realms should be kept carefully locked!

The functions of and the relationship between the two legal professions are very much the same as in England and it must therefore suffice if I describe them briefly under the headings which now follow –

The Solicitors of Northern Ireland By a Royal Charter granted in 1922 an existing body called the Northern Law Society and certain other solicitors were incorporated under the name of The Incorporated Law Society of Northern Ireland. This Society now exercises, as respects the solicitors of Northern Ireland, functions similar to those formerly exercised by the Incorporated Law Society of Ireland. Its statutory powers were subsequently increased by various Acts of the Parliament at Stormont and are now contained in an Order in Council made on April 12, 1976. (1976 No 582 (NI12)). The Society acts through an elected council; controls the educational and other qualifications for admission to the profession; and is empowered to regulate the professional practice, conduct and discipline of solicitors. The number of solicitors entitled to practise in Northern Ireland in 1977 was 656; and it is now customary for new solicitors to be admitted formally by the Lord Chief Justice at a ceremony in one of the principal courts.

In addition to its other duties the Society like its English counterpart also administers the Legal Aid and Advice Scheme which was initiated by an Act passed at Stormont in 1965.

The Bar of Northern Ireland Before October 1921 the Irish Bar had been regulated and controlled by the Benchers of King's Inns, Dublin, and for some years after that a Northern Committee of the Benchers took charge of matters affecting students for the Bar of Northern Ireland. By 1926, however, this arrangement had run into difficulties and early in that year, at a meeting of the Bench and Bar of Northern Ireland, the Inn of Court of Northern Ireland was established and assumed functions and powers as respects Northern Ireland similar to those of King's Inns. In 1927 a Royal Licence conferred the style of 'The Honorable Society of the Inn of Court of Northern Ireland'; but the new Inn was soon faced with several serious problems. It had no premises, few books and no readily available means of providing for the education and examination of its students. These difficulties have been surmounted sufficiently to enable the new Inn to discharge its functions, albeit in an unostentatious way. The Judges' Assembly Room in the New Supreme Court building – a room of many uses – has given the benchers a meeting place, and a long gallery overlooking the central hall has been converted and furnished to provide accommodation for members of the Inn and a place where its property (mostly pictures and documents) may be kept on view.

Life as a barrister in Northern Ireland is markedly different in some respects from that at the English Bar. There is no chambers system. Following the usage in Dublin and, I understand in Edinburgh also, there is a Bar Library in the precincts of the Supreme Court where the barrister works when not in court. Another difference is that there is much less specialisation than at the English Bar. Work for a comparatively small number lies more in one branch of the law than another, but by and large the total volume of work allows few of those who have to make a living the chance of confining themselves strictly to a single field.

A further difference lies in the fact that, as was and is the case in Dublin, the barrister's clerk is unknown. This lack of someone to fix fees and arrange the day's engagements seems, more than anything else, to surprise members of the English Bar. But the Library system affords less use for clerks, and their absence from the scene causes little difficulty or embarrassment. That system, moreover, has special advantages for a small jurisdiction. It promotes a camaraderie which helps and does not hinder the administration of justice, and novices of quality probably get better known and find their feet sooner than they would in chambers.

Junior barristers, at any rate in their early years, must be prepared to appear before any court or tribunal in which they have a right of audience, and to do any class of work; but the practice of Her Majesty's counsel, who constitute the Inner Bar, is generally more closely confined to the Supreme Court and the courts of Assize. Admission from the Junior or Outer Bar to the Inner Bar is granted by warrant on the recommendation of the Lord Chief Justice and the consequences of taking this step – which is irrevocable – are much the same as in England.

The volume of work has shown a marked increase during the last 25 years, though this has been on the common law rather than on the Chancery side, and patent suits and commercial cases are still few and far between. But the biggest increase of recent years has been in criminal proceedings. This has arisen almost entirely from the emergency, for before that the incidence of crime in Northern Ireland was comparatively low notwithstanding much unemployment, particularly in the North-West.

Recruitment for the Bar did not at first keep pace with the rising tide of litigation and it was not until 1969 that the yearly intake of students for the first time exceeded a score. Since then numbers have increased rapidly, but for a time too many briefs were chasing too few counsel. Now (December 1978) the active Bar consists of 25 Queen's Counsel and 134 Junior counsel; these are all barristers practising in the jurisdiction and the numbers therefore exclude those who have been called but who normally practise elsewhere or not at all. This comparatively sudden influx has raised two problems. The first, which time alone can cure, lies in the lack of experience of many junior counsel, for of the 134 practising juniors 99 are of five years' standing or less. The other problem also affects the junior Bar. The Library and its adjoining rooms only provide desks for 108 barristers which means that at present 51 barristers are without places of their own. Though there is seldom a full muster of 'seated' barristers in the Library at any given time this problem may be worse before it is better: and better it ought to be if the Library is to function at its best.

The General Council of the Bar of Northern Ireland oversees a wide range of matters, including professional conduct, access to the Bar Library and its amenities, and relations between the Inner and Outer Bar. It consists of a Chairman, Vice-Chairman, nine elected members and two co-opted. The Attorney-General for Northern Ireland is an *ex officio* member of the Council. The Chairman is elected by the Bar by secret ballot and holds office for two years. The Vice-Chairman is elected annually by the Council. Of the nine elected members three more are from the Inner Bar and six from the Outer Bar and all are elected by the Bar by secret ballot.

An arrangement has long been in existence with the English Bar for reciprocity of call in respect of those who have been in practice for three years and are of good standing. A similar arrangement which was made in 1976 now operates between members of King's Inns, Dublin, and the Inn of Court of Northern Ireland.

Two further matters call for mention on account of their importance for both legal professions. The first followed a Report presented to the Parliament of

Northern Ireland in April 1971 by a Working Party on Public Prosecutions (Cmd 554). In December of that year a Bill to give effect to its main recommendations was introduced at Stormont but had not completed its Parliamentary course when Direct Rule intervened. It then, in its substance, was made law by an Order in Council dated March 30, 1972. This Order abolished the offices and functions of the Crown solicitors throughout the jurisdiction and made provision for the appointment of a Director and Deputy Director of Public Prosecutions with powers to organise and conduct public prosecutions throughout Northern Ireland, but subject always to the superintendence and directions of the Attorney-General and to the qualifications on appointment for the Director and Deputy Director being not less than ten years and seven years' practice respectively at the Bar of Northern Ireland or as a solicitor of its Supreme Court. These officers were appointed shortly after the Order was made, the Director from the Inner Bar and his deputy from the solicitors' profession; and the reorganisation throughout all areas was accomplished shortly thereafter.

The second of the matters mentioned was the appointment of the Attorney-General for England and Wales as the Attorney-General for Northern Ireland. This was first done by the Northern Ireland (Temporary Provisions) Act 1972 and was later re-enacted by section 10 of the Northern Ireland Constitution Act 1973. While responsibility for law and order remains at Westminster this provision is understandable as the Attorney-General is available there to answer for the discharge of his Northern Ireland duties as a Member of Parliament. But no matter how well those duties are discharged, difficulties may arise if this situation lasts indefinitely; most independent Bars are the better for a resident leader of high status, such as a Law officer, and there seems no reason to think that, as the years pass, the Bar of Northern Ireland will prove itself exceptional in this respect.

Education and Training Changing circumstances have brought the legal education and training of those seeking admission to both professions under close scrutiny during the last decade and led to the setting-up of two important Committees. The first, under the chairmanship of Mr Justice Ormrod (as he then was), was appointed by the Lord Chancellor in relation to England and Wales at the end of 1967 and reported in January 1971. The second, under the chairmanship of Sir Arthur Armitage, Vice-Chancellor of Manchester University (who had served on the Ormrod Committee), was appointed in relation to Northern Ireland by its Minister of Education in February 1972, and reported in May 1973.

While each of Northern Ireland's professional bodies had for years required its students to possess an approved degree (not necessarily a law degree) of a recognised university before admission or call, increasing difficulties had arisen for the solicitors' profession in providing an effective training by means of the three years' apprenticeship which was then obligatory; and the benchers had had to end their educational arrangements with the Inns of Court in London on account of

changes made there after the Ormrod Report which could not well be applied to students residing in Northern Ireland. And over and above all this two other matters had to be taken into account. Public opinion was strengthening in favour of the view that the student on attaining professional status as a lawyer – the solicitor on admission and the barrister on call – should, in addition to the essential requirement of an academic knowledge

of the principles of law, possess a fair working knowledge of the practical procedures and techniques of his vocation, in other words, of the law in action. And, secondly, trained teachers of law and its practice were scarce and it was recognised that more could be done, and better done, if the two branches of the profession in this small jurisdiction made more use of the same teachers. However different the functions of each

branch might be, there was much in common to be learnt and mastered at student level.

The main recommendations of the Armitage Committee were accepted by the Government, the Queen's University of Belfast and the two legal professions; and the central feature of its Report, the Institute of Professional Legal Studies, was established in December 1975 as a part of the Queen's University.

Under the new scheme each professional body retains its present powers respecting the admission of students. Before qualification, whether as a solicitor or barrister, the student must ordinarily possess an approved degree of a recognised university. If this is a law degree covering certain 'core' subjects it will normally satisfy the academic requirements of the profession concerned. But if the student's degree is not of this kind, the student to gain his academic qualifications will generally have to take and pass at the Institute a two-year course designed for this purpose.

The student seeking to become a solicitor will no longer have to serve an apprenticeship, but he and the Bar student will have to take and pass at the Institute one year's vocational course of the kind mentioned earlier. If the student qualifies in this vocational training and has also got his academic qualification he is then ready to be admitted or called as the case may be: but the tenor of the Report indicates that ordinarily this will not be the end of his professional preparation for practice, and that the new solicitor on admission will have to act as an assistant solicitor for three years before practising alone or in partnership, while the new barrister will have to spend a specific period in pupillage before taking work on his own account.

The Report also envisages a third stage in legal education for which it considers the Institute should be responsible. This is called 'continuing education' and would provide, on a self-financing basis, for refresher courses, lectures on new subjects, information on recent research, etc.

The Report recommends further 'an adequate system of grants to ensure that the profession is open to all.' It is understood that the expense of the scheme to the Queen's University, including such grants, will be re-imbursed by the Government as part of its annual grant to that university, and that entitled students will be eligible for awards or bursaries while at the Institute. This agreed scheme became operative in October 1977.

As I write, the first vocational course has started and the problems which attend every new development of this kind – such as the provision of transitional arrangements – are under close study. My conclusion is that the Institute should get beyond such teething troubles as it may experience and prove itself a growing source of strength not only for the entire legal profession but for the entire community as well. This optimism springs from the co-operative spirit already shown by the bodies and individuals most concerned; and, no less, from the resolve and tenacity of purpose which the lawyers of Northern Ireland have manifested in face of the difficulties and distractions of a grave and lengthy emergency.

7
ENGLISH LAW ABROAD

Rival representatives of law and order at Shanghai 1900. The most prominent figures in the procession are the executioner and his deputy. The explanation of the presence of an English policeman is that the procession was passing the British settlement where in 1900 the law was administered entirely by the British

English Law and the Commonwealth

S W Magnus QC

The Spread of English Law 'I have often criticised Britain in the past', said President Kaunda of Zambia to me, 'and shall no doubt criticise them again in the future. But there is one thing that I will always be grateful to Britain for – the institutions they have given us; the courts and judiciary, their system of law and the civil service.' It was during one of our frequent talks that he made this observation. I was, at the time, first a Member of Parliament in the Zambian National Assembly (which was a direct derivation, both in form and procedure, from the Mother of Parliaments at Westminster), and latterly a member of the judiciary as puisne judge of the High Court and later as Justice of Appeal in the Court of Appeal, both modelled on the English courts. And, indeed, the influence of English law and the British system of government on the former colonies and dependencies of what used to be called the British Empire is profound, and still persists after most of these territories have achieved independence as states of their own within what is now known as the Commonwealth, even where, as in some cases, countries have continued their independent existence outside the Commonwealth. An outstanding example is, of course, the United States of America the basis of whose system of law is the common law of England. In more recent times, there have been the examples of Burma and Pakistan, which seceded from the Commonwealth and Israel, which was never in the Commonwealth, but where, in all cases provision was made for the continuation of the legal system, at least for a transitional period.

How English law was extended to these countries has been best summed up in *Halsbury's Laws of England* (5 Halsbury's Laws (3rd edn), pp 691, 692) as follows:

The extent to which English law is introduced into any particular territory varies according to the manner in which that territory is acquired. There is an essential difference between a possession acquired by conquest or cession, in which an established system of laws of European type exists, and one acquired by the settlement of British subjects in territory which is unoccupied, or occupied only by uncivilised inhabitants, and therefore without an established legal system. In a third type of case a possession may have been acquired by conquest, and at the time of annexation there may have existed a system of law which, though adapted to the requirements of the native population, was insufficient for and unsuitable to the requirements of the European settlers.

An example of the first type of case is that of the former Union of South Africa, now, as the Republic of

South Africa, an independent republic outside the Commonwealth. The system of law established there by the original Afrikaner settlers was that of Roman-Dutch law brought by those settlers from the Netherlands, where they originated. That system was extended to Southern Rhodesia, Bechuanaland (now Botswana) and the High Commission Territories, all of which were then administered from South Africa, and the position now is that, in Africa, the basic system in that part of the Continent south of the Zambezi River is Roman-Dutch law, with a parallel system, as in the rest of Africa, of native customary law for the indigenous inhabitants.

This last-mentioned system exemplifies to some extent the third type of case cited by *Halsbury,* and in most of the former African colonies and dependencies, as well as in most of the former colonies and dependencies elsewhere, native customary law was preserved, as far as it was consistent with the English system superimposed in those territories and was not opposed to public policy or natural justice, for the benefit of the indigenous inhabitants.

Roman-Dutch law was applied in Ceylon (now Sri-Lanka), but English legal doctrines also had a powerful influence, as well as that system of customary law called Tesawalamai, in the case of Hindus in the north, and Islamic law in the case of personal relationships for the Muslim inhabitants. Before 1917, British Guiana (now Guyana) had Roman-Dutch law applied, but this was abrogated by the Civil Law of British Guiana Ordinance 1916, and English common law applied. The Code Napoleon was also once applied to Mauritius and the Seychelles and to the Province of Quebec. Spanish law formerly prevailed in Trinidad and Gibraltar.

In the main, however, the law of England was applied in one way or another in most of the former colonies and dependencies. In general, the law so applied was the common law of England and the statute law existing at the time of its application. English statutes enacted subsequent to that time did not apply unless they were expressly so applied.

The Zambian Experience In Northern Rhodesia (now Zambia), the Northern Rhodesia Order in Council 1924 (SR and 0 1924 No 324) provided that the law of England was to apply save so far as it was inapplicable, but that no Act of Parliament passed after August 16, 1911 was to apply unless by express enactment (*ibid,* Art

27 (2)). Special provision was made, as was essentially made in most of the other African territories, for the indigenous population so that in all civil cases and in minor criminal cases to which natives were parties the courts were to be guided by native law so far as it was applicable and was not repugnant to justice and morality or inconsistent with any positive legislation (*ibid* Art 36).

The Code Although the general principle was the application of English law as at the relevant date, subject to the restrictions and modifications referred to, in practice the law was codified in Ordinances, originally promulgated by the Government, but later enacted by the legislature of the territory, usually known as the Legislative Council. Using Northern Rhodesia again as an example (as being the former colonial territory most familiar to me, but a fairly typical example), these Ordinances were contained in a code known as the Laws of Northern Rhodesia, which continued after independence as the Laws of Zambia, but side by side (untypically in this case) with the former legislation of the Federation of Rhodesia and Nyasaland, of which Northern Rhodesia was part between 1953 and 1963, so far as it still remained in force after the dissolution of the Federation at the end of 1963. These Ordinances were, on the whole, simply codifications of English law on their particular subject. Thus, there was a Penal Code which largely repeated English criminal law as it was at the time of the enactment of that Code with minor variations to adapt it to local conditions. These adaptations sometimes took curious forms. For example, the Penal Code made it an offence to maim a camel, although it is unlikely that a camel had ever set foot in Northern Rhodesia.

Parallel with the Penal Code was a Criminal Procedure Code which governed the procedure of the criminal courts on the lines of procedure of criminal courts in England, adapted, as we shall see, to the needs of the territory. On the civil side, there was a High Court Ordinance and a Subordinate Courts Ordinance, dealing, as their names imply, with the procedure of the High Court and the subordinate courts, with which I shall deal presently.

Ordinances also made individual provision for various matters. Thus the Companies Ordinance dealt with company law, which was still largely based on the Companies (Consolidation) Act 1908, being the last British Companies Act to be passed before August 16, 1911. The Marriage Ordinance provided for marriages between Europeans and such other residents as chose to avail themselves of its terms, which were similar to those of the Marriage Act in England and made similar provision for the registration of marriages. Indigenous persons could, however, marry under their own tribal laws, which permitted, in most cases, polygamous marriages. Once, however, an indigenous person had chosen to marry under the Marriage Ordinance, that marriage became monogamous and a party thereto could not remarry without previously divorcing his or her marriage partner, as one Zambian cabinet minister found to his cost, when he was convicted of bigamy and sentenced to two years' imprisonment. Divorce, incidentally, was governed by the law relating to matrimonial causes for the time being applied in England. This was English post–1911 legislation expressly applied.

Except for indigenous persons, where tribal customary law prevailed, land law was based largely on the pre–1925 property legislation in England, again, however, adapted to local conditions. Except for a short period, when legislation was introduced to provide for freehold tenure, land could only be acquired on 99–year leases, except for agricultural land, which could be held on 999–year leases. Freehold tenure was abolished by the Government of the Republic of Zambia soon after independence.

Courts and the Judiciary The courts consisted of a High Court, subordinate courts and native courts. In my time in Northern Rhodesia and Zambia, the High Court sat in the capital, Lusaka, and in the Copperbelt at Ndola, while judges went at set times on circuit to other centres of population, where they held assizes, exactly in the

Below: The Speaker and Members of the National Assembly of Zambia outside the old Parliament building in about 1966

Bottom: Members of the High Court of Zambia with President Kaunda outside State House in 1968. Mr Justice Magnus is second from the right

same way as in England before 1972 and the Courts Act. The High Court consisted of a Chief Justice and six puisne judges, of whom two were resident in Ndola. At one time, appeals from the High Court were heard at Pretoria in South Africa, but after the Federation of Rhodesia and Nyasaland was created in 1953, a Federal Supreme Court was set up in Salisbury for the hearing of appeals from the High Court of all the three constituent territories which made up the Federation. Appeal from that Court lay to the Privy Council.

With the dissolution of the Federation, the Federal Supreme Court also came to an end and Zambia set up a Court of Appeal, which originally consisted of the Chief Justice, a Justice of Appeal and any of the puisne judges whose judgment was not the subject of appeal. A separate Court of Appeal was set up in 1971, consisting of a President, the Chief Justice and two Justices of Appeal. Latterly, it has been set up as a Supreme Court, with an original and an appeals division but on the same lines as previously, the only difference being one of nomenclature. Appeal to the Court of Appeal was final, appeals to the Privy Council having been abolished, in accordance with the prevailing trend in Commonwealth countries.

The judges of the High Court were appointed in origin from the Colonial Legal Service but are now appointed by the President on the recommendation of an independent Judicial Service Commission. They have all the powers and jurisdiction of a High Court judge in England, but, unlike their counterparts in England, who tend to specialise in one of the three divisions of the High Court, a High Court judge in Zambia has to deal with all branches of law, so that I would find myself in one day with, say, a petition to wind up a company in the morning, followed by one to wind up a marriage later on and with a criminal case in the afternoon. Or I might be taking a criminal list one week and find myself dealing with an intricate Chancery action the following week, followed, perhaps, by an action for breach of contract the week after that. Occasionally, one would find oneself faced with a constitutional problem which would not arise in England, which has no written constitution and Parliament is supreme, such as the time when I made an order of *mandamus* to the Speaker of the National Assembly to comply with a constitutional requirement arising out of a member of the opposition crossing the floor of the House to join the Government majority party. I was faced with the problem which might arise if the Speaker refused to comply, when I would have had no option but to commit him for contempt. Fortunately, at the last moment, the Speaker did as I told him!

The subordinate courts were a cross between English magistrates' courts and the county court and had both criminal and civil jurisdiction. The limit of the criminal jurisdiction was roughly the same as that of the magistrates' courts and that of civil jurisdiction similar to that of the county courts. They were presided over by resident magistrates, originally appointed from the Colonial Legal Service, but latterly on the recommendation of the Judicial Service Commission. Only magistrates of the first class had the full jurisdiction, magistrates of the second and third class having a more limited jurisdiction, both in civil and criminal cases. High Court judges had a supervisory jurisdiction over every subordinate court and could review any decision and vary the sentence. An appeal lay from the subordinate court to the High Court and thence to the Court of Appeal.

There was, and still is, as I have already indicated, a third system of courts, the urban or native courts. These are a development of the chiefs' courts and are presided over by tribal magistrates who are experts on their own tribal law. There are 73 district tribes in Zambia and each has its own language and its own system of law. The jursidiction of these courts is confined to cases, both civil and criminal, where indigenous persons are concerned and the criminal jurisdiction is limited. Appeal lies to a subordinate court and thence to the High Court, but when such an appeal comes before such a court, the magistrate or the judge concerned sits with native assessors, who give him the benefit of their expert knowledge on the law concerned.

Influence of English Law It is interesting to note that the general scheme of law and administration in Zambia continues to be based on the United Kingdom pattern which prevailed before independence. In fact, the Zambia Independence Act 1964 expressly provided that:

Subject to the following provisions of this Act, on and after the appointed day all laws which, whether being a rule of law or a provision of an Act of Parliament or of any other enactment or instrument whatsoever, is in force on that day or has been passed or made before that day and comes into force thereafter, shall, unless and until provision to be contrary is made by Parliament or some other authority having power in that behalf, have the same operation in relation to Zambia, and persons and things belonging to or connected with Zambia, as it would have apart from this subsection if on the appointed day Northern Rhodesia had been renamed Zambia but there had been no change in its status.

Of course, the Zambian National Assembly continued to legislate for its own purposes, as had the Legislative Assembly and Legislative Council before it, but, during the time that I was concerned in the administration of justice in Zambia (until the middle of 1971), that administration had, and continued to have, a strong flavour of English law and, despite constitutional changes that have since occurred, I understand it still continues to have that flavour.

The foregoing is but a brief survey of the subject which does not profess to give more than a superficial sketch and is intended to indicate the very great extent to which the law of England has influenced the law and practice in countries of the Commonwealth. As more and more of these countries achieve independence, there is a tendency in each of these countries to adopt more specialist legislation in conformity with the special need of the country concerned or in line with policies which a particular government may seek to follow, and, to that extent, their legal system may diverge from that of the mother country. There is, however, little sign that they intend to divorce themselves entirely from the heritage which we have handed down, and the English common law is likely to continue as the basis and foundation of their systems.

Below: The High Court of Nigeria where, as the accompanying pictures demonstrate, the influence of English Legal administration is evident

Bottom: A barrister and judges of the Nigerian High Court wear traditional wigs and robes

The Chief Justice of the Federal Supreme Court of
Nigeria, Sir Adetokunboh Ademola presides over a
one week session of the Court holding in Enugu
Below: Sir Adetokunboh inspects a guard of honour
Bottom: The judges take the salute in front of the
court building

171

A facsimile of the Constitution of the United States of America; "We the people of the United States, in order to form a more perfect Union, establish Justice, insure domestic tranquility, provide for the common defence, promote the general welfare and secure the Blessings of Liberty to ourselves and our Posterity do ordain and establish this Constitution for the United States of America"

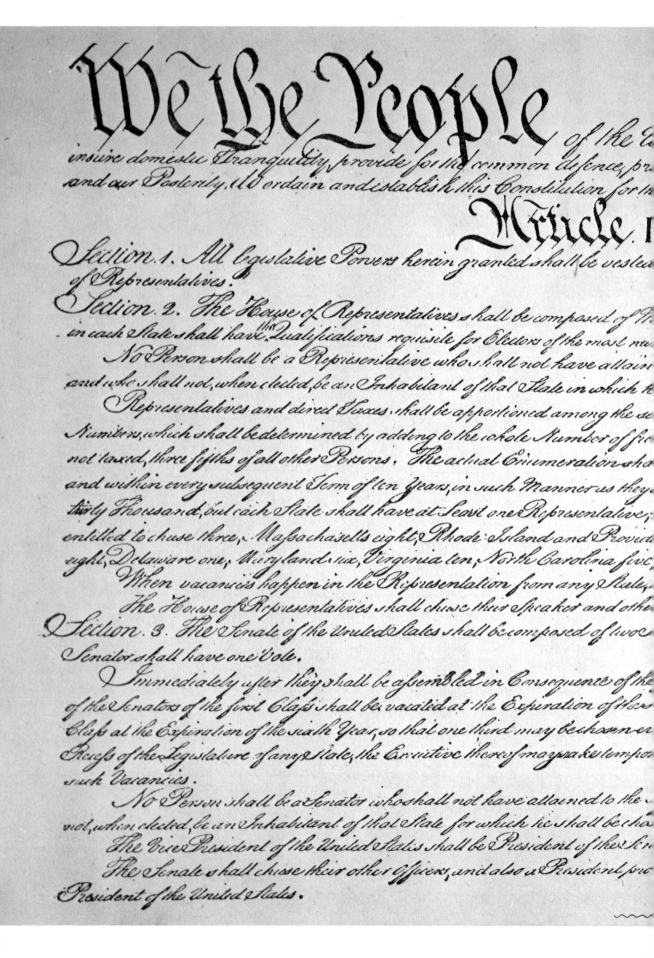

English and American Law

Professor Harry W Jones

States, in Order to form a more perfect Union; establish Justice;
general Welfare, and secure the Blessings of Liberty to ourselves
States of America.

gress of the United States, which shall consist of a Senate and House

hosen every second Year by the People of the several States, and the Electors
ranch of the State Legislature.
Age of twenty five Years, and been seven Years a Citizen of the United States,
chosen.
les which may be included within this Union, according to their respective
including those bound to Service for a Term of Years, and excluding Indians
e within three Years after the first Meeting of the Congress of the United States,
Law direct. The Number of Representatives shall not exceed one for every
l such enumeration shall be made, the State of New Hampshire shall be
tations one, Connecticut five, New York six, New Jersey four, Pennsylvania
Carolina five, and Georgia three.
ive Authority thereof shall issue Writs of Election to fill such Vacancies.
and shall have the sole Power of Impeachment.
on each State, chosen by the Legislature thereof, for six Years, and each

ition; they shall be divided as equally as may be into three Classes. The Seats
r, of the second Class at the Expiration of the fourth Year, and of the third
d Year; and if Vacancies happen by Resignation, or otherwise, during the
intments until the next Meeting of the Legislature, which shall then fill

ty Years, and been nine Years a Citizen of the United States, and who shall

all have no Vote, unless they be equally divided.
in the Absence of the Vice President, or when he shall exercise the Office of

Below: The building of the Supreme Court, Washington, DC

Bottom: The membership of the Supreme Court in 1899. From left, standing: Justices Peckham, Shiras, White and McKenna. Sitting: Justices Brewer, Harlan, Chief Justice Fuller, Justices Gray and Brown

Thomas Jefferson was an early convert to the idea that separation of the American colonies from the British Crown was necessary and historically inevitable, but even he was not entirely happy when the full break came. The next to last paragraph of the Declaration of Independence refers sadly, and I think with complete honesty on Jefferson's part, to our English brethren and to 'the ties of our common kindred'. Before the long and bitter War of Independence was over, most American patriots had come to think of it as a struggle against a foreign enemy, but in its inception it was essentially a civil war, a war within the common law family.

The outbreak of hostilities in 1775 followed more than a decade of formal protests that the colonists of British North America were being deprived of rights to which they were entitled by virtue of the British constitution and the common law of England. The men who wrote the Resolutions of the Stamp Act Congress (1765), the Declaration and Resolves of the First Continental Congress (1774), and even the Declaration of the Causes and Necessity of Taking Up Arms (1775) were British subjects, thought of themselves as heirs equally with Englishmen in England of the Bill of Rights of 1689, and expressed their increasingly indignant remonstrances in terms of traditional English legality.

It is, I suppose, a paradox that Americans had never before been and never again would be quite as English in their political style and rhetoric as in the years immediately preceding the break with England. James Otis's renowned argument in 1761 in the *Writs of Assistance Case (Paxton's Case,* Quincy's Reports 51) was above all a constitutional argument. Otis had no quarrel with the British constitution; his influential pamphlet, *The Rights of the British Colonies Asserted and Proved* (1764), says of that constitution that it is 'the most free one, and by far the best, now existing on earth.' His basic contention in the *Writs of Assistance Case* was simply that official action that would be unconstitutional in England must be illegal in America, too. Similarly, English legal institutions are appealed to and claimed for British subjects in the colonies throughout the 1774 Declaration and Resolves. The colonists are declared to be 'entitled to all the rights, liberties, and immunities of free and natural-born subjects, within the realm of England,' and to be 'entitled to the common law of England, and more especially to the great and inestimable privilege of being tried by their peers of the vicinage, according to the course of that law.'

Political and Legal Freedom One could make a pretty good case that the American Revolution would never have come about, or would have come about differently and far later, if English legal and political institutions had been less valued than they were in the colonies. The American patriots were sensible men. They knew that liberties were far more secure in England than anywhere else in the eighteenth century world, just as they knew perfectly well that the colonies of British North America enjoyed incomparably more political and legal freedom than any other European colony of the time. The ferocity of the indictment of George III in the

Declaration of Independence was a plea to the jury of world opinion; George III was no tyrant guilty of 'cruelty and perfidy scarcely paralleled in the most barbarous ages,' and the ministries of Charles Townshend and Lord North were not the malevolent, freedom-threatening conspiriacies they were made out to be on this side of the Atlantic. But Americans of the years preceding the Revolution were touchy where their political and legal rights were concerned and not disposed to think that half a loaf of liberty, or even nine tenths of a loaf, was better than none. They valued the traditional English liberties so profoundly that they insisted on having them all.

The mother country in a sense had been too good a teacher. The colonies, now grown to adolescence, felt that the lessons of liberty were fully as well understood in Boston and Williamsburg as in London and York, and they had grown impatient with instruction from England as to how the constitution and the common law were to be interpreted for American purposes. The Bill of Rights of 1689 had declared taxation to be 'illegal' without 'grant of Parliament.' The inescapable inference from this, contended American patriot lawyers, was that taxes could not be imposed on Americans without the consent of their own parliamentary equivalents, the colonial general assemblies. Parliament in London could not be representative of British subjects an ocean away; Americans were British subjects only in the sense that they owed allegiance to the Crown. *Ergo:* exercise of legislative jurisdiction in the colonies by Parliament was unconstitutional and mere 'illegal' usurpation.

The constitutional issues in contest were close ones. The American interpretations, although certainly self-serving, were not unreasonable or irrational by common law standards. Neither were the opposed interpretations embodied in the Declaratory Act of 1768 by which Parliament explicitly asserted its 'full power and authority to make laws and statutes of sufficient force and validity to bind the colonies and people of America ... in all cases whatsoever.' A good advocate, if not too personally identified with one cause or the other, would have enjoyed arguing either side of the case. But does this consitutional rhetoric seem an unduly legalistic way to deal with an explosive dispute between a great power and a disaffected, potentially rebellious colony? Not when we remember that the opposing contentions were being formulated, on both sides of the Atlantic, by men who shared the traditions and the habits of thought of the common law.

Common Faith and Common Law Jefferson had many things in mind when he referred in the Declaration to 'our British brethren' and to 'the ties of our common kindred.' One of these was certainly the tie of a shared legal tradition, and this has proved to be the most durable tie of all. By renouncing their allegiance to the Crown, the colonies of British North America seceded from the British Empire. But they did not secede from the common law family of nations. English and America law and legal institutions are very different now, after two hundred years of political separation.

But American law still bears the marks of its English origins. We are reminded of this every time we speak of Anglo-American legal history. 'The provisions of the Constitution of the United States,' wrote Holmes, 'are organic legal institutions transplanted from English soil.' It is in recognition of this historic and still enduring tie that the American Bar Association took as its bicentennial theme in 1978, 'Common Faith and Common Law: A Declaration of Kinship of the English and American Legal Professions.'

When one says – and it is by no means a loose or meaningless statement – that England and the United States are both 'common law countries,' more is meant than that English and American lawyers work at times with similar structural concepts: consideration, trust, nuisance, and the like. 'Common law,' as used in the characterization 'a common law country,' signifies also and far more significantly a distinctive mode of reasoning, one in which decisions are guided and structured by precedent. And there are certain procedures and arrangments that we associate with the 'common law' way of doing things – the adversary system of proof and legal argument, for example, or the institution of trial by jury. So the story of the common law in the United States has to be more than an account of the American reception and reshaping of English case law principles. That is an important part of it but only a part. The continuity of American law with its common law past is also a continuity of techniques, values, and institutions.

The Declaration and Resolves of the First Continental Congress included a sturdy assertion 'That the respective colonies are entitled to the common law of England.' How is this claim to be interpreted? We can assume that it was not a demand that Americans be enabled to enjoy the aesthetic delights of common law pleading or the blessings of such doctrinal intricacies as the Rule in *Shelley's Case*. The principal reference was not to the corpus of English case law doctrine but to such profoundly valued common law procedures and arrangements as trial by jury, the independence of the

judiciary, and the subjection of governmental power to what John Locke had called 'standing laws.' Magna Carta, the Petition of Right, the Bill of Rights of 1689, and the Act of Settlement of 1701 were all, by the accepted usage of the time, thought of as ingredients of 'the common law of England.' This identification of the common law with historic liberties is one of the principal reasons that the estrangement of Americans from Great Britain, which long survived the end of the Revolutionary War, did not seriously interrupt the reception by American courts of common law principles.

Americans of the Revolutionary generation not only received what they thought of as the essential safeguards of the common law; they wrote them into their state constitutions of 1776 and 1777 and, when the time came, into the Constitution of the United States. They wanted to be sure about the independence of the judiciary, which had been made a principle of the British constitution by the explicit provision of the Act of Settlement of 1701 that 'judges, commissions be made *quamdiu se bene gesserint* and their salaries ascertained and established.'

The Massachusetts Constitution of 1780 borrowed the English idea but recast it in the American idiom: 'It is the right of every citizen to be tried by judges as free, impartial and independent as the lot of humanity will admit. It is, therefore ... for the security of the rights of the people and of every citizen, that the judges of the supreme judicial court shall hold their offices as long as they behave themselves well, and that they should have honorable salaries ascertained and established by standing laws.'

The Act of Settlement, perhaps through this Massachusetts constitutional provision, is the ancestor of the corresponding tenure provision in Article III of the Constitution of the United States. The British and American documents are stylistically different but equivalent in substance: tenure during good behavior, with judicial independence secured both against arbitrary removal and against the threat of punitive salary reduction.

The common law institution of jury trial was even more highly valued; indeed, Americans of the latter half of the eighteenth century put trial by jury first in the hierarchy of values they associated with the common law. The successive steps that led in ten years from loyal colonial protest to outright American rebellion are recorded in a series of great political documents, beginning with the Resolutions of the Stamp Act Congress in 1765 and ending with the Declaration of Independence. Every one of these documents makes explicit and resolute mention of the institution of jury trial. In the Resolutions of the Stamp Act Congress, trial by jury is proclaimed to be 'the inherent and inviolable right of every British subject in the colonies.' It is given first place in the Declaration and Resolves of 1774 by the statement that 'the respective colonies are entitled to the common law of England, and more especially to the great and inestimable privilege of being tried by their peers of the vicinage.' One of the factors cited in the Declaration of the Causes and Necessity for Taking Up Arms is that 'statutes have been passed for ... depriving us of the accustomed and inestimable privilege of trial by jury, in cases affecting both life and property,' and the Declaration of Independence makes it one of the counts in its indictment against George III that he had given his assent to legislation 'for depriving us, in many cases, of the benefits of trial by jury.'

Small wonder, then, that every one of the eleven state constitutions adopted in the years 1776 and 1777 provided explicitly for jury trial in both criminal and civil cases, a pattern followed in virtually every state constitution adopted since then. Small wonder, too, that the Constitutional Convention of 1787, although it decided against the incorporation of a specific Bill of Rights in the original Constitution recommended to the states for ratification, took pains to specify in Article III that:

'The trial of all crimes, except in cases of impeachment, shall be by jury; and such trial shall be held in the States where the said crimes shall have been committed.' Even this was not enough. The right to jury trial is reaffirmed for criminal cases in the Sixth Amendment and extended to civil causes by the Seventh.

It is something of an anomaly that jury trial in civil cases persists in its adoptive country long after its virtual disappearance in the land of its origin. Although the institution retains its full vitality in English criminal proceedings, trial by the court alone has become the norm in English civil litigation. There are a few exceptions, most notably defamation suits and cases in which fraud charges have been made, but there is no right to jury trial in other civil cases. It is as if Shakespeare's plays – or would the analogy be better suited to the works of Gilbert and Sullivan? – had become rarities on the London stage but were still regularly performed in every American theatre. Is there something different in English and American attitudes toward legal institutions that accounts for this variation in contemporary practice? Or is the survival of jury trial in American civil litigation simply an example, perhaps the most striking example, of what happens when an old idea or institution is written into a fixed and judicially enforceable constitution and so made relatively invulnerable to legislative change?

The idea of the 'rule' or, as it is more often expressed in America, the 'supremacy' of law, is the most important of America's legacies from the common law of England. As understood in England and in the countries that share the English legal tradition, the principle of the rule of law has certain distinctive meanings and associations. These reflect the historical fact that the principle did not come into being in England by one dramatic announcement from on high but by a long case-by-case process of common law decision. In his approach to the rule of law, the common lawyer, whether English or American, takes it for granted that there must be standing laws of general application to which all members of society, government officials and private persons, are equally responsible. But common law training and tradition have made him incurably procedural in emphasis; there is no budging him from the ingrained common

law idea that there is no meaningful right if there is no effective remedy to vindicate it. So it is not enough for the common lawyer and common law judge that the supremacy of law be formally acknowledged as an abstract proposition. They insist that the legal system provide effective procedures to keep public power within its fixed legal limits. And the typical common lawyer can never quite be persuaded that there is a better way to keep public power within bounds than by empowering the 'ordinary courts,' courts of general jurisdiction as distinguished from specialized public law tribunals, to require public officials to justify the legality of what they have done.

Judicial Review and Constitutionality American history and the logic of American constitutional federalism made it virtually certain that the rule of law, in its American version, would come to mean not merely the supremacy of the law enacted by the legislature but the supremacy of the federal or state constitution, as interpreted by the courts, over any statute the legislature may enact. The institution of judicial review is incomparably the most striking American variation on the English theme of the rule of law. Constitutionality, on our side of the Atlantic, is an issue for court adjudication. On the home grounds of the common law, it remains an issue for profound public debate, for the question period in the House of Commons, and for ultimate decision by Parliament. This difference in constitutional practice touches and concerns almost everything that judges, legislators, and lawyers do in the two countries. Great issues of public policy – abortion, capital punishment, fair treatment of minorities, to mention only three – on which Parliament has the last and authoritative say in the United Kingdom—are constitutional issues here and so for ultimate, or virtually ultimate, judicial resolution.

The range of our present-day judicial review must be an amazing phenomenon to an English lawyer accustomed, as Englishmen have long been, to the peaceful coexistence of the institution of parliamentary supremacy and the principle of the rule of law. We are often too ready to identify the supremacy of the law with judicial supremacy. Individual liberty can be maintained without the institution of judicial review of legislation – the vigour of English constitutionalism is proof enough of that – but the survival of freedom is at best precarious without the rule of law.

'No strangers these, but kinsmen' In 1930 Chief Judge Cardozo, as he then was, greeted a visiting delegation from the English Bench and Bar as 'no strangers these, but kinsmen of the blood who have kept alive traditions that were born long ago when their law was one with ours. American lawyers and their English legal kindred share more than common problems. They also share principles and legal values that are deeply rooted in the long history of the common law, and they have a common faith that the institutions, traditions, and pragmatic modes of thought of the common law are as good a means as men have yet devised to achieve the reality of justice in human affairs.

What Joining Europe Means to Britain

L W Melville

The Background In the aftermath of the Second World War the realisation that militarism was no longer a means of solving the problems of today led many statesmen to advocate a new initiative in international co-operation. The League of Nations had failed to prevent the Second World War, and the new United Nations, though it was to have a form of international 'police force' (a joint military force under the control of the Security Council which never materialised except in the form of *ad hoc* arrangements), and has various other, no doubt very useful, agencies to promote unity in various walks of life, still lacked that degree of political effectiveness which many felt was needed. In particular European statesmen felt the need for a new order based on legally enforceable commitments.

Nevertheless voluntary organisations, however valuable, can never form the backbone of a social order. If effective co-operation among nations is to become a reality a legal order must be established. A start was made with the formulation of the Council of Europe at the Congress held at The Hague in May 1948 under the chairmanship of Winston Churchill. Contemporaneously Belgium, Netherlands and Luxembourg ('Benelux') set up a common customs union between them which eventually matured into a treaty of economic union in 1960.

Coal and Steel Meantime the European states continued to work towards some form of closer relationship. Since coal and steel are the essential raw materials of armaments it was urged by Robert Schumann that if the control of the manufacture of steel and the mining of coal could be brought under a common European organisation, war between the states involved would be virtually impossible. A treaty to that effect was entered into between France, Germany, Italy and the Benelux countries in 1951 of which the High Authority (under Jean Monnet) has considerable legislative power in these fields.

Treaties of Rome 1957 Two Treaties were signed at Rome in 1957 in furtherance of the intention of setting up legally enforceable structures that would lead to harmonisation among the states of Europe. One dealt with atomic energy and the other with the formation of an economic union. The latter was far the most important since a common market touches on almost all the business activities of the parties to it, and many other activities as well. These Treaties were entered into in March 1957 between the same parties as above, and by a Merger Treaty (entered into in 1965) common institutions for all three communities – Coal & Steel, Atomic Energy and the Common Market were agreed. These comprise an Assembly or Parliament, a Council and a Commission. In addition the European Court of Justice (set up under the earlier Treaties) had the task assigned to it of the supervision of the fulfilment of the Treaties.

Britain's Hesitation From having been in the forefront of the European Movement and the setting up of the Council of Europe at Strasbourg, Britain held back when invited to become legally committed to any form of integration with the European nations even though limited to functional activities without full federalism. The reason is not hard to seek. In the first place though hard hit by the war she was the victor and her way of life remained unimpaired in principle. Moreover she still had close trade and cultural connections with her Commonwealth. Europe had twice cost her dear in two world wars, in addition to which there were significant cultural differences between her and Europe. It may well have been felt that Britain had enough to do to repair her own towns and cities without taking on as a partner countries much more devastated than herself.

It was the changed economic climate throughout the world that eventually made Britain realise that she had lost her pre-war position as a world leader added to which some of her Commonwealth partners had formed different alliances in the meantime. Meanwhile, in the 1960's, the Common Market was proving more successful than had been expected so that it gradually became evident that Britain was more a part of Europe than she had ever been in the past and that integration with Europe was a natural step for her to take. There was yet another reason: the threat of war has still not receded sufficiently for Europe not to feel the need to pool its military resources to match so far as it can the other superpowers, and an attempt to set up a European Defence Community Treaty in the early 1950's was made. Unfortunately it failed since when the will for the members of the EEC to combine their forces has been lacking. Not all nations have recognised the failure of militarism to solve problems which are essentially political or economic. Nevertheless, even without a European Military Treaty the closer our ties with other European nations can be made the better we should be able to co-operate with them in standing up to threats from powerful states.

There were problems: not the least of which would be language, but it is doubtful whether the different systems of law were in themselves any reason for us to hesitate. The only law additional to our own which is applicable is the Community law applicable only where there is a European element and this applies equally to the other nations. On the other hand the fields in which Community law affects our own law, though primarily concerned with trade between member states, extends to such matters as the movement of people and a common agricultural policy and transport policy. Then again, this country's attitude to competition law differs in many respects from the European (and the American).

All this leads to uncertainty. The changes will probably be slow and subtle, but change there will be. Each member will, of course, have some influence in determining those changes which, hopefully, will be determined on the basis of what is best.

Effect on English Law The effect on English law has been commented on by Lord Denning, the Master of the Rolls. In *H P Bulmer Ltd & anor v J Bollinger SA & others* (1974) his Lordship pointed out that in interpreting the Community law the English judges are no longer the final authority: the supreme tribunal is the European Court. The principles of interpretation are different:

Judges from nine countries make up the bench of the
Court of Justice of the European Communities,
Luxembourg

instead of looking for the precise grammatical meaning of an enactment the judges, guided by European legal principles, look to the spirit of the provisions in question and the purpose and intent. If they find a gap in the law they must fill it. Then again, in *Application des Gaz v Falk Veritas* (1974), the Master of the Rolls accepted that the Treaty of Rome creates rights in private citizens which they can enforce in the national courts. He was referring particularly to the effect of Articles 85 and 86 and he stated that in effect these Articles of the Treaty of Rome create new acts of a tortious nature and he gave them appropriate names based on the basic provisions of each of those Articles. The first tort he called 'undue restriction of competition within the Common Market' that being based on Article 85; and the second one he named 'abuse of a dominant position in the Common Market' referring there of course to Article 86.

Thus where Community laws and regulations have any application to activities in the member state they will override any provision in the national law which is incompatible with those laws or regulations. To that extent our national law is overriden by the provisions of the Treaty of Rome. An example of the sort of situation that can arise is provided by Case 40/69 *H Z A v Bollman,* a decision of the European Court of Justice, where a customs officer who found it necessary to interpret a Customs and Excise Regulation was held to be required to follow the interpretation accepted or imposed upon the whole community under the relevant provision of the European Customs Tariff and not to exercise the discretion based on his own judgment, which, prior to the operation of the Treaty of Rome, it had been a practice recognised and accepted for a customs officer to follow.

A Referendum It will be recalled that in January 1972 following our signature to the Treaty of Accession to the European Communities (together with the Irish Republic and Denmark), and the commencement of our membership on January 1, 1973, nevertheless in less than two years thereafter, so far as the United Kingdom was concerned, the question whether we should remain a member was debated and eventually settled by a referendum held on June 5, 1975. There was a two-to-one majority in favour of remaining a member.

Treaties entered into by the Government do not form part of the law of England until an Act of Parliament adopts their provisions. The Act passed for this purpose is the European Communities Act 1972. By section 2, it is enacted that 'All such rights, powers, liabilities, obligations and restrictions from time to time created or arising by or under the Treaties . . . are without further enactment to be given effect or used in the United Kingdom, shall be recognised and available in law. . . .' Under section 4, various existing statutes were amended as a step towards harmonisation of our laws with the Community's.

The Institutions of the Community It is not proposed in this summary to deal at any length with the institutions other than the Court of Justice. A few words must, at the least, be devoted to the other institutions, namely, the Assembly or Parliament, the Council and the Commission.

European Parliament Until recently there were 198 members of the European Parliament representing the member-states and set up under the provision of Article 137 of the Rome Treaty, but with effect from June 1979 the number was increased to 410 and these

representatives are now directly elected by the electorate in each member state.

The powers of the European Parliament are not very extensive. It has an advisory power to give opinions on projects submitted to it prior to any action being taken by the Council, but it does not have the same control over the activities of the Commission. Under Budget Treaties of 1970 and 1977 it has been given substantial budgeting powers. In any event the Council is not bound to follow Parliament's advice. Parliament also has some supervisory power: for example, it may put questions to the Council and it may put questions to the Commission, and, in each case, on any subject; the Commission is bound to reply but the Council is not bound to reply. In addition Parliament may (under Article 144) pass a motion of censure on the activities of the Commission but this power has been seen to be an impractical form of control. It is a fair inference that when the directly elected Parliament begins to operate it will seek more extensive powers.

The Council This is made up of representatives from each of the member states. They are necessarily Cabinet Ministers chosen according to the subject matter of any particular meeting. The Council is the place where national interests have to be reconciled with community interests. There is a committee of permanent representatives, and that committee is responsible for the preparatory work on matters to be discussed in Council. This is an important body, and it may well be that its full potential has not yet been achieved.

The Commission The functions of the Commission are set out in Article 155 of the EEC Treaty. This body is a form of civil service, and it is the most active body of the various institutions. It can initiate activities, and it normally has a programme drawn up for a four year period covering the matters which it intends to pursue. Under Article 157, its members have to be completely independent of the member states, and although that provision is followed, commissioners tend to represent the national interests of the countries appointing them. The tasks of the Commission as set out in Article 155 include the duty to ensure the implications of the provisions of the treaty; they are to formulate recommendations or opinions on the subject matter of the Treaty or in those matters where the Commission considers it necessary; they have a power of decision and participation in the preparation of the acts of the Council and Parliament. In particular, the Commission has the power under Articles 85 to 89 of the EEC Treaty to investigate, adjudicate upon, and in the end, prohibit concerted practices affecting trade between member states which have as their object or effect the prevention, restriction or distortion of competition, and any abuse of a dominant position; where an offence has been committed they have power to impose substantial fines. The procedure is embodied in Regulation 17 of 1962.

The Commission and the Council jointly are empowered under Article 189 to adopt regulations and directives, make decisions and formulate recommendations or opinions. The regulations are to have general application, and these regulations are to be binding in every respect in each member state. It must be appreciated that these powers represent legislation which applies directly and immediately in every member state and which are to be applied and enforced by national courts and executive organs. The Council and Commission can also issue directives to the Governments of member states requiring them to take legislative action or other actions within a specified time. In so far as they make decisions, these are binding on the body or bodies to whom they are addressed. However, recommendations and opinions are not binding.

Under Article 190, regulations, directives and decisions must be supported by reasons which are set out in a preamble and they must be related to the Treaty. Article 192 requires the member states to enforce decisions of the Council or of the Commission where they contain a pecuniary obligation on persons other than states.

Court of Justice This is composed of nine judges. Although they do not have to be nationals of the member states, nor is it a requirement that each member state be represented on the Bench, in practice each member state appoints one or more of its nationals. They are appointed for a term of six years. There is power to appoint persons known as Advocates General, under Article 166. Their number is four, and their duty is to present publicly with complete impartiality, reasoned conclusions on cases admitted to the Court of Justice with a view to assisting the latter in the interpretation and application of the Treaty.

The Task of the Court The Court has to supervise the adherence of the various bodies, ie the Council, the Commission and Parliament to the various Community Treaties. This is an extremely important function since to the extent that the Treaties override national sovereignty it is essential for the members of the Treaties to ensure that the organisations do not exceed their powers. It must also be appreciated that some of the activities of the Treaty are carried out by member states rather than by the institutions of the Community, so that the actions of member states also are liable to come under review by the Court of Justice.

Because of its supervisory powers which are to some extent regulatory, the Court is often acting more in an administrative capacity than a judicial capacity, for example it sometimes has to decide whether a decision of a Commission of the Community is general or individual in its application because the right to bring an action against general acts is more restrictive than that in individual cases. In the *ERTA* case (22/70) the Court was concerned with the right of instituting proceedings against any EEC act which has legal effect. This is based on Article 173 which imposes on the Court a duty to review the lawfulness of acts of the Council other than recommendations or opinions. Since recommendations and opinions are excluded by that Article it was reasonable to conclude that everything else is to have legal effect.

An important function of the Court is contained in Article 177 of the EEC Treaty, which confers upon the

Court jurisdiction to give preliminary rulings concerning the interpretation of the Treaty, the validity and interpretation of acts of the institutions of the Community, and the interpretation of statutes of bodies established by the Council where such provision is made. In these cases where any such question arises before any court or tribunal of a member state that Court may, if it considers it necessary to enable it to give judgment, request the Court of Justice to give a ruling thereon; unless the court is one against whose decision there is no judicial remedy, in which case the question must be referred to the Court of Justice for a ruling.

Procedural Arrangements The procedure established for the Court hearings is based on that of the French courts and the language used is generally French. The emphasis is upon written pleadings, written statements of the parties and written arguments of counsel. There may be an oral hearing but it tends to be formal and perfunctory.

Attempts to compare the hearings of the Court with those of the English courts must take into account, if they are to be fair, the substantially different task that European Court has to fulfil. Its interpretation of the Treaties is concerned with the interpretation of what is, in effect, a written constitution which England does not have. Then again, some of its work is of an administrative nature, such as is the concern of the French Conseil d'Etat, when exercising jurisdiction under Articles 173–175. Even when hearing submissions on references under Article 177 for a preliminary ruling, it does not hear the parties, or investigate facts, but merely considers the abstract questions of interpretation of Community Law which the national court has submitted to it.

The procedure is typical of that of courts established in countries whose law is based on a written constitution and written codes of law. Because the law is intended to be comprehensively covered by the codes, the role of the judge is little more than that of a civil servant speaking for the government: indeed the judges are a branch of the civil service recruited from law students – an enormous contrast with England where judges are appointed from among the senior and successful practising barristers. In the codified legal systems the writings of professors are accorded more respect than the judgments of the courts. Judgments tend to be formalised in structure, each following the same sequence under stylised headings, and the language is terse, restrained, stilted and minimal: a typical civil service document designed to give nothing away and not to expose the originator to any sort of liability.

Bearing in mind the importance of the matters coming before the Court of Justice and that its rulings will affect a population of some 300 million people, it may be assumed that the style and content of its decisions have been the subject matter of much thought. They follow in fact the style mentioned above to be found in countries whose law is based upon codes, though we must qualify that to some extent, which will be done later.

One important feature is the principle adopted of giving only one judgment and disallowing dissenting judgments. It has been suggested that the reason for this stems from the fact that there is no really effective legislative machinery for the Communities: if there were, that legislature could amend the law or fill gaps as required from time to time; but as there is not, the task has to be undertaken by the Court, and for reasons of certainty it was thought desirable that dissenting judgments should be avoided. Another reason may have been that if dissenting judgments were allowed the public might seize on the nationality of the dissenting judge or judges and this might create divisions throughout the Community.

Expressing a personal view, the author disagrees with this line of argument. He believes that the Court's reputation would be enhanced by allowing dissenting opinions. Even a court of nine experienced judges may sometimes come to a wrong conclusion, and if that should happen there will always be someone to point out by logical argument the defect in the Court's ruling. If such a ruling is apparently backed by all nine judges we should have good ground for feeling disturbed; whereas if it were a 5:4 majority decision there would be little cause for concern. No one respects claims by humans to infallibility: greater respect is accorded to a man who admits to an error of judgment (to which we are all prone) than to he who refuses such an admission even where it can be seen to be unsatisfactory. In the writer's philosophy certainty for the future is not within the grasp of the human judgment.

There is an alternative, though it is not readily available to the Court of Justice: that is to adopt a system under which a case is reviewed by a committee advising a single judge, who then gives his judgment based on that advice, but not necessarily following the majority view where there is not unaninimity. This is the position of the Privy Council in England on matters arising in the Commonwealth outside the jurisdiction of Parliament but within the jurisdiction of the monarch.

Comparison with the Anglo-Saxon Procedure In the English courts the role of the court is to a large extent passive. This arises from the adoption of adversary presentation of cases. It is for the parties each in turn to present their case to the court and carry it forward to a hearing at which they will appear by themselves and/or their counsel and the facts and arguments will be fully debated in oral proceedings. In a case of first instance witnesses will be present to give oral evidence which can be challenged in cross-examination of the witness. It is a firm belief of the Anglo-Saxon lawyer that cross-examination by counsel for the opposing party is an important method of getting at the truth. By the very nature of the thing one cannot adopt that procedure where evidence is presented in written form.

Judges will often take part in the debate: this is particularly the case in appeals heard by the House of Lords. Written arguments will have been provided beforehand by the parties' counsel. Such hearings are characterised by a sharp cross-fire of question and answer from the judges (usually five) to counsel at a high intellectual level, and woe betide the barrister who is not fully conversant with his case.

The result of these differences shows itself in the very

different form of judgment that emanates from English courts. The judgments are in effect an essay which reviews the facts and the previous law and then proceeds to deduce reasons why the decision should be whatever the judge has concluded as appropriate. The contrast with the terse judgments of the Court of Justice could hardly be greater. In this connection it is fair to say that not all continental courts adopt the terse form found in Luxembourg. Notably the German and the Netherlands courts usually produce judgments not unlike the English and even tend to adopt the doctrine of precedent.

The contrast between the two systems is of course historical. English law was originally based upon custom as interpreted by the cases, and in this way a body of law grows up from a collection of case decisions on a purely practical basis. For the court can only lay down rules in cases that come before it and these tend to be the problems of significance. As the years go by the law tends to follow the changing nature of society and to grow with it.

In general terms the English system with its unwritten constitution and its common law based on case decision is an open-ended system that adapts itself to the needs of the times, and where the courts play a dominant role and must perforce justify their rulings by fully expounding their reasons. By contrast a system based on written codes is a closed system wherein the ruling for any particular case must be found inside the code, so that the code plays a dominant role and the court a minor one.

It seems to follow that in so far as the Court of Justice is required to take the place of an absent legislative body, it should have followed the English pattern.

An appraisal Expressing a personal view of what is believed to be the general reaction in this country to the system in operation among the various institutions set up under the Treaties, whose powers when exercised will affect this country, it may be said that the English lawyer is particularly conscious of the 'foreign' style of the court reports emanating from Brussels and Luxembourg.

It is important to mention both Brussels and Luxembourg. Brussels is the seat of the Commission and that body gives legally binding decisions on agreements coming before it under the provisions of Regulation 17 where such agreements may fall within the scope of Articles 85 and 86 of the EEC Treaty concerned with competition policy. These are necessarily commercial agreements of importance. The way in which this basically civil service type organisation decides what agreements are allowable and what are not appears to indicate in some cases an absence of understanding of the business considerations involved, particularly in the field of technology agreements. Here again it is fair to point out that we cannot give any praise to the United Kingdom legislation on restrictive trade practices, for this equally is drawn in terms that show an unfamiliarity with the reality of competition.

So far as Luxembourg is concerned there seems no ground for criticism of the efficiency of the Court of Justice: quite the contrary. There is however a belief that the reliance on written submissions rather than oral argument is a less satisfactory proceeding for arriving at a decision. In cases where evidence from a witness is needed oral cross-examination should always be allowed. Since a change in the rules in 1974, cross-examination has been possible within the limitations of European procedure, ie in Chambers. It is a start.

As to the Advocates General, their role of supervising each case from the outset can, no doubt, only be beneficial, but their right to give the final opinion seems less justified, except perhaps in cases of public law as protectors of the public interest. In the latter role we should welcome their presence and set about copying the system in England in those branches of the law which are classed as 'public law', but as advocates addressing the court we should like to see them as having no greater right or standing that the advocates for the parties in matters which are adversary in nature. A somewhat similar role is played in England by the *amicus curiae* in important cases, and by the Comptroller General of Patents in cases where the continued existence of a patent is in issue.

Best of Both Worlds? Having looked at the differences between the English common law legal system, and, in a very generalised way, at the type of legal system on which the European Institutions are based, we may well ask ourselves whether we cannot so contrive further development of those Institutions as to gain the best from each.

The English lawyer may be puzzled by the role of the Advocate General, but we may safely assume that the Scottish lawyer would not, but would recognise him as the equivalent (to some extent) of their procurator fiscal, who carries out an investigatory task in criminal cases as an independent official concerned with the interests of the public. And if we look at some of the recent public investigations into English criminal law we will see criticism of English procedure in this branch of the law with recommendations that the benefits of adopting Scottish procedure in this field, or the French equivalent known as the *juge d'instruction,* should be considered.

A more trenchant comment on the way in which society has changed in its need for legal regulation, and how the common law has failed to meet the needs of the day – not for want of the will to do so, so much as not having the right tools to do the job – is to be found in the Hamlyn lecture by Lord Scarman. He points to the need for the legal control of administrative tribunals which are a common feature of much social legislation and the control of other aspects of public law – of which the common law has little to say apart from *habeas corpus* which is of very limited application – and concludes that there is a pressing need for a Bill of Rights to guard against a weak Parliament failing to protect the public weal by yielding to pressure from a determined active minority.

The form and style of the decisions of the European Court and of the EC Commission is that of one single and necessary lengthy sentence in classical, Ciceronian form, always following the same order of content. The necessary result is a straitjacket rigidity, all cases being

as alike as peas in a pod except for size. The overall effect is mechanistic: as though decisions are arrived at by computer. The effect is unreal and only serves to emphasise the suppression of dissenting views, and is seen as a straining after that degree of certainty beyond human power – striving for infallibility which is not to be had even by pretence, coupled with dehumanisation.

It is inconsistent with the insistence on an uneven number of judges, with the Court's power to refuse to follow its earlier decisions, and with its occasionally rejecting the advice of the Advocate General.

It is easy for an outsider to be critical. With nine judges each brought up in a different legal tradition and in the absence of a universally common language, some compromise is clearly necessary. But the one chosen as a result of unsuccessful attempts to try others is too defensive, moat-like, as though the Court had retreated to an ivory tower. The denouement is in the style of the gods on the heights of Olympus dispensing oracular pronouncements which can never be gainsaid.

Surely it would be preferable for each judgment to be framed in a style which takes account of the nature of the case, and for the judges to select one of their number to frame the judgment in whatever style appeals to him – his native style perhaps, at the same indicating how large a majority of the nine agrees with him. Dissenting judgments could be given anonymously and these could be in a standard form so as not to reveal the nationality of the dissenters. Such judgments would be more believable and so of greater authority, more palatable and easier to understand.

In addition attempts to obtain guidance from decisions in the European Court have not proved very inspiring. In *James Buchanan & Co v Babco Forwarding and Shipping* (1977), a case heard by the Court of Appeal, the Master of the Rolls indicated a willingness to adopt what he considered to be methods of interpretation generally used on the Continent. He was referring in particular to the teleological approach (which is one of the principles of interpretation that the European Court adopts). He pointed out that that approach was one which gives the Court freedom to avoid the literal meaning or the grammatical structure of the sentence (the usual English approach) which was criticised as narrow or pedantic, and instead to look behind the actual words used and ascertain its design or purpose. When that case was appealed to the House of Lords their Lordships rejected that approach. The Law Lords did not accept that English principles of interpretation were unduly narrow, inflexible or pedantic. Lord Wilberforce referred to some cases (which had not been quoted to the Court of Appeal) where on a similar point the courts on the Continent had made a different ruling. He therefore pointed to the logical conclusion that there was no universal wisdom available across the Channel upon which our insular minds can draw. Their Lordships also were able to refer to the case of *Ulster-Swift v Taunton Meat Haulage* (1977). This was another case which came before the Court of Appeal (where the Master of the Rolls was not a member of that Court). The main judgment was given by Lord Justice Megaw. In this case the court was faced with a situation in relation to which there had been thirty previous cases decided by European tribunals and it was found on analysis that they could be analysed into twelve different rulings. The judge wittily remarked that on this analysis the cases could be regarded as virtually 'encircling the clock' so that all directions were open; there was therefore no clear guidance to be obtained on the correct directions to take.

The more we study the differences between the different legal systems within the countries of the Common Market and the institutions set up to operate it, the more we realise that each has something to learn from the other. It appears propitious that we should have allied our country to countries which have legal features that are needed in our own society: such as a system of public legal protection (similar to the role of the procurator fiscal) such as the continental *juge d'instruction*, and a Bill of Rights with entrenched clauses, inspired by the role played by the Court of Justice in supervising adherence to a written constitution.

That we can work with our continental friends harmoniously is evidenced by the work of bodies of the Council of Europe, namely the Committee on Legal Co-operation and the European Committee on Crime Prevention. In spite of the differences of legal systems, language and procedure, in practice a surprising amount of consensus emerges in the end, even though sessions are necessarily protracted. There arises what has been described as 'underlying the whole operation ... some indefinable will to advance pan-European solutions to common problems. Not the least of the reasons for the final consensus at committee level is the guidance given continuously and discreetly by the Director of Legal Affairs and his team of lawyers, operating from the headquarters of the Council of Europe at Strasbourg'.

If these committees can work harmoniously in those circumstances there is no reason why others drawn from the member-states should not be able to do the same.

Human Rights in Europe The history of mankind is replete with examples of the tug-of-war between the demands of freedom for the individual and the subjection of the individual to the claims of the community. Both in politics and religion there is, on the one hand, advocacy for the individual to make this own decisions and accept responsibility for the consequences, and, on the other hand, totalitarian paternalism demanding obedience to a hierarchy which offers to take care of all major problems for those who obey. Whatever merits there may be in a totalitarian community it produces a hierarchy which is usually irremovable and a division of the community into classes with different privileges. If it is to work the upper echelons need to be of noble character whose private lives are above suspicion for the temptations of power corrupt all but the angels. And if one looks at the list of human rights set forth below it is the exception for items 3, 6, 7, 9, 11, 12, 13, 16, 17 and 18 to be granted in those societies.

The proposition that every individual has certain fundamental rights by nature or some other source became a general topic of discussion throughout Europe towards the end of the 18th century. It was originally propounded in 1690 by John Locke, in 1750 by J J Rousseau and in 1791 by Tom Paine; both the newly formed American States in 1787 and the French Assembly after the fall of the Bastille and the 'night of the 4th August' in 1789 proposed that a Declaration of the Rights of Man should be incorporated in a new Constitution.

After the Second World War the nations of the world, so far as represented at the Assembly of the United Nations in 1948, thought it necessary to declare adherence to an extended version of the Rights of Man and the Council of Europe determined to draw up a European Convention on the matter. The first meeting took place in 1950 at Strasbourg, which has become the centre from which the Council of Europe operates. In November of that year a convention was signed at Rome which came into force on September 3, 1953. By

that time ten ratifications had been obtained and by 1978 the number had risen to 18, namely: Austria, Belgium, Cyprus, Denmark, France, West Germany, Greece, Iceland, Ireland, Italy, Luxembourg, Malta, Netherlands, Norway, Sweden, Switzerland, Turkey and the United Kingdom. Spain and Portugal are expected to add their signatures and yet others may do so too.

The rights and freedoms protected by the convention as extended by further protocols, may be summarised, in a simplified form, as follows:

Rights to:
1 Life
2 Liberty and security of person
3 Fair trial
4 Privacy, family life, home and correspondence
5 Marriage and family
6 A remedy where rights are violated
7 Property
8 Education
9 Free elections
10 To enter one's own country and remain there
11 Equal treatment irrespective of sex, race, colour, religious faith and so on

Freedom from:
12 Torture or inhuman treatment
13 Slavery or forced labour
14 Imprisonment for civil debt

Freedom of:
15 Thought, conscience and religion
16 Expression
17 Assembly
18 Movement and choice of residence

Protection against: 19 Retroactivity of civil law

Prohibition of: 20 Collective expulsion of aliens

Not all of these features have been accepted by all member states.

European Commission of Human Rights To implement the Convention a Commission of Human Rights was set up consisting of one member from each of the High Contracting Parties. Any state may refer to the Commission particulars of an alleged breach of the Convention, but not much use has been made of this power because the purpose of the Convention is to protect individuals rather than condemn any particular member state. There have been a few inter-state cases.

Under the rules of public international law, it has been established that an individual cannot have rights which can be asserted by him personally against a state; but that it is for his government to take action on his behalf. This rule presents difficulties if there is to be a remedy in a situation where it is his own government. Therefore the Commission had to abrogate the earlier rule, and institute a procedure whereby an individual can complain to an international body against the conduct of a government, even though it is his own, and it is to the credit of the members of the Council of Europe that 11 of its members have accepted that rule, namely: Austria, Belgium, Denmark, West Germany, Iceland,

Ireland, Luxembourg, Netherlands, Norway, Sweden and the United Kingdom. Subsequently France also ratified in part. Moveover, the Netherlands have extended their application to the Netherlands Antilles and the United Kingdom to 22 dependent territories. Thus the Commission has jurisdiction to receive petitions from several hundred million inhabitants of these member states and their dependent territories.

Position of the Individual The enforcement of human rights by an individual does not apply to all the rights listed above, and he cannot go to the European Court direct. Moreover, he cannot enforce rights under the Convention until all domestic remedies have been exhausted. What happens is that a sub-committee of the Commission on Human Rights considers the matter with a view to establishing whether a violation has occurred, and if it is satisfied that that is the case, then it issues an opinion on the matter, and it lays down for the offending member state a limited period within which to effect a remedy.

Commencing Proceedings in the Court The Commission's opinion on the case which comes before them is the basis on which proceedings may be commenced in the European Court of Human Rights. That Court has been established by the Council of Europe. It has its seat at Strasbourg, which is where the Council of Europe itself and the Commission have their headquarters. The European Court on Human Rights has one member per country, so that at present there are 18 judges (19 when Portugal signs). Its jurisdiction calls for the consent of the parties so that it resembles arbitration. Eleven of the contracting states have accepted jurisdiction as compulsory. If the Commission decides to take a case to the European Court, then although the individual concerned is not strictly a party, he may on special occasions be allowed to be heard if the Commission thinks that his evidence would be useful. The Court's decision is binding on the parties who must implement the ruling, and a committee of the ministers of the Council of Europe will supervise proper fulfilment of the terms of the judgment.

The question whether our joining Europe will prove beneficial is still, in these early years, debated. It is equally important to consider whether it will be beneficial for Europe. Will there be a fusing of cultural concepts so that Britain will cease to have any distinctive features in a homogeneous conglomeration of peoples?

On the latter point we might look at the Scots and note that their union with England has not driven out the bagpipes or the kilt, nor the Scottish caution combined with enterprise; on the contrary, these features are if anything encouraged all the more. So it should be with the United Kingdom in Europe; we shall, in all probability, soon see the bowler hat, pin stripe suit and rolled umbrella increasingly in evidence in London; and see it spread to other cities. We shall nurture our wry sense of humour, our even-tempered, phlegmatic attitude to the vicissitudes of life, our inventiveness and our so-called eccentricity, the latter being nothing more than the application of inventiveness to new ways of doing things and of living.

As to the effect on Europe it is a question of the defence of common interests in our form of democratic government. Our very freedom allows the existence in our midst of militant extremists determined to stamp out individualism in personal life and in business and to replace it with totalitarian nationalisation. By supporting a movement devoted to the defence of freely elected governments we help other European nations and they help us, and thereby we mutually reduce the significance of any threat from those quarters. Not surprisingly the European Movement is attracting other like-minded nations wanting to join.

Conclusion Britain's adherence to the Community Treaties and the Human Rights Convention will make a significant difference to the law of this country. So far as Community law is concerned the effect will be limited to circumstances where there is a European content to the matter. I do not think that the new arrangements will lead to full federalism: our cultural heritage is sufficiently different from that of others – and theirs from ours – to make it unacceptable. Moreover it is desirable that the principle of Treaties which are legally enforceable but limited to certain inter-state functions ('functional federalism') should be extended to as many democratic countries as is reasonably practicable, whereas full federalism among nations of diverse languages and culture cannot extend so far.

There is a move towards the enacting of a European Bill of Rights with entrenched clauses enforceable in the European Court of Justice so far as not covered already by Article 164 EEC and supplementing the jurisdiction of the Court of Human Rights at Strasbourg thereby guaranteeing a true democracy throughout those States acceding to the EEC Treaties. This should cover not merely the right to vote but the duty of any Parliament to offer itself for re-election in competition with any alternative government willing to take power on the same terms.

The United Kingdom was in the forefront of the beginnings of these arrangements, convention and treaties from the establishment of the Council of Europe to the setting up of the Human Rights Court. With hindsight we may judge that she should have been a founding member of the Common Market, but at least she has belatedly joined. Part of the reason for her hesitancy lies in the feature which makes membership worthwhile: legal enforceability of inter-State traffic, even though at the present time the Court of Justice does not have its own powers of enforcement but relies on the adherence to its pronouncements by the member-States. Democracy is being challenged by the totalitarian states whose lip-service to democratic principles is the extent of their commitment to individual freedom. The European experiments are essential to the survival of a true democracy and their extension to other sympathetic states should be encouraged.

Acknowledgements

A great many people have helped me produce this book. To them all I express my gratitude. They all lead busy lives so their time, energy and advice have been given through kindness and generosity.

Most particularly I wish to thank Sir Basil Nield for his great support and patience. The book would not have been produced without his help. He has eased my path, enabling me to cover events and places that would otherwise have remained closed.

I am immensely grateful to Judy Hodgson for editing the book and to Julian Allason for much of the photography. Both have given of themselves beyond their initial terms of reference as have Paul Watkins, who designed the book, and Tom Williams who researched the illustrations.

Lord Elwyn-Jones, who as Lord Chancellor wrote the Foreword, saw the book in proof. I wish to thank him and his Private Secretary, I H Maxwell, for their advice and suggestions.

All the contributors have been most generous – inserting the writing of their chapters into extremely busy schedules. It is an honour that they have given the book so much consideration. I should like especially to thank Lord Rawlinson and Francis Cowper for practical assistance in addition to their published contributions.

Lord Justice Willmer, Lady Willmer, Lt Col J H Allason, Sue Lloyd-Roberts, Michael Braid and Brian Clifford have my thanks for help in the planning. For assistance in the execution I owe gratitude to the Sub-Treasurer of Middle Temple, Capt J B Morrison and the Under Treasurers of Inner Temple, Gray's Inn and Lincoln's Inn, Commander R S Flynn, Christopher Hughes and Lt Col E R Bridges; also the librarians of all four Inns, Miss E McNeill, Messrs. W W S Breem, P C Beddingham and R Walker; from the Bar Senate Sir Arthur Power and the late Philip Gaudin; from the Law Society, Graham Lee; from the Royal Courts of Justice, Maurice Cockrem; from the Central Criminal Court, Jack Gamble; to all those I am grateful and to many others including Ronald Allison, B Beaumont-Nesbitt, Mrs S Blick, D M M Carey, K Chard, Timothy Daniell, Jane Davan-Wetton, Robert Dudley, Ian Elder, Ruth Eldon, Andrew Graham, W T Harland, Susan Hirst, Thomas E Johnson, Heather Mitchell, Stephen O'Malley, A H Pasmore, Christine Reeves, G Wiegand, Paul Wigby and David M Young.

Finally to Mrs Cynthia Lewis, many thanks for the typing.

John Stidolph July 1979

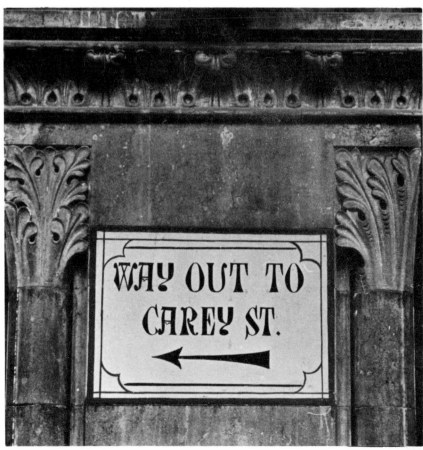

The following list of books, while no means comprehensive, contains suggestions for further reading on subjects covered in this book

R J Walker and M G Walker, *English Legal System.* 4th ed. 1976. Butterworths.

P S James, *Introduction to English Law.* 9th ed. 1976. Butterworths.

J H Baker, *Introduction to English Legal History.* 2nd ed. 1978. Butterworths.

S F C Milsom, *Historical Foundations of the Common Law.* 1969. Butterworths.

G W Keeton, *Harvey the Hasty – A Mediaeval Chief Justice.* Barry Rose (Publishers) Ltd.

R F V Heuston, *Lives of the Lord Chancellors.* Reprinted 1976. Wildy.

Lord Denning, *The Discipline of Law.* 1979. Butterworths.

T Daniell and J M B Crawford, *The Lawyers.* 1976. Wildy.

R Hazell (ed), *The Bar on Trial.* 1979. Quartet.

H Kirk, *Portrait of a Profession – A History of the Solicitors Profession 1100 to the Present Day.* 1976. Oyez.

G M Sanctuary, *Before You See A Solicitor.* 1977. Oyez.

D N MacCormick (ed), *Lawyers in their Social Setting.* 1976. W Green.

M Zander, *Lawyers and the Public Interest: A Study of Restrictive Practice.* 1968.

B Abel-Smith and R Stevens, *Lawyers and the Courts.* 1967. Heinemann Educational.

G D Squibb, *Doctors' Commons.* 1978. Clarendon Press.

Sir R E Megarry, *Inns Ancient and Modern.* 1972. Selden Society.

F Topolski and F H Cowper, *Legal London Illustrated.* 1961. Stevens & Sons.

F H Cowper, *A Prospect of Gray's Inn.*

T Daniell, *The Inns of Court.* 1971. Wildy.

Legal Action Group. *Legal Services: A Blueprint for the Future.* Available from 28A Highgate Rd., London NW5 IN5.

M Zander, *Legal Services for the Community.* 1978. Temple Smith.

J Baker, *Neighbourhood Advice Centre: A Community Project in Camden.* 1978. Routledge & Kegan Paul.

H Cecil, *The English Judge.* 1970. Hamlyn Lecture. Stevens & Sons.

J A G Griffith, *Politics of the Judiciary.* 1978. Fontana.

JUSTICE, *The Judiciary,* (Report of a Justice Sub-Committee). 1972. From JUSTICE, Carey Street, London WC2.

S Shetreet, *Judges on Trial.* 1976. North Holland Publishing Co.

S Pollock, *Legal Aid: The First 25 Years.* 1978. Oyez.

F S Turner, *May It Please Your Lordship?* 1971. Michael Joseph.

H Cecil, *Tipping the Scales.* 1964. Hutchinson.

D Barnard, *The Criminal Court in Action.* 1974. Butterworths.

D Barnard, *The Civil Court in Action.* 1977. Butterworths.

R M Jackson, *Machinery of Justice in England.* 7th ed. 1977. Cambridge University Press.

Sir Basil Nield, *Farewell to the Assizes.* 1972. Garnstone Press.

H G Hanbury, *English Courts of Law.* 4th ed. 1977. Oxford University Press.

L Blom-Cooper and G Drewry, *A Study of the House of Lords in its Judicial Capacity.* 1972. Oxford University Press.

F L Morrison, *Courts and the Political Process in England.* 1973. Sage Publications.

G Drewry, *Law, Justice and Politics.* 1975. Longmans.

Law Commission, *Jurisdiction of Certain Ancients Courts.* Law Com No 72. 1976. HMSO.

B F Harrison and A J Maddox, *The Work of a Magistrate.* 3rd ed. 1975. Shaw & Sons.

J Baldwin and M McConville, *Jury Trials.* 1979. Oxford University Press.

J Baldwin and M McConville, *Negotiated Justice.* 1978. Martin Robertson.

N Underhill, *The Lord Chancellor.* 1978. Terrence Dalton Ltd.

P Archer, *Role of the Law Officers.* Fabian Research Series.

J le J Edward, *The Law Officers of the Crown.* 1964. Sweet & Maxwell.

A James, *Media and the Law.* 1977. Brennan Publications.

R Callender Smith, *Press Law.* 1978. Sweet & Maxwell.

W M Gwag and R C Henderson, *Introduction to the Law of Scotland.* 7th ed. 1968. W Green & Sons.

Scottish Office, *Legal System of Scotland.* 2nd ed. 1977. HMSO.

D N A Walker, *Scottish Legal System.* 4th ed. 1976. W Green & Sons.

Report of Committee on the Supreme Court of Judicature of Northern Ireland. 1970. Cmnd 4292. HMSO.

Report of the Diplock Commission on Legal Procedures to deal with Terrorism in Northern Ireland. 1972. Cmnd 5185. HMSO.

Report of the Cardiner Committee on measures to deal with terrorism in Northern Ireland. 1975. Cmnd 5847. HMSO.

The Constitution of Northern Ireland (being the Government of Ireland Act 1920 as amended to 1964). HMSO, Chichester St, Belfast.

W J Trimble, "The Judgments Enforcement Office", 21 NILQ 357.

Northern Ireland Office, *Northern Ireland and the EEC.* 1977. HMSO.

A Allott, *New Essays in African Law.* 1970. Butterworths.

Sir Ivor Jennings, *Constitutional Laws of the Commonwealth.* 3rd ed. 1957. Cambridge University Press.

B O Nowaubeze, *Constitutionalism and the Emergent States.* 1978. C Hurst.

F Phillips, *The Evolving Legal Profession in the Commonwealth.* 1978. Oceana (New York).

D Lasok and J W Bridge, *Law and Institutions of the European Communities.* 2nd ed. 1976. Butterworths.

L Neville Brown and F Jacobs, *The Court of Justice of the European Communities.* 1977. Sweet & Maxwell.

H G Schermers, *Judicial Protection in the European Communities.* 1977. Stevens & Sons.

Manual of the Council of Europe. 1970. Stevens & Sons.

A H Robertson, *European Institutions.* 3rd ed. 1973. Stevens & Sons.

E H Wall, *Court of Justice of the European Communities.* 1966. Butterworths.